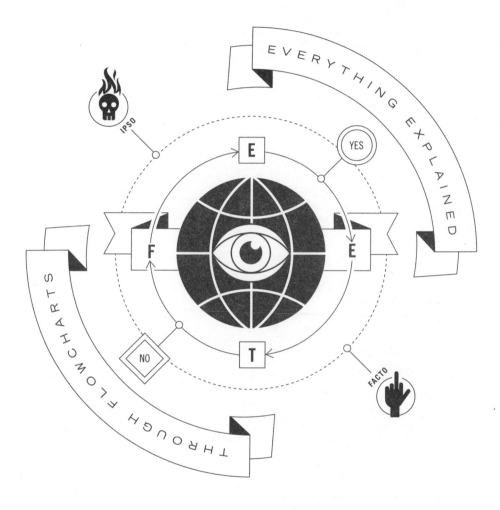

EVERYTHING
EXPLAINED
THROUGH FLOWCHARTS

BY DOOGIE HORNER

HARPER

NEW YORK · LONDON · TORONTO · SYDNEY

HarperCollins books may be purchased for educational, business, or sales promotional use. For information please write: Special Markets Department, HarperCollins Publishers, 10 East 53rd Street, New York, NY 10022.

FIRST EDITION

Designed and illustrated by Doogie Horner

Library of Congress Cataloging-in-Publication Data has been applied for.

ISBN 978-0-06-182660-3

10 11 12 13 14 CW 10 9 8 7 6 5 4 3 2 1

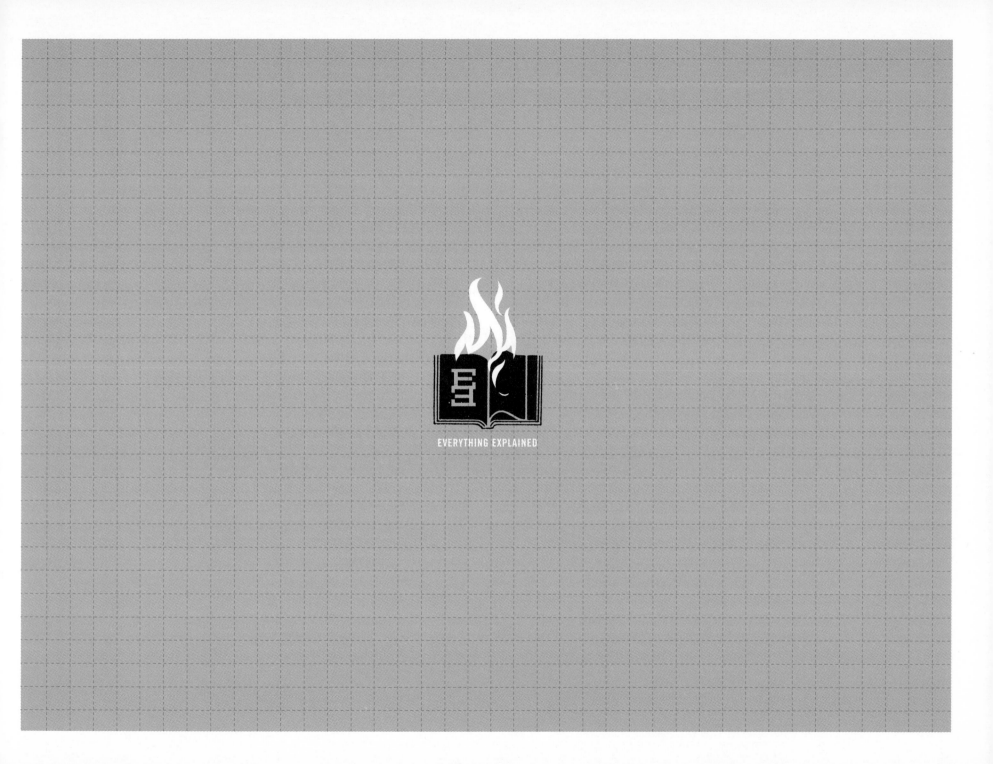

EVERYTHING EXPLAINED

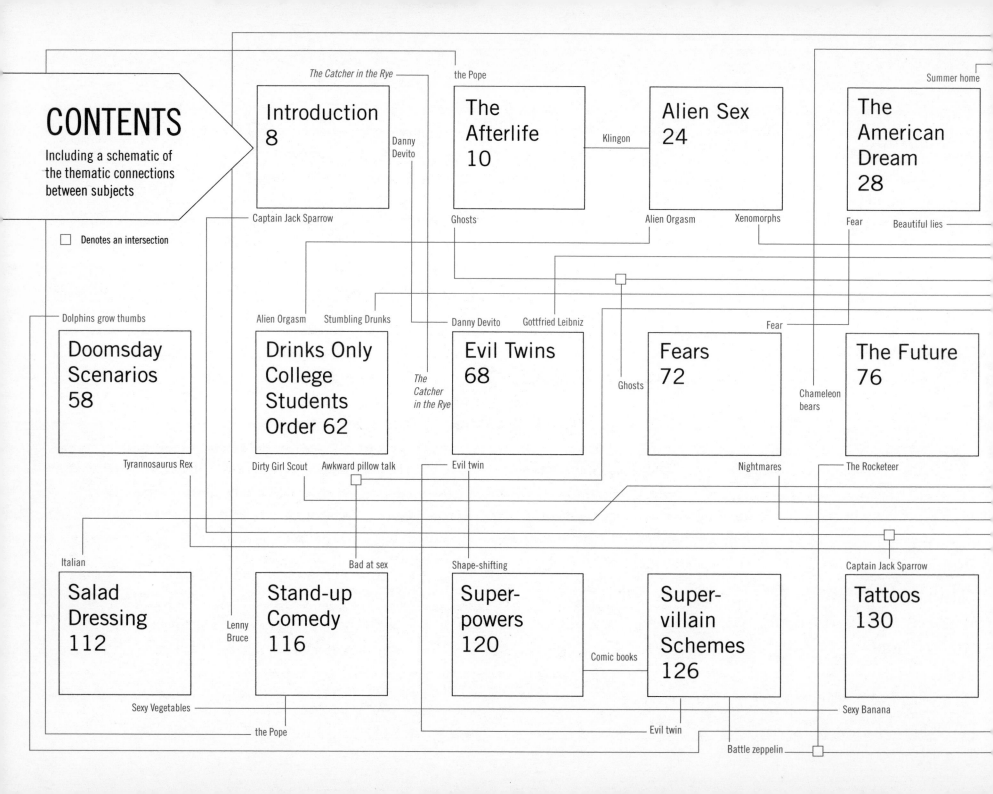

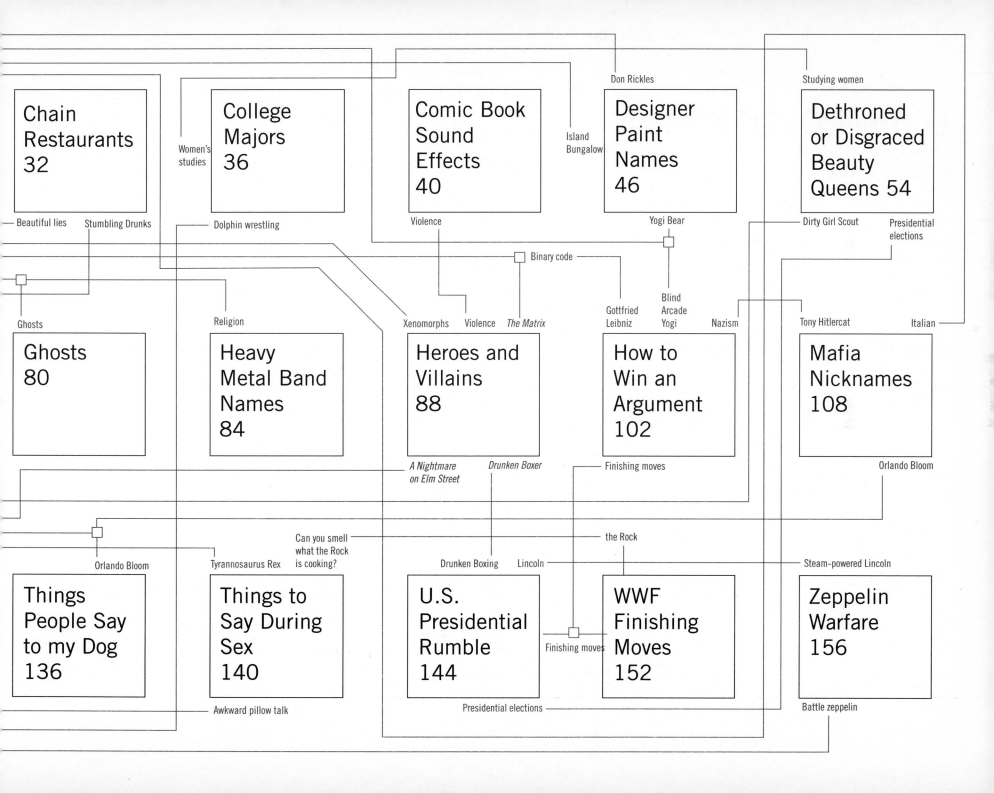

INTRODUCTION

IF YOU'RE A WRITER[1] and your book has a misleading title, the introduction is typically used to clear things up. Some good examples are J. D. Salinger's introduction to *The Catcher in the Rye*, where he explains that the title is a metaphor and there are no actual rye fields in the book, or the introduction to *Moby Dick*, where Melville explains that the title is not supposed to be funny, and that the book is about a big whale (he goes on to recommend that you skip the whole middle part). *(See Figure 1: Classic Book Titles Modified to be More Accurate.)* Not to brag or anything, but the title of this book is crystal clear, so luckily I don't have to waste space belaboring the obvious: that the book is an extended equation for the unified field theory (along with some humorous illustrations). *What?* Everything Explained. *How?* Flowcharts. Introduction done! Now we can spend the rest of these two pages exploring different types of common introductions:

---

(1) I am too! We should hang out.

FIGURE 1: CLASSIC BOOK TITLES MODIFIED TO BE MORE ACCURATE

- *Of Migrant Workers and Mentally-Challenged Men*
- *The Sun Also Rises, and Also Sets Again, and Repeats That Cycle Until Someday the Sun Burns Out*
- *Moby Whale*
- *Only a Douchebag Would Kill a Mockingbird*
- *Gatsby*
- *On the Road With Potheads and Beautiful Winos*
- *Lolita the Sexy Twelve-Year-Old Nymphette*
- *Where the Red Fern Grows: Between the Graves of Two Dogs Named Old Dan and Little Ann*
- *The Wizard of Oz is Just a Man Behind a Curtain in a Dream*
- *And Then There Were None, Because Justice Wargrave Killed Them All*

COMMON INTRODUCTIONS

Written by a celebrity: Doogie didn't ask me to write this introduction, I asked him. "You saved my career, it's the least I can do for you," I told him. We first met on the set of *Pirates of the Carribean*. It was our second day of shooting, and I was having difficulty finding my character's voice. Doogie pulled me aside and said, "I think you're approaching your character's name too literally. I don't think Captain Jack Sparrow has to behave like an actual sparrow. It might be better if you just acted like a pirate . . . or maybe Keith Richards."

Written by someone who acts like a celebrity, although you've never heard of them: I know what your first question is going to be, because people always stop me on the street and ask: "When you were Bob Ukerack's motorcycle stunt-double for the famous 'tarantula jump' scene in the hit film *Spider Rider III*, how did you keep track of which tarantulas you could safely punch, because they were drugged, and which ones were wild?" Well the answer is simple: Doogie charted the whole scene—and probably saved my life.

Written by another celebrity who offered to write the introduction, but was turned down, and now is

pissed he got snubbed (introduction appears on the celebrity's blog, not in the actual book): Doogie didn't ask me to write this introduction, I asked him. And he said, "No thanks, we'd rather have Johnny Depp write the introduction, because we're stupid, and we think *Edward Scissorhands* was a better movie than *Throw Momma' From the Train*." Was Johnny Depp in *One Flew Over the Cuckoo's Nest*? Does he direct his own films? Does he have his own brand of Limoncello? No, he doesn't. But I guess some publishing bigwigs think his name on the cover will sell more books than mine, Danny Devito.

Simple country talkin': I remember my grand-daddy used to have a chart for near about everything. I'd sneak a peek into his workshop when he was out raking leaves or draining possum blood for the winter, and I'd see all the charts lined up on his bench there, or hanging by hooks from the rafters. They smelled like sawdust, and when I got up the courage to scurry in and run my hands over their rough-hewn edges, the corkboard and hand-molded square nails felt more real and true than anything I'd felt before or since. Did they just appear to glow in the slanting light of Indian summer, or was there some magic in them too? Shucks, I don't know.

Needlessly literal: When I first presented the idea of a book of charts to my editor, he said, "That sounds like a good idea." So I got to work. After the first chart, I made another one, and then I kept making them until I had enough charts to fill a book, plus one extra chart. Then I got rid of that chart, because it was extra, and there wasn't room for it in the book.

Confusing metaphor: Writing a book is akin to giving birth, except that writing a book is far more painful, and there's a lot more (metaphorical) blood. As in pregnancy, there is a defined period of gestation during which you get to know this "baby" growing inside your "womb," but it is a child of words, and its heartbeats are dreams of the future. We are here today at that book child's christening, in the church of human understanding, to breath those dreams awake.

The acknowledgments page masquerading as the introduction: This book would not have been possible without the kind (but stern) guidance of my beautiful wife Jen, who put up with my odd working hours (thanks Honey-bear!) and an upsetting trip to the zoo to do some fact-checking (fact checked: monkey's *do* fling feces when they get angry!). Also a big thanks to Zits for reading the first draft, and of course John K., Steve G., and Chip C. Mike, I bet you think I'm going to forget to mention you, don't you? *Well I am!* (Just kidding.)

The Ultimate Warrior Masquerading as the Introduction *(see WWF Finishing Moves on page 152)*: When my opponent said a book of charts would not be a good book, I said, "Load the spaceship with the rocket fuel and fly it into the sun!" I need not the Normals to protect me! These charts are the charts of your destruction. I have injected fire poison into your veins with the power of the Warrior, and there is only one antidote: Walk with me to the edge, AND LOOK BEYOND YOUR FEARS, IF YOU DARE!

Ironically detached meta-introduction: You just read it! Whoah, it just became even more meta![2]

---

(2) CAUTION: Don't hold this introduction up to a mirror, or it could create a meta-awareness vortex that frees your shadow-self from the multiverse.

THE AFTERLIFE

I'D LIKE TO BEGIN this section by politely requesting that any religious zealots who are reading this book not murder me or my family (also, I'm sorry I called you a "zealot"). As much as I would like to be mentioned in the same sentence as Salman Rushdie, I'd prefer it to be because we both won the Booker Prize or dated Padma Lakshmi, and not because both of us have had fatwas declared against us. Also, if there are any gods reading this text, please do not send me to hell. Despite these risks, I'd like to discuss religion, because it is *fascinating*. If you don't believe me, just ask one of the approximately 5 billion people who adhere to it in some form.

Although this is primarily a humor book, I've exerted all my willpower not to make any jokes in these charts [1] because I do respect the religious beliefs of other people [2] *(See Figure 1: Things I Don't Respect in Other People.)* Religion has been a stabilizing and helpful force

FIGURE 1: THINGS I *DON'T* RESPECT IN OTHER PEOPLE

- Their taste in music.
- Their taste in films.
- Their right to not have anyone sneak a look at their diary if they're foolish enough to leave it sitting out.
- Their right to not invite me to a party if they're my next door neighbor.
- Their right to tell me what they think of my beard when I didn't ask for their opinion.
- Their right to form a militia. (The problem is that none of the people who *want* to be in a militia are people that *should* be in a militia.)

in my own life, and I'm not presumptuous enough to dismiss the validity of other religions that I only came in contact with while I lived on the International Exchange floor of my college dorm [3] Therefore I've tried to eliminate any editorial slant from these charts and present the data as objectively as possible. So if at any point it seems like I'm poking fun at a particular feature of that religion, I assure you, I'm not—unless it's one of those dumb religions (you know the ones I'm talking about).

Why only focus on the afterlife in each of these religions? Because religion is a massive and amorphous subject, and charts become more accurate the more specifically you filter their data. Also, the

---

(1) Although I do make a joke about Sekhmet's hat in the Ancient Egyptian chart. I also take a rather arch tone in the atheism chart, but atheism is more of a philosophy than a religion, so I don't feel guilty. Screw empiricism!

(2) Except for religions that were created by science-fiction writers or motivational speakers. And no, I don't count Jesus or Mohammed as motivational speakers.

(3) If I was to make presumptions based solely on my experiences with religious adherents I knew in college, here is what a few would be: Buddhists are tidy, Mormons touch your elbow too much when they're trying to make a point, and Taoists like to play track 3 on *Dark Side of the Moon* over and over and over again.

afterlife lends itself nicely to the flowchart format: if you do this you go to heaven, if you don't you go to hell (or maybe get reincarnated as a hungry ghost—it's complicated).

Perhaps I'm being unreasonably cautious and apologetic in this introduction, but you don't know how many problems I've had with these charts. I showed the Buddhism chart to a couple Buddhists, and here's what they said:

Buddhist 1: This is completely inaccurate.
Me: What should I change?
Buddhist 1: All of it.

Buddhist 2: This is accurate. However, making the cycle of reincarnation a circle is misleading, because there's no permanent self, no recurring soul.
Me: What shape would be more accurate?
Buddhist 2: A line that never ends.
Me: That won't fit in the book.

Buddhist 3: This chart should really just be a blank page.
Me: . . .

However, it's not just Buddhists that have given me attitude. I've had similar problems with all the other religions, and there are multiple reasons. First of all, some religions, such as Buddhism, Klingon, or Chinese Folk Religion, don't have a single sacred text that they're based on, so it's hard to find consistent doctrine. Chinese Folk Religion is especially difficult to define, since it's a catch-all phrase for an unofficial mixture of Taoism, Confucianism, Buddhism, and folklore. Secondly, even when a religion does have a primary sacred text, such as the Bible in Christianity or the Qur'an in Islam, that text is still open to multiple interpretations. And finally, people are just touchy about the afterlife; a lot of religions don't want to say "Do this and you'll go to hell." (Rich people are especially touchy about that line in the Bible that says it's easier for a camel to pass through the eye of a needle than it is for them to enter the kingdom of heaven. *See Billionaire Pet Peeves #42 on page 12.*)

The religions chosen for this section are skewed more toward afterlife paths that I found interesting, and don't reflect an inclusive survey of all world religions. Here are some notable exclusions:

Hinduism: Although it's the third largest religion in the world, its afterlife mechanics are kind of similar to Buddhism; also, it's really confusing.

Christianity (not Catholicism): There are minor differences among denominations, but their afterlife is still super simple: If you accept Jesus Christ as Your Saviour and try to obey his teachings, you go to heaven. And Jews probably go to heaven too, because they're God's chosen people. (And possibly other people too, if they're good people.)

Scientology: Scientology doesn't have an official belief about the afterlife, although they believe in reincarnation.

Various Folk/Indigenous Religions: These are difficult to chart because their tradition is passed down orally; there's no single religious text or doctrine. However, I have represented this category in Chinese Folk Religion.

Whatever religion you are: Your religion is too awesome to be in my lame book. Please don't kill me.

(from Afterlife essay, page 11)

BILLIONAIRE PET PEEVES

---

1. Trophy wife's opera career not taking off
2. Trophy wife uses your yacht to hold charity fundraisers, and all the wheelchairs scuff the deck
3. Michael Moore always wants to interview you
4. Wawa can't break a million-dollar bill
5. Moon vacations overpriced
6. Nuveau riche
7. Your greedy relatives hovering around you like a pack of vultures, waiting for you to die.
8. Good help hard to find
9. Butler not British enough
10. Nothing left to buy!
11. Poor people
12. People always get you cheap birthday presents
13. Wallet is too thick to fit into your expensive trouser pockets
14. Constantly finding diamonds in your bed
15. Taxes! Especially the luxury tax
16. Universal Healthcare
17. Anti-Trust laws
18. The middle class always striving in new and annoying ways
19. Limo jet's poor gas mileage
20. Getting lost in your house's many rooms
21. Can't remember which mansion you left your keys in
22. Trillionaires won't let you sit at their table in the cafeteria
23. People asking you how many zeros are in a billion
24. Inconvenient locales for secret Illuminati meetings
25. Gold toilet becoming tarnished
26. Running out of $1000 bills to wipe your ass with and having to use $100s
27. Central American military junta you funded is going "against the game plan"
28. President of United States makes you hang on a second because he's on the other line with the UN
29. Africa slow at repaying loans
30. Not allowed to show anyone the centaur you genetically engineered, because it's a "sin against god," or something
31. That engine that runs on water that some enterprising inventor keeps discovering every couple years
32. That billionaire who always has one dollar more than you do
33. Millionaires acting like they're rich
34. Not able to brag about how you're the Grand Master of the Shadow Government, because it's supposed to be a secret
35. When you have an itch on the bottom of your foot, but you can't scratch it because you're wearing a solid pewter suit of armor and sitting on a horse, posing for an equestrian portrait
36. Poets harping about all the stuff money can't buy
37. The noise styrofoam makes as it rubs together when you're unpacking the latest Picasso you just bought
38. When you take a chick into the White House to have sex on the desk of the Oval Office, and discover the President is working late, so you have to tell him to beat it, and he leaves immediately but by then the mood is ruined, so you have to hop into a helicopter and have sex in the torch at the top of the Statue of Liberty
39. The endangered animal whose skin you use for all your underwear becomes extinct
40. Man in red bowtie at auction house who always seems to outbid you
41. Ghost of Christmas Past
42. That line in the Bible that compares a rich man trying to enter the kingdom of heaven to a camel trying to pass through the eye of a needle
43. Billy Joel always throws loud parties next door and never invites you
44. Fox hunt rained out
45. Money doesn't keep you warm on cold winter nights . . . oh wait, you can buy a blanket—the warmest blanket known to man, woven from alpaca fur. Never mind.
46. Daughter wants to marry a commoner
47. Human being you're hunting for sport proves to be surprisingly resourceful
48. Lucky dime constantly stolen
49. Robin Hood
50. The difficult to open packaging that ostrich eggs come in

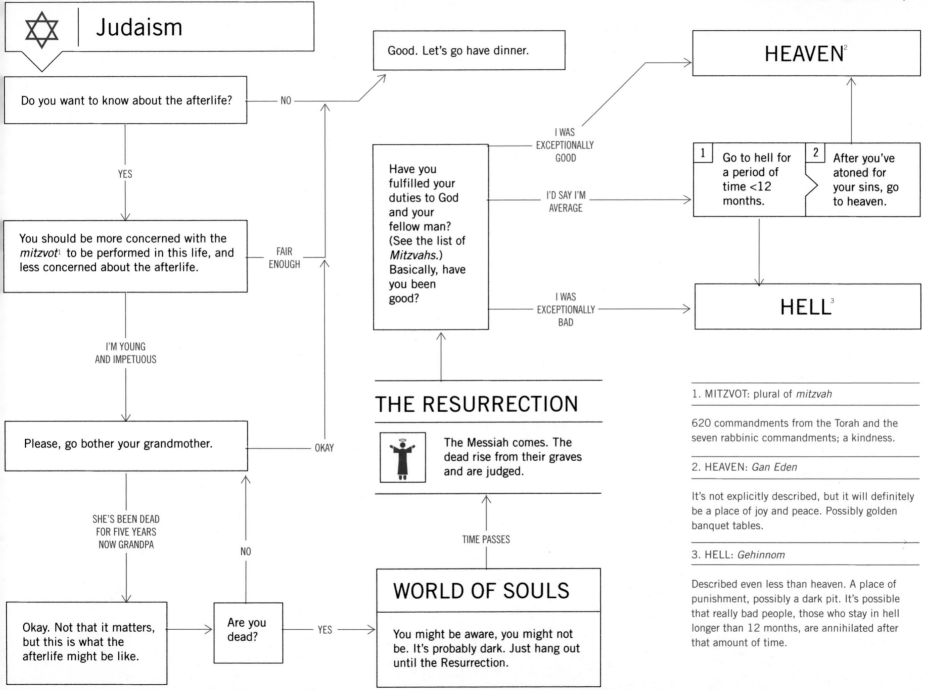

Judaism

Do you want to know about the afterlife? — NO → Good. Let's go have dinner.

YES ↓

You should be more concerned with the *mitzvot*[1] to be performed in this life, and less concerned about the afterlife.

— FAIR ENOUGH →

I'M YOUNG AND IMPETUOUS ↓

Please, go bother your grandmother.

— OKAY →

SHE'S BEEN DEAD FOR FIVE YEARS NOW GRANDPA ↓

Okay. Not that it matters, but this is what the afterlife might be like.

→ Are you dead? — NO ↑

— YES →

WORLD OF SOULS

You might be aware, you might not be. It's probably dark. Just hang out until the Resurrection.

TIME PASSES ↑

THE RESURRECTION

The Messiah comes. The dead rise from their graves and are judged.

↑

Have you fulfilled your duties to God and your fellow man? (See the list of *Mitzvahs*.) Basically, have you been good?

— I WAS EXCEPTIONALLY GOOD → HEAVEN[2]

— I'D SAY I'M AVERAGE →

| 1 | Go to hell for a period of time <12 months. | 2 | After you've atoned for your sins, go to heaven. |

→ HELL[3]

— I WAS EXCEPTIONALLY BAD → HELL[3]

---

1. MITZVOT: plural of *mitzvah*

620 commandments from the Torah and the seven rabbinic commandments; a kindness.

2. HEAVEN: *Gan Eden*

It's not explicitly described, but it will definitely be a place of joy and peace. Possibly golden banquet tables.

3. HELL: *Gehinnom*

Described even less than heaven. A place of punishment, possibly a dark pit. It's possible that really bad people, those who stay in hell longer than 12 months, are annihilated after that amount of time.

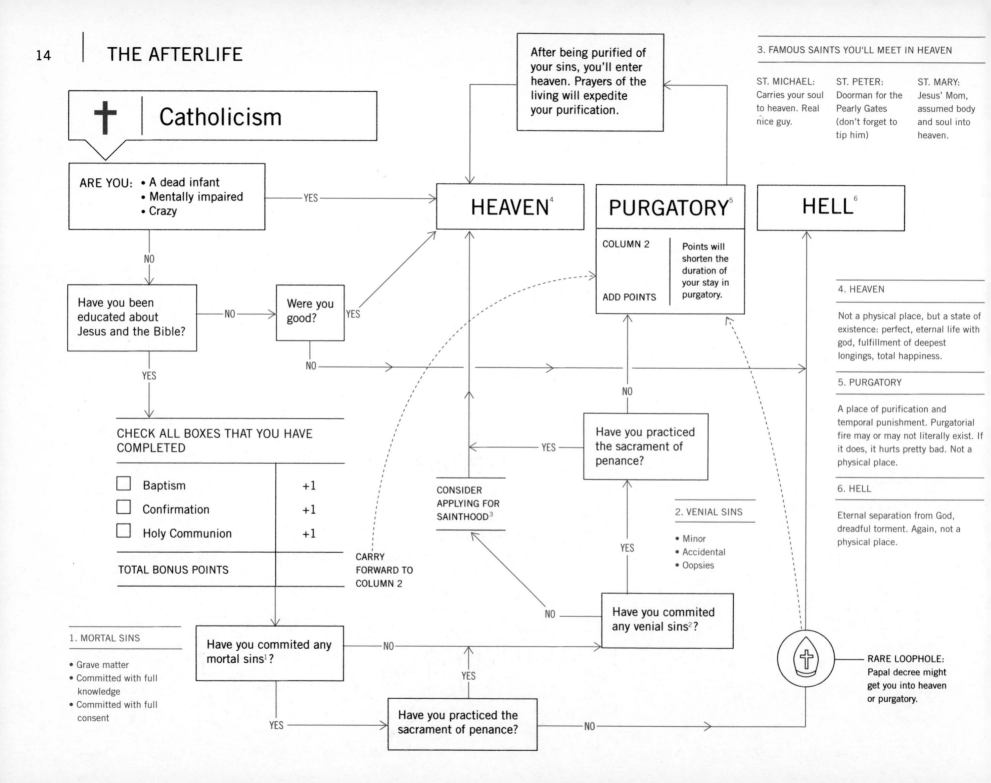

Catholicism

After being purified of your sins, you'll enter heaven. Prayers of the living will expedite your purification.

ARE YOU:
• A dead infant
• Mentally impaired
• Crazy

— YES →

NO ↓

Have you been educated about Jesus and the Bible?

— NO → Were you good?

YES ↓

CHECK ALL BOXES THAT YOU HAVE COMPLETED

☐ Baptism +1
☐ Confirmation +1
☐ Holy Communion +1

TOTAL BONUS POINTS

NO (Were you good?) →

HEAVEN[4]

PURGATORY[5]

COLUMN 2 | Points will shorten the duration of your stay in purgatory.
ADD POINTS

HELL[6]

CONSIDER APPLYING FOR SAINTHOOD[3]

Have you practiced the sacrament of penance?

— YES →
NO ↓

2. VENIAL SINS
• Minor
• Accidental
• Oopsies

YES ↓

Have you commited any venial sins[2]?

— NO →

CARRY FORWARD TO COLUMN 2

1. MORTAL SINS
• Grave matter
• Committed with full knowledge
• Committed with full consent

Have you commited any mortal sins[1]?

— NO →

YES ↓

Have you practiced the sacrament of penance?

— NO →

3. FAMOUS SAINTS YOU'LL MEET IN HEAVEN

ST. MICHAEL: Carries your soul to heaven. Real nice guy.

ST. PETER: Doorman for the Pearly Gates (don't forget to tip him)

ST. MARY: Jesus' Mom, assumed body and soul into heaven.

4. HEAVEN

Not a physical place, but a state of existence: perfect, eternal life with god, fulfillment of deepest longings, total happiness.

5. PURGATORY

A place of purification and temporal punishment. Purgatorial fire may or may not literally exist. If it does, it hurts pretty bad. Not a physical place.

6. HELL

Eternal separation from God, dreadful torment. Again, not a physical place.

RARE LOOPHOLE: Papal decree might get you into heaven or purgatory.

THE SEVEN DEADLY SINS

In 590 AD Pope Gregory I classified the seven deadly sins to help the pious avoid the most serious mortal sins. Since then the Deadly Seven have also proved an invaluable tool for creative mass murderers, cruise ship event planners, and ad executives. The following radial scatter charts dissect the deadly sins further and chart their following aspects:

1. EASY: How easy is it to commit the sin?
2. FUN: How much fun is committing the sin?
3. COMMON: How commonly is the sin committed by the average person?
4. BAD FOR YOU: How harmful is the sin to your own well-being?
5. BAD FOR OTHERS: How harmful is the sin to the well-being of others?

All numbers have been calculated in reference to the other sins' ratings, and based on the sinning habits of a hypothetical "average" person that is certainly not me. Pride's very high "bad for you" rating is due to the fact that it is the only sin from which all the others can stem.

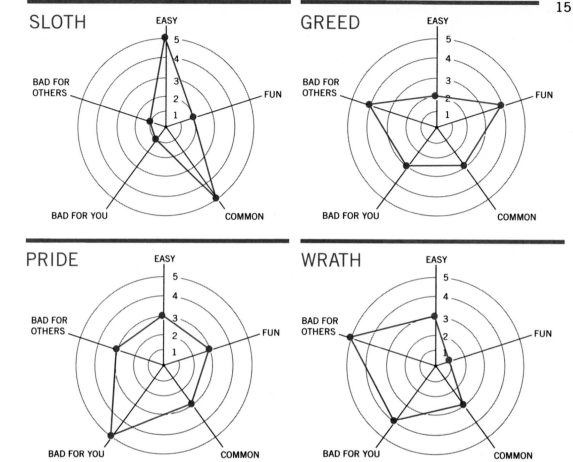

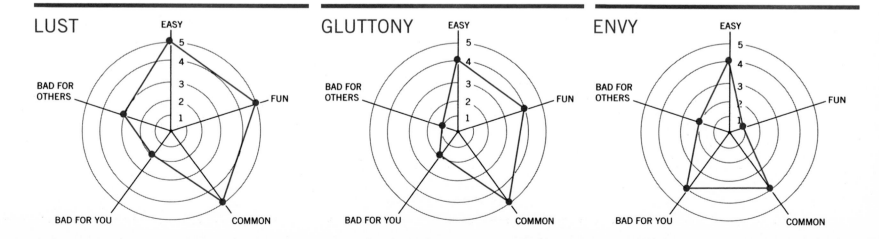

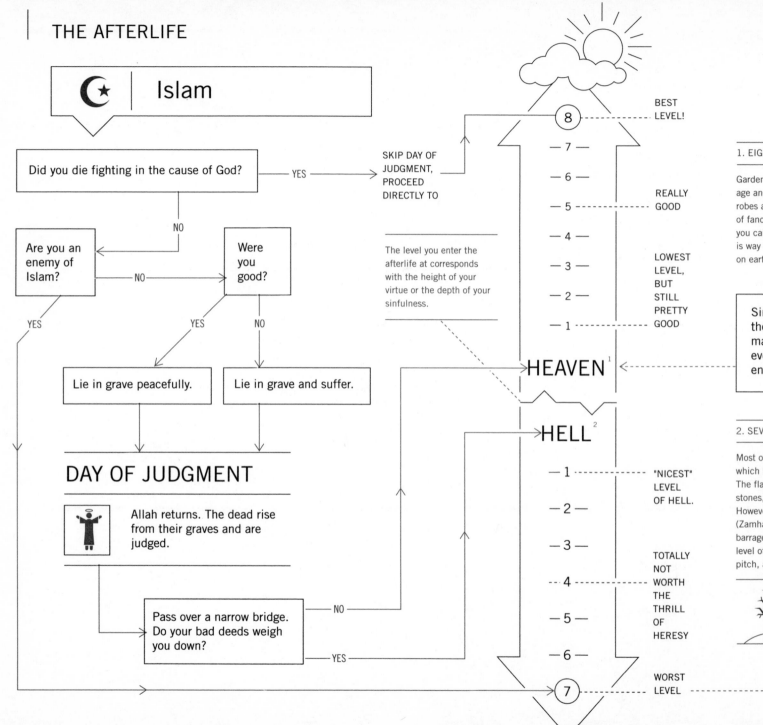

Islam

Did you die fighting in the cause of God? — YES → SKIP DAY OF JUDGMENT, PROCEED DIRECTLY TO

NO

Were you good?

Are you an enemy of Islam? — NO →

YES (Are you an enemy of Islam?)

YES (Were you good?) → Lie in grave peacefully.

NO (Were you good?) → Lie in grave and suffer.

The level you enter the afterlife at corresponds with the height of your virtue or the depth of your sinfulness.

DAY OF JUDGMENT

Allah returns. The dead rise from their graves and are judged.

Pass over a narrow bridge. Do your bad deeds weigh you down? — NO

YES

8 — BEST LEVEL!

— 7 —
— 6 —
— 5 ------- REALLY GOOD
— 4 —
— 3 ------- LOWEST LEVEL, BUT STILL PRETTY GOOD
— 2 —
— 1 ------- GOOD

HEAVEN¹

HELL²

— 1 ------- "NICEST" LEVEL OF HELL.
— 2 —
— 3 —
— 4 ------- TOTALLY NOT WORTH THE THRILL OF HERESY
— 5 —
— 6 —
7 ------- WORST LEVEL

1. EIGHT LEVELS OF HEAVEN:

Gardenlike. Everyone is the same age and height, and wears costly robes and perfumes. There are lots of fancy banquets, and also virgins you can have sex with—and the sex is way better than the sex you had on earth.

Since Allah is merciful, there's a chance you may enter heaven eventually after doing enough time in hell.

2. SEVEN LEVELS OF HELL:

Most of hell is filled with hellfire, which burns hotter than regular fire. The flames are fuelded by people, stones, and false gods and idols. However, one level of hell (Zamhareer) is extremely cold, and barraged by blizzards. The deepest level of hell is a cauldron of boiling pitch, and holds the Zaqqum tree.

ZAQQUM TREE

POSSIBLE LOOPHOLE!

Buddhism

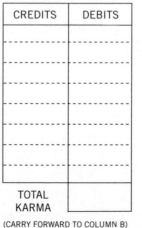

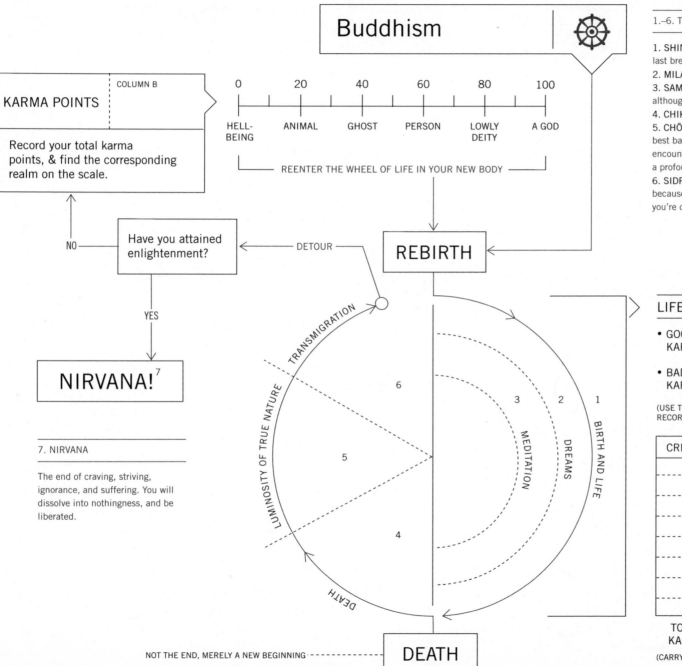

KARMA POINTS | COLUMN B

Record your total karma points, & find the corresponding realm on the scale.

| 0 | 20 | 40 | 60 | 80 | 100 |

HELL-BEING | ANIMAL | GHOST | PERSON | LOWLY DEITY | A GOD

REENTER THE WHEEL OF LIFE IN YOUR NEW BODY

NO

Have you attained enlightenment?

DETOUR

REBIRTH

YES

NIRVANA![7]

TRANSMIGRATION

LUMINOSITY OF TRUE NATURE

6

5

4

MEDITATION

DREAMS

BIRTH AND LIFE

3

2

1

DEATH

7. NIRVANA

The end of craving, striving, ignorance, and suffering. You will dissolve into nothingness, and be liberated.

NOT THE END, MERELY A NEW BEGINNING ----- **DEATH**

1.–6. THE SIX BARDOS

1. **SHINAY:** Birth and life, from conception until your last breath.
2. **MILAM:** Dreams.
3. **SAMTEN:** Usually only attained through meditation, although it sometimes occurs spontaneously.
4. **CHIKKHAI:** Death.
5. **CHÖNYID:** Luminosity of true nature. This is the best bardo, in my opinion. You see a bright, clear light, encounter various deities and visions, and are awash in a profound sense of peace.
6. **SIDPAI:** Transmigration. I hope you enjoyed chönyid, because this is the part where you may find out that you're coming back to earth as a worm.

LIFE: BARDOS 1-3

- GOOD DEEDS GAIN YOU KARMA POINTS.

- BAD DEEDS COST YOU KARMA POINTS.

(USE THE SPACE BELOW TO RECORD YOUR KARMA POINTS)

CREDITS	DEBITS
TOTAL KARMA	

(CARRY FORWARD TO COLUMN B)

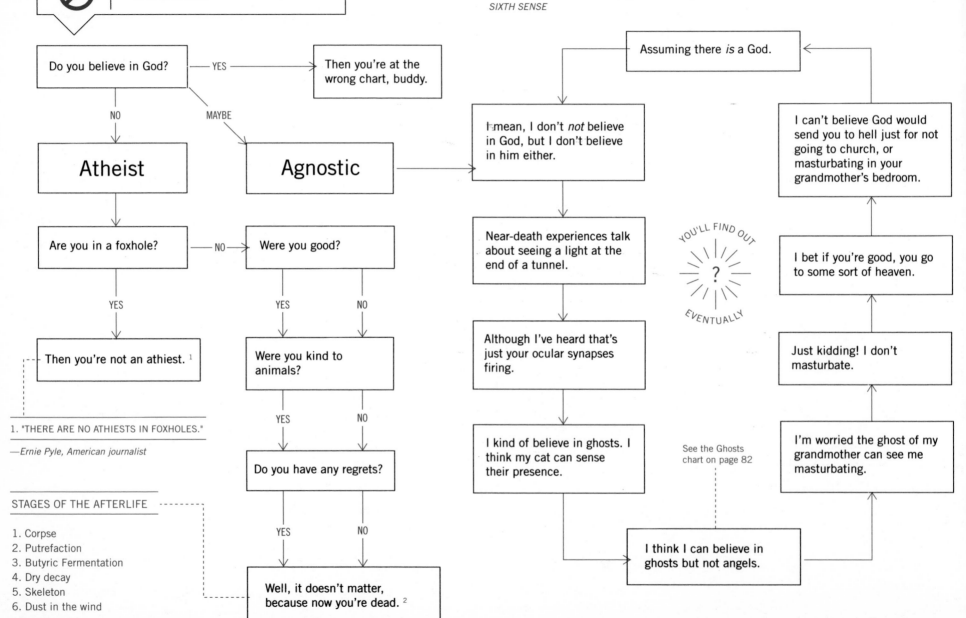

Secular

ALL DOGS GO TO HEAVEN, ALMOST AN ANGEL, ALWAYS, BEETLEJUICE, COCCOON, FIELD OF DREAMS, FLATLINERS, GHOST, GHOST BUSTERS, GHOST DAD, THE FRIGHTENERS, THE SHINING, THE SIXTH SENSE

Do you believe in God? —YES→ Then you're at the wrong chart, buddy.

NO ↓   MAYBE ↘

Atheist   **Agnostic**

Are you in a foxhole? —NO→ Were you good?

YES ↓   YES ↓   NO ↓

Then you're not an athiest. [1]

Were you kind to animals?

YES ↓   NO ↓

Do you have any regrets?

YES ↓   NO ↓

Well, it doesn't matter, because now you're dead. [2]

1. "THERE ARE NO ATHIESTS IN FOXHOLES."
—*Ernie Pyle, American journalist*

STAGES OF THE AFTERLIFE

1. Corpse
2. Putrefaction
3. Butyric Fermentation
4. Dry decay
5. Skeleton
6. Dust in the wind

Assuming there *is* a God.

I mean, I don't *not* believe in God, but I don't believe in him either.

Near-death experiences talk about seeing a light at the end of a tunnel.

Although I've heard that's just your ocular synapses firing.

I kind of believe in ghosts. I think my cat can sense their presence.

YOU'LL FIND OUT ? EVENTUALLY

See the Ghosts chart on page 82

I think I can believe in ghosts but not angels.

I can't believe God would send you to hell just for not going to church, or masturbating in your grandmother's bedroom.

I bet if you're good, you go to some sort of heaven.

Just kidding! I don't masturbate.

I'm worried the ghost of my grandmother can see me masturbating.

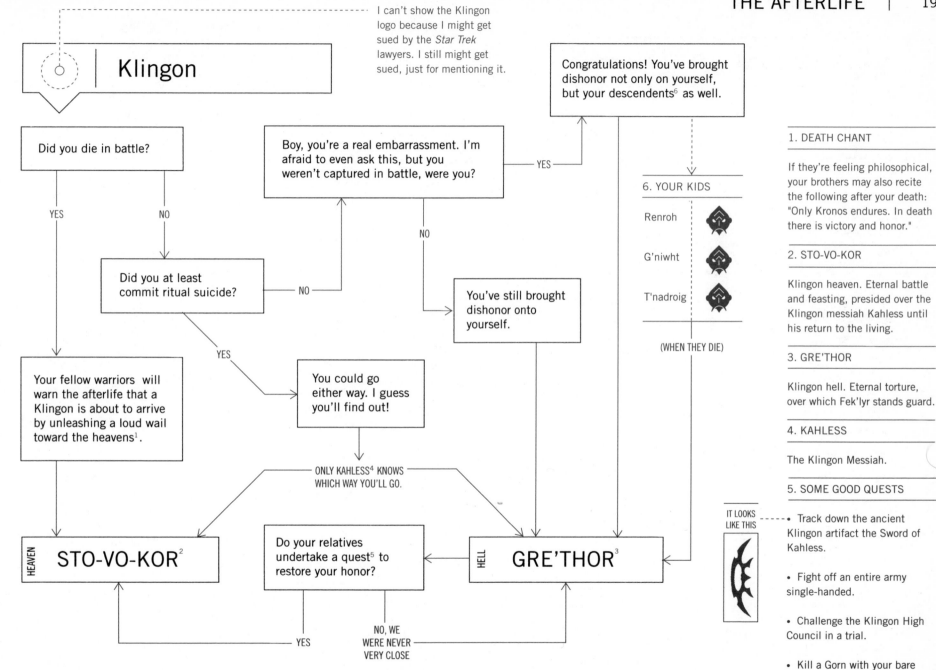

Klingon

I can't show the Klingon logo because I might get sued by the *Star Trek* lawyers. I still might get sued, just for mentioning it.

Did you die in battle?

YES → NO

Did you at least commit ritual suicide?

Boy, you're a real embarrassment. I'm afraid to even ask this, but you weren't captured in battle, were you?

Congratulations! You've brought dishonor not only on yourself, but your descendents[6] as well.

YES

NO

NO

You've still brought dishonor onto yourself.

Your fellow warriors will warn the afterlife that a Klingon is about to arrive by unleashing a loud wail toward the heavens[1].

YES

You could go either way. I guess you'll find out!

ONLY KAHLESS[4] KNOWS WHICH WAY YOU'LL GO.

HEAVEN STO-VO-KOR[2]

Do your relatives undertake a quest[5] to restore your honor?

HELL GRE'THOR[3]

YES

NO, WE WERE NEVER VERY CLOSE

6. YOUR KIDS

Renroh

G'niwht

T'nadroig

(WHEN THEY DIE)

1. DEATH CHANT

If they're feeling philosophical, your brothers may also recite the following after your death: "Only Kronos endures. In death there is victory and honor."

2. STO-VO-KOR

Klingon heaven. Eternal battle and feasting, presided over the Klingon messiah Kahless until his return to the living.

3. GRE'THOR

Klingon hell. Eternal torture, over which Fek'lyr stands guard.

4. KAHLESS

The Klingon Messiah.

5. SOME GOOD QUESTS

IT LOOKS LIKE THIS

• Track down the ancient Klingon artifact the Sword of Kahless.

• Fight off an entire army single-handed.

• Challenge the Klingon High Council in a trial.

• Kill a Gorn with your bare hands, and eat its still beating heart.

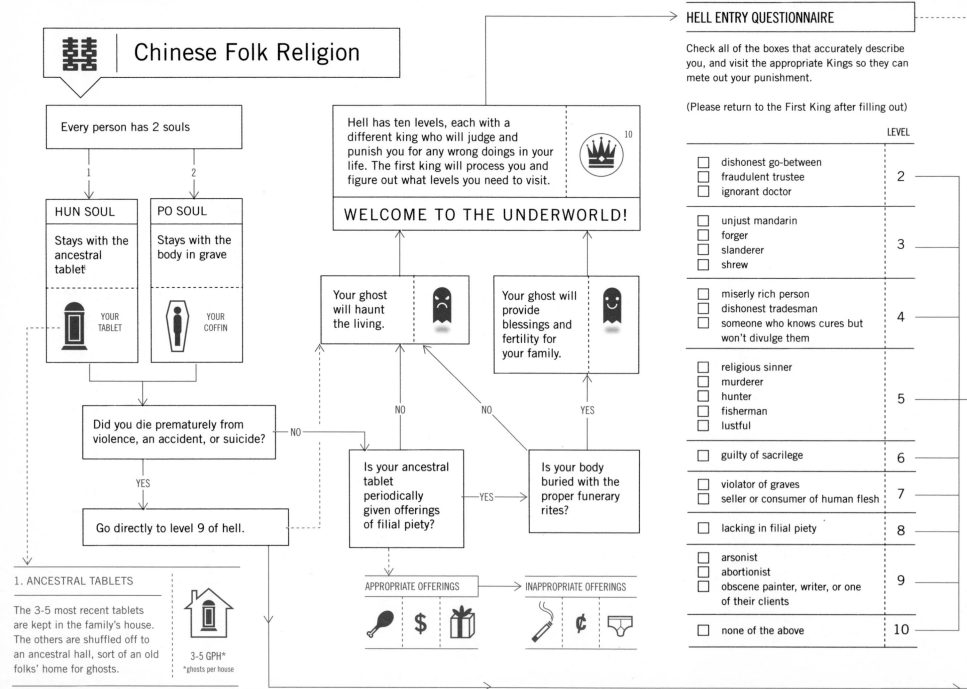

Chinese Folk Religion

Every person has 2 souls

1 → **HUN SOUL**
Stays with the ancestral tablet[1]

YOUR TABLET

2 → **PO SOUL**
Stays with the body in grave

YOUR COFFIN

Did you die prematurely from violence, an accident, or suicide?

YES → Go directly to level 9 of hell.

NO → Is your ancestral tablet periodically given offerings of filial piety?

NO → Your ghost will haunt the living.

YES → Is your body buried with the proper funerary rites?

NO → Your ghost will haunt the living.

YES → Your ghost will provide blessings and fertility for your family.

WELCOME TO THE UNDERWORLD!

Hell has ten levels, each with a different king who will judge and punish you for any wrong doings in your life. The first king will process you and figure out what levels you need to visit.

10

APPROPRIATE OFFERINGS → INAPPROPRIATE OFFERINGS

1. ANCESTRAL TABLETS

The 3-5 most recent tablets are kept in the family's house. The others are shuffled off to an ancestral hall, sort of an old folks' home for ghosts.

3-5 GPH*
*ghosts per house

HELL ENTRY QUESTIONNAIRE

Check all of the boxes that accurately describe you, and visit the appropriate Kings so they can mete out your punishment.

(Please return to the First King after filling out)

LEVEL

☐ dishonest go-between
☐ fraudulent trustee
☐ ignorant doctor
2

☐ unjust mandarin
☐ forger
☐ slanderer
☐ shrew
3

☐ miserly rich person
☐ dishonest tradesman
☐ someone who knows cures but won't divulge them
4

☐ religious sinner
☐ murderer
☐ hunter
☐ fisherman
☐ lustful
5

☐ guilty of sacrilege
6

☐ violator of graves
☐ seller or consumer of human flesh
7

☐ lacking in filial piety
8

☐ arsonist
☐ abortionist
☐ obscene painter, writer, or one of their clients
9

☐ none of the above
10

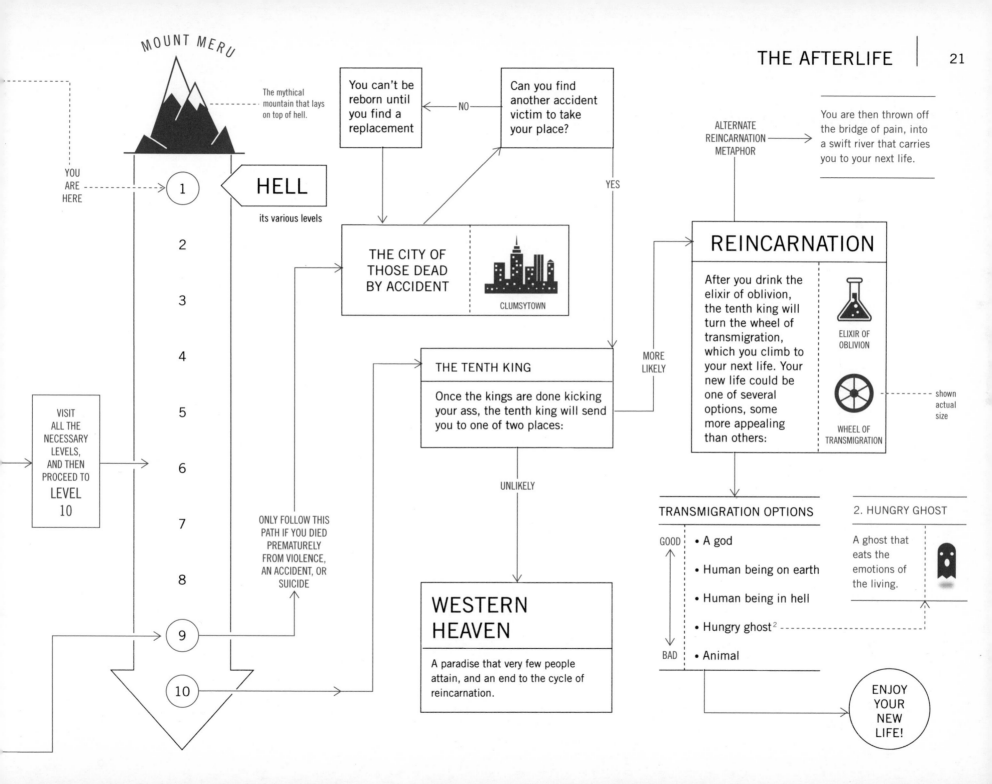

MOUNT MERU

The mythical mountain that lays on top of hell.

YOU ARE HERE

HELL

its various levels

1
2
3
4
5
6
7
8
9
10

VISIT ALL THE NECESSARY LEVELS, AND THEN PROCEED TO LEVEL 10

ONLY FOLLOW THIS PATH IF YOU DIED PREMATURELY FROM VIOLENCE, AN ACCIDENT, OR SUICIDE

You can't be reborn until you find a replacement

Can you find another accident victim to take your place?

NO

YES

THE CITY OF THOSE DEAD BY ACCIDENT

CLUMSYTOWN

THE TENTH KING

Once the kings are done kicking your ass, the tenth king will send you to one of two places:

MORE LIKELY

UNLIKELY

WESTERN HEAVEN

A paradise that very few people attain, and an end to the cycle of reincarnation.

ALTERNATE REINCARNATION METAPHOR

You are then thrown off the bridge of pain, into a swift river that carries you to your next life.

REINCARNATION

After you drink the elixir of oblivion, the tenth king will turn the wheel of transmigration, which you climb to your next life. Your new life could be one of several options, some more appealing than others:

ELIXIR OF OBLIVION

WHEEL OF TRANSMIGRATION

shown actual size

TRANSMIGRATION OPTIONS

GOOD
• A god
• Human being on earth
• Human being in hell
• Hungry ghost [2]
BAD
• Animal

2. HUNGRY GHOST

A ghost that eats the emotions of the living.

ENJOY YOUR NEW LIFE!

Ancient Egyptian (Middle Kingdom or later)

During the Old Kingdom, it was believed that only pharaohs had an afterlife; commoners just died.

Every person has 2 souls

1 → **KA** — Your life force

2 → **BA** — Your unique personality

Was your body mummified?

— NO → **Every night your ba returns to the body to gain new life. If your body isn't preserved, your ba can't do this.**

— YES →

Is your ka given offerings of food?

— NO → **Just as your ka needed food during life to surivive, it needs to feed on the spiritual energy of food after life. Without food offerings it will die.**

CLIFF!

FIRE!

DEMONS!

DEAD END!

FIRE!

WELCOME TO THE UNDERWORLD!

But be careful, the underworld is treacherous, and you have to travel a long way to reach the Hall of Truths (the Hall of Maat).

FORK!

Were you buried with a copy of the Book of the Dead, a map that explains how to avoid the perils of the underworld?

NO → **It will be more difficult for you to make it through the underworld's many perils.**

YES →

PERIL!

Begin your long journey.

HELL

• Outer darkness. Primeval chaos.

• Demons will hack you up and roast your flesh.

• The god Shezmu will chop your head off and squeeze it like a grape to make blood wine that the gods drink.

— ALSO →

• You're forced to walk upside down.

• Forced to eat your own poop.

• Your shadow is stolen.

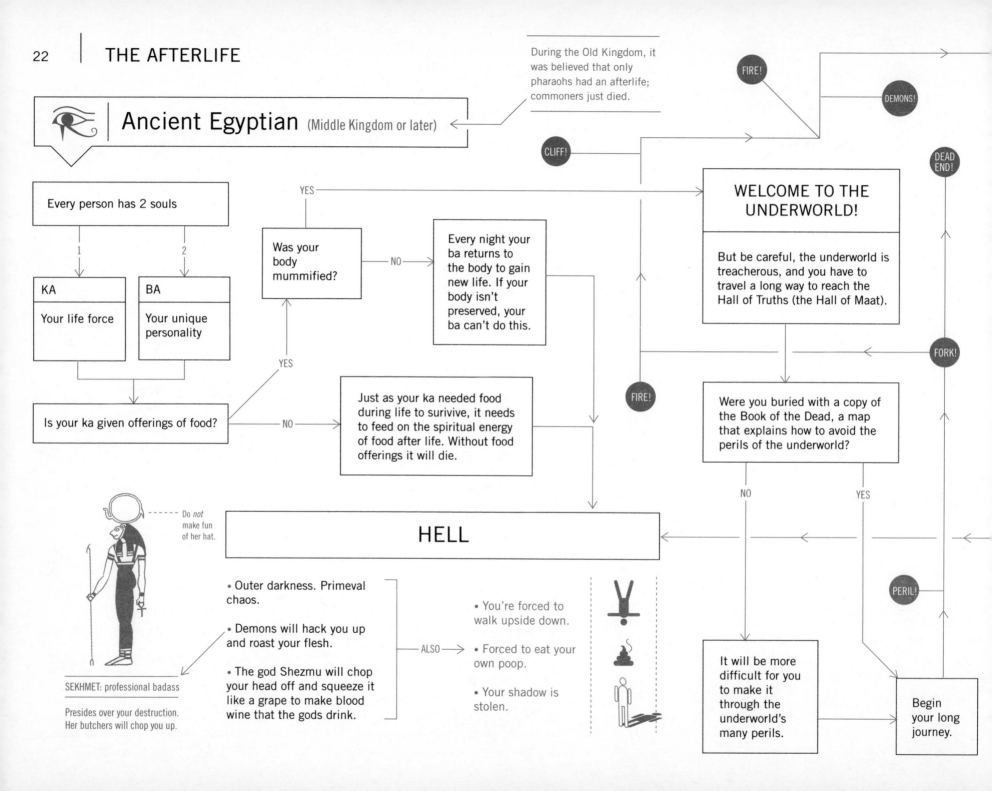

Do not make fun of her hat.

SEKHMET: professional badass

Presides over your destruction. Her butchers will chop you up.

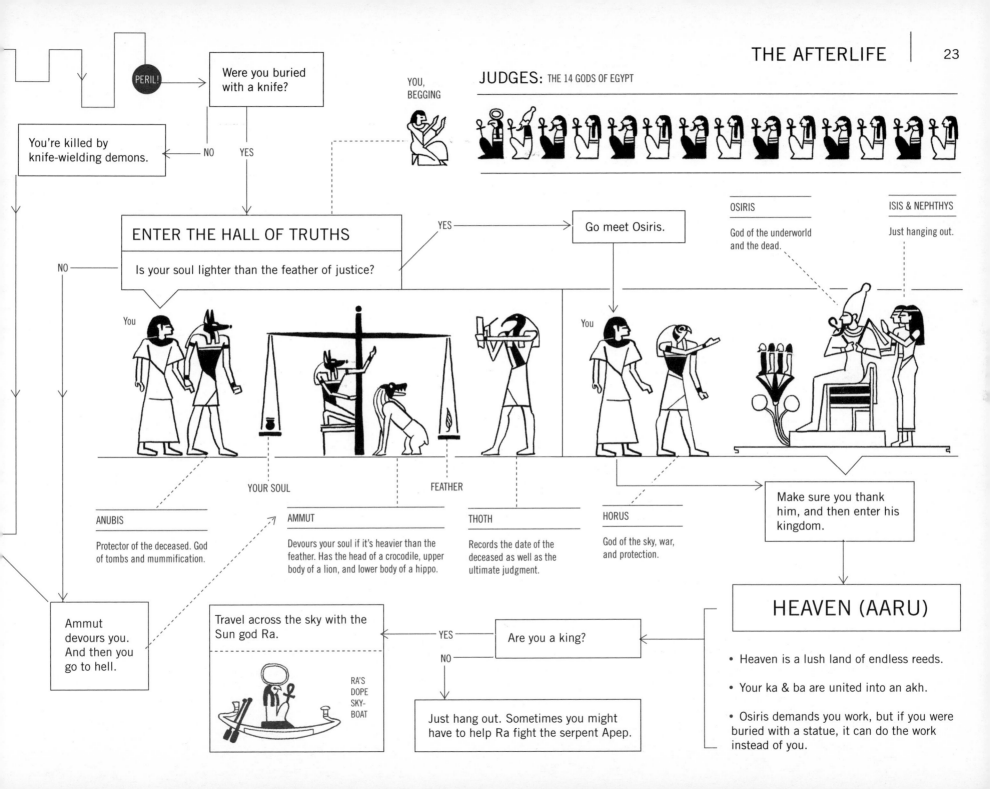

PERIL!

Were you buried with a knife?

You're killed by knife-wielding demons.

NO   YES

YOU, BEGGING

JUDGES: THE 14 GODS OF EGYPT

ENTER THE HALL OF TRUTHS

Is your soul lighter than the feather of justice?

YES → Go meet Osiris.

NO

OSIRIS

God of the underworld and the dead.

ISIS & NEPHTHYS

Just hanging out.

You

YOUR SOUL

FEATHER

You

Make sure you thank him, and then enter his kingdom.

ANUBIS

Protector of the deceased. God of tombs and mummification.

AMMUT

Devours your soul if it's heavier than the feather. Has the head of a crocodile, upper body of a lion, and lower body of a hippo.

THOTH

Records the date of the deceased as well as the ultimate judgment.

HORUS

God of the sky, war, and protection.

Ammut devours you. And then you go to hell.

Travel across the sky with the Sun god Ra.

RA'S DOPE SKY-BOAT

YES ← Are you a king? ←

NO

Just hang out. Sometimes you might have to help Ra fight the serpent Apep.

HEAVEN (AARU)

• Heaven is a lush land of endless reeds.

• Your ka & ba are united into an akh.

• Osiris demands you work, but if you were buried with a statue, it can do the work instead of you.

ALIEN SEX

INSIDE A TOP SECRET BUNKER in Area 51, The United States Air Force has photographs, documents, and forensic evidence which irrefutably prove that on July 9th, 1947, in Roswell, New Mexico, an unidentified flying aircraft crash-landed, and the alien astronauts inside (commonly referred to as "grays") liked to have sex using the extremely difficult Kneeling Pretzel position. At this point, nobody except the White House Press Secretary and Sagittariuses (the most skeptical of all the signs) still claim that the alien orgasm is a myth (and even *they* don't deny the existence of the Alien Orgasm alcoholic shot, which will seriously mess you up). *(See Drinks Only College Students Order, page 64).*

Earthlings' preoccupation with alien sex is embarrassingly evident after even a cursory examination of extraterrestrials in popular culture. *(See Figure 1: Top Three Alien Pornos.)* This is a little sad, because it offers compelling evidence that if humanity were given the opportunity to communicate with aliens, instead of asking them how to create renewable energy resources or end world famine, we'd ask what their turn-ons are. Luckily, their turn-ons are *fascinating*. Also, some bold young scientists are tinkering with the idea that alien orgasms—if their power could be harnessed—might one day be used as a renewable energy resource, and power hoverboards, moon colonies, and yes, even washing machines.

Although humans put undo emphasis on the sexual component of alien encounters, real-life extraterrestrials certainly aren't helping to dispel these stereotypes, since every time they show up on earth they're wearing skintight silver jumpsuits and anally probing hillbillies. To be fair, aliens aren't *always* trying to have sex with humans—sometimes they're trying to kill or enslave us. *(See Figure 2: What are Aliens Doing on Earth?)* But how can you tell if an alien encounter is going to end in death or an awkward intergalactic breakfast?

FIGURE 1: TOP THREE ALIEN PORNOS

1. ALIEN: A crew of spacemen get face-raped and impregnated by an alien whose head is shaped like a giant phallus, and whose blood is made of acidic sperm.

2. EARTH GIRLS ARE EASY: Aliens cross the galaxy to have sex with Geena Davis. The amorous invaders discover that Earth girls are indeed easy, assuming you look like Jeff Goldblum.

3. MEN IN BLACK: Will Smith and Tommy Lee Jones star in this sizzling summer blockbuster about secret agents who police alien activity on earth. If you want to see some real sizzling, check out the director's cut, which includes a scene where Jones has to suck the venom out of a poisonous alien bite on Smith's tongue.

Step 1: Visually match your alien with one of the extraterrestrials on the Alien Identification Chart. Step 2: Locate their corresponding number on the Alien Aggression and Hornyness Diagram to gauge the level of danger you're in and plan an appropriate response. *(See Figure 3.)*

FIGURE 3: ALIEN IDENTIFICATION / AGGRESSION AND HORNYNESS COMPARISON CHART

1. REPTILIAN	2. PURE ENERGY	3. COMMON GRAY	4. BORG	5. ? ? ?

FIGURE 2: WHAT ARE ALIENS DOING ON EARTH?

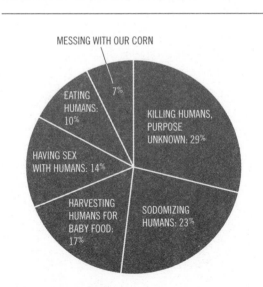

MESSING WITH OUR CORN: 7%

EATING HUMANS: 10%

KILLING HUMANS, PURPOSE UNKNOWN: 29%

HAVING SEX WITH HUMANS: 14%

HARVESTING HUMANS FOR BABY FOOD: 17%

SODOMIZING HUMANS: 23%

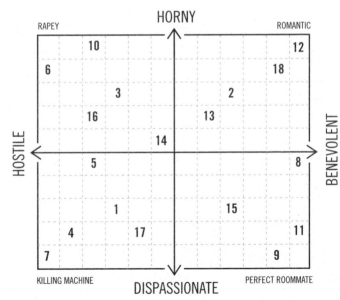

HORNY

RAPEY — ROMANTIC

HOSTILE ← → BENEVOLENT

KILLING MACHINE — PERFECT ROOMMATE

DISPASSIONATE

MORE ALIENS:

6. Xenomorphs (*Alien*)
7. the Predator
8. Antereans (*Cocoon*)
9. "Fix-Its" (*Batteries Not Included*)
10. Sil (*Species* alien)
11. E.T.
12. Starman (Jeff Bridges in *Starman*)
13. Alf
14. Jeriba Shigan (*Enemy Mine*)
15. Spock
16. Jabba the Hutt
17. V'ger (*Star Trek*)
18. Mork (*Mork and Mindy*)

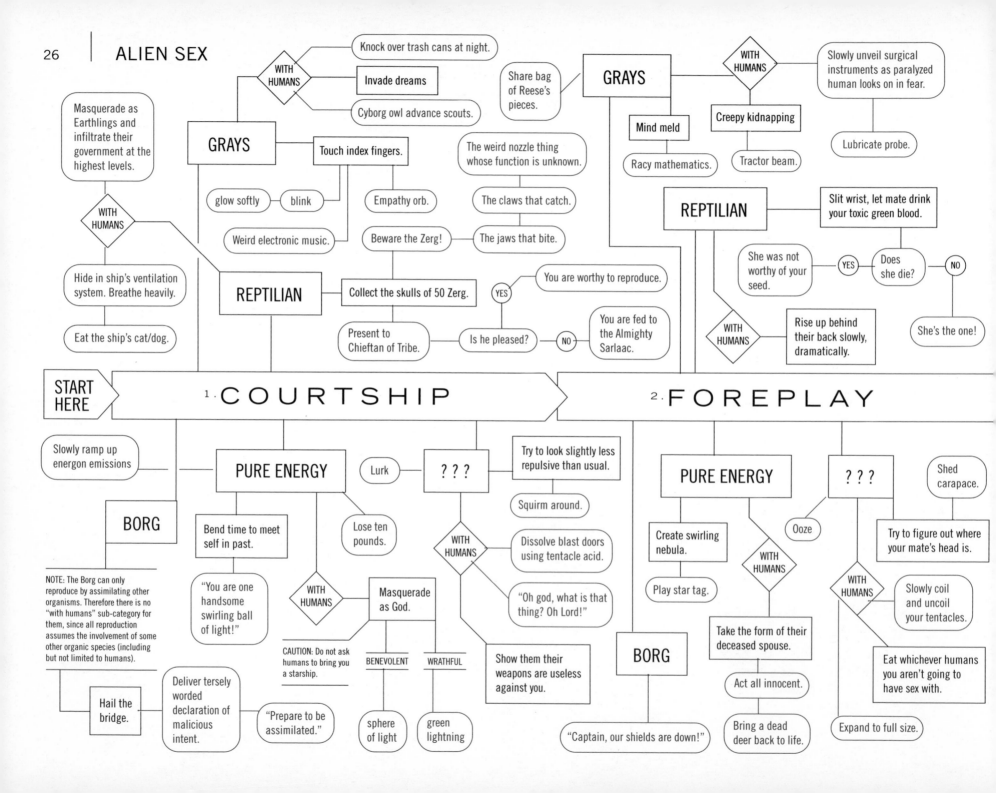

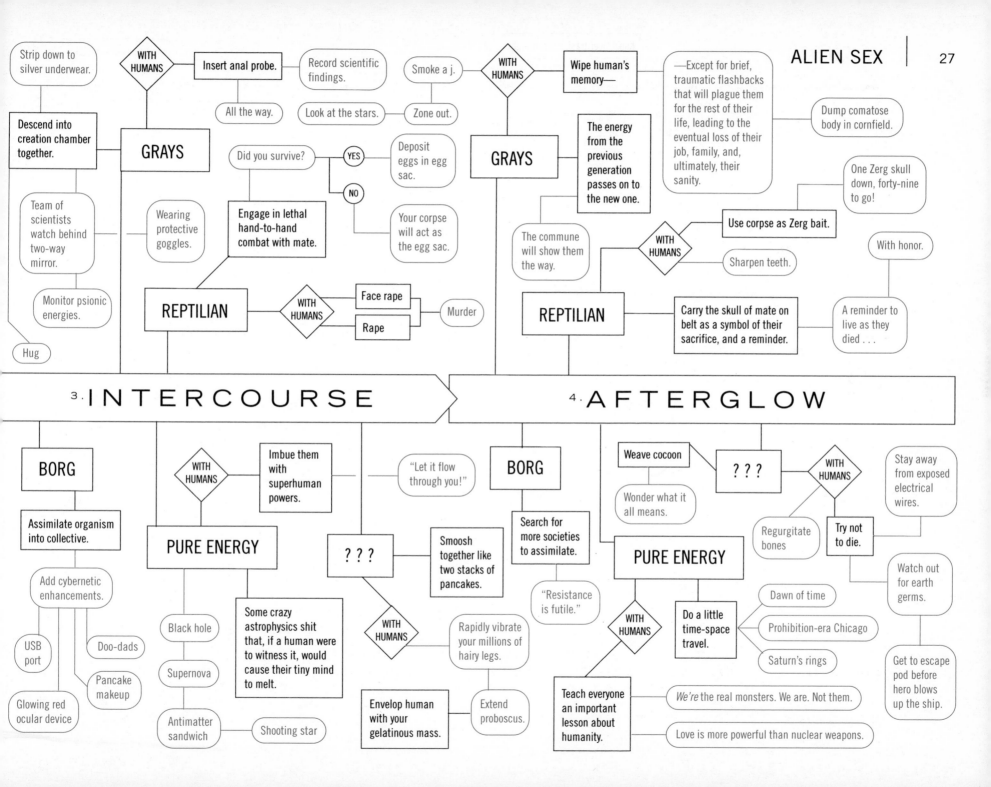

Strip down to silver underwear.

WITH HUMANS

Insert anal probe.

Record scientific findings.

All the way.

Descend into creation chamber together.

GRAYS

Smoke a j.

WITH HUMANS

Wipe human's memory—

—Except for brief, traumatic flashbacks that will plague them for the rest of their life, leading to the eventual loss of their job, family, and, ultimately, their sanity.

Look at the stars.

Zone out.

Dump comatose body in cornfield.

Team of scientists watch behind two-way mirror.

Did you survive?

YES

Deposit eggs in egg sac.

GRAYS

The energy from the previous generation passes on to the new one.

One Zerg skull down, forty-nine to go!

Wearing protective goggles.

NO

Monitor psionic energies.

Engage in lethal hand-to-hand combat with mate.

Your corpse will act as the egg sac.

The commune will show them the way.

Use corpse as Zerg bait.

With honor.

WITH HUMANS

Sharpen teeth.

Hug

REPTILIAN

WITH HUMANS

Face rape

Rape

Murder

REPTILIAN

Carry the skull of mate on belt as a symbol of their sacrifice, and a reminder.

A reminder to live as they died . . .

3. INTERCOURSE

4. AFTERGLOW

BORG

WITH HUMANS

Imbue them with superhuman powers.

"Let it flow through you!"

BORG

Weave cocoon

???

WITH HUMANS

Stay away from exposed electrical wires.

Assimilate organism into collective.

Wonder what it all means.

Regurgitate bones

Try not to die.

Add cybernetic enhancements.

PURE ENERGY

???

Smoosh together like two stacks of pancakes.

Search for more societies to assimilate.

PURE ENERGY

Watch out for earth germs.

USB port

Doo-dads

Black hole

Some crazy astrophysics shit that, if a human were to witness it, would cause their tiny mind to melt.

"Resistance is futile."

Do a little time-space travel.

Dawn of time

Prohibition-era Chicago

Glowing red ocular device

Pancake makeup

Supernova

WITH HUMANS

Rapidly vibrate your millions of hairy legs.

WITH HUMANS

Saturn's rings

Get to escape pod before hero blows up the ship.

Antimatter sandwich

Shooting star

Envelop human with your gelatinous mass.

Extend proboscis.

Teach everyone an important lesson about humanity.

We're the real monsters. We are. Not them.

Love is more powerful than nuclear weapons.

THE AMERICAN DREAM

I THINK IT'S WORTH NOTING that our national ethos is not called the American Realistic Expectation. As far as government-sponsored propaganda goes, the American Dream's name is astonishingly frank; it clearly advertises itself as a false hope, a long shot, a delusion. But even if it had been named the American Lie, the myth would've proven just as effective at motivating poor Americans to work hard, because the American Dream is the kind of beautiful lie that everyone wants to believe.

Just in case this book's pages are your toilet paper in a North Korean prison, or you found it buried in a bunker in some Brave New World version of the United States a hundred years hence, let me explain: The American Dream (which I will capitalize, like the name of God, throughout this essay) is the promise of prosperity for anyone—regardless of their social, economic, or racial status—provided they're willing to work hard. *(See Figure 1: Recurring American Dreams and*

Their Meanings) The genesis of the American Dream can be found in the second sentence in the Declaration of Independence:

We hold these Truths to be self-evident, that all Men are created equal, that they are endowed by their Creator with certain unalienable Rights, that among these are Life, Liberty and the pursuit of Happiness.

It's significant what the founding fathers did not mention in that famous sentence; they did not mention anything about the pursuit of possessions. Yet the American Dream and its promise of equality and freedom quickly became confused with the pursuit of wealth and possessions. Replacing happiness with money as a central pillar of the American Dream wasn't a malicious decision; it wasn't even a conscious *decision*. It was simply a result of the natural association between wealth and success, coupled with the

FIGURE 1: RECURRING AMERICAN DREAMS AND THEIR MEANINGS

- **AMERICA** is eating brunch with a bulldog and an Italian Greyhound. They're eating crepes, when suddenly all of America's teeth start to fall out.
  MEANING: America is self-conscious about the dollar's declining value compared to the Euro.

- **AMERICA** is lost at the zoo. A man in a black dress, his face obscured by shadows, asks America if it would like an ice cream cone. America takes the cone, but realizes it's covered in ants.
  MEANING: America doesn't know whether it should commit more troops to the war in Afghanistan.

- **AMERICA** is falling, but wakes up right before it lands.
  MEANING: America is afraid it might be gay, because it secretly finds Canada's majestic forests attractive, but can't tell if Canada is a guy or a girl.

- **AMERICA** is in a nightclub, dancing to a song with a loud, pulsing techno beat.
  MEANING: America's alarm clock is going off.

- **AMERICA** pulls a coffee mug out of its kitchen cabinet and is shocked to find a cockroach inside it. America wakes up. The next day it opens its kitchen cabinet, pulls out a coffee mug, and finds a cockroach inside.
  MEANING: Nothing—just a coincidence.

unbridled capitalism that was so instrumental in our young country's growth and eventual ascension as a world power.

Whether or not the American Dream is as attainable as the average American believes, there's no denial that it has been an advantageous national ethos. Not only has it served as a unifying, nationalistic force, but it has motivated U.S. citizens to work hard, even without receiving immediate compensation. *(See Figure 2: How are We Motivating Our Workers?)*

The American Dream is premium grade fuel for Capitalism, the thrumming engine that runs our hot-rod country. Capitalism and the American Dream both promote competition by promising rewards to the most industrious person; indeed, the economic system and ethos have almost become interchangeable.

Although the American Dream is not a total fabrication, its central pursuit of materialism—rather than happiness—is a fatal flaw that will inevitably lead to its extinction as a realistic ideal. Because while happiness is an inexhaustible commodity, money is not. If everybody is rich, then nobody is rich; scarcity is what gives money its value. There is a finite amount of money that can be distributed in various proportions, and every year that money is distributed less equally, as it's aggregated in the hands of a wealthy few.

While the actual attainability of the American Dream has fluctuated wildly over the past century, our national perception of its accessibility has remained remarkably steady *(See Figure 3: Attainability of the American Dream: Perceived and Actual)*, and the hope will persist until the ever-widening chasm between the haves and have-nots grows too wide to be bridged by empty platitudes.

FIGURE 2: HOW ARE WE MOTIVATING OUR WORKERS?

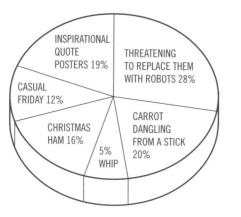

FIGURE 3: ATTAINABILITY OF THE AMERICAN DREAM: PERCEIVED AND ACTUAL

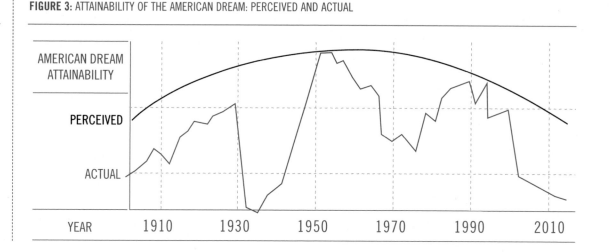

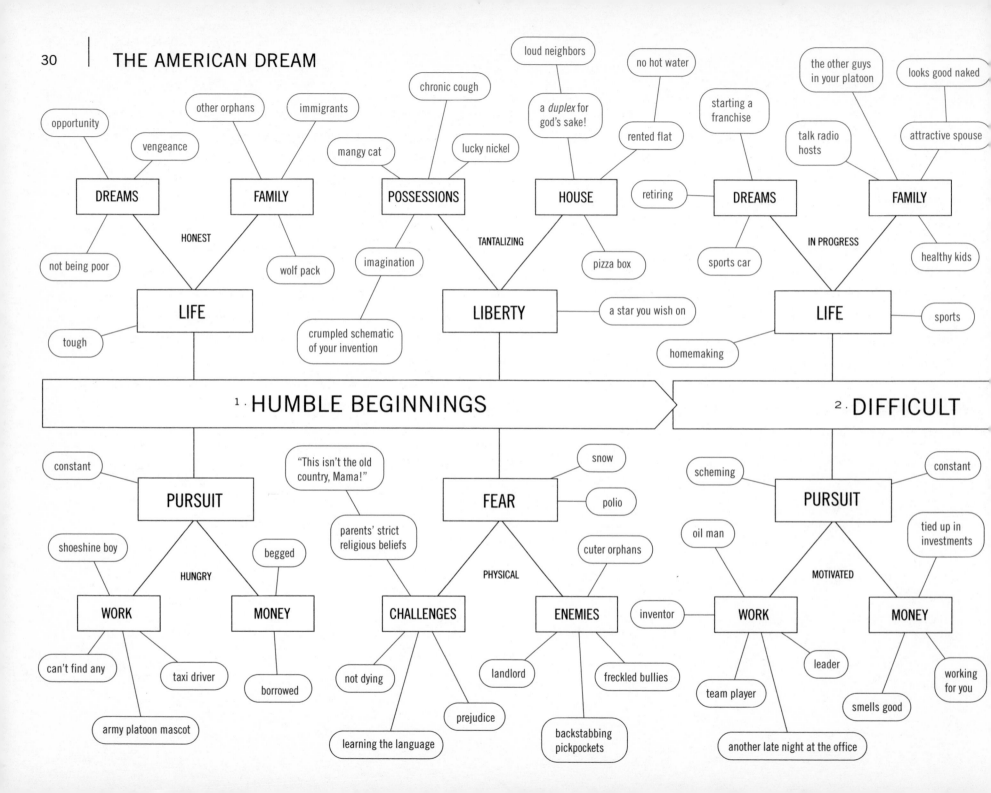

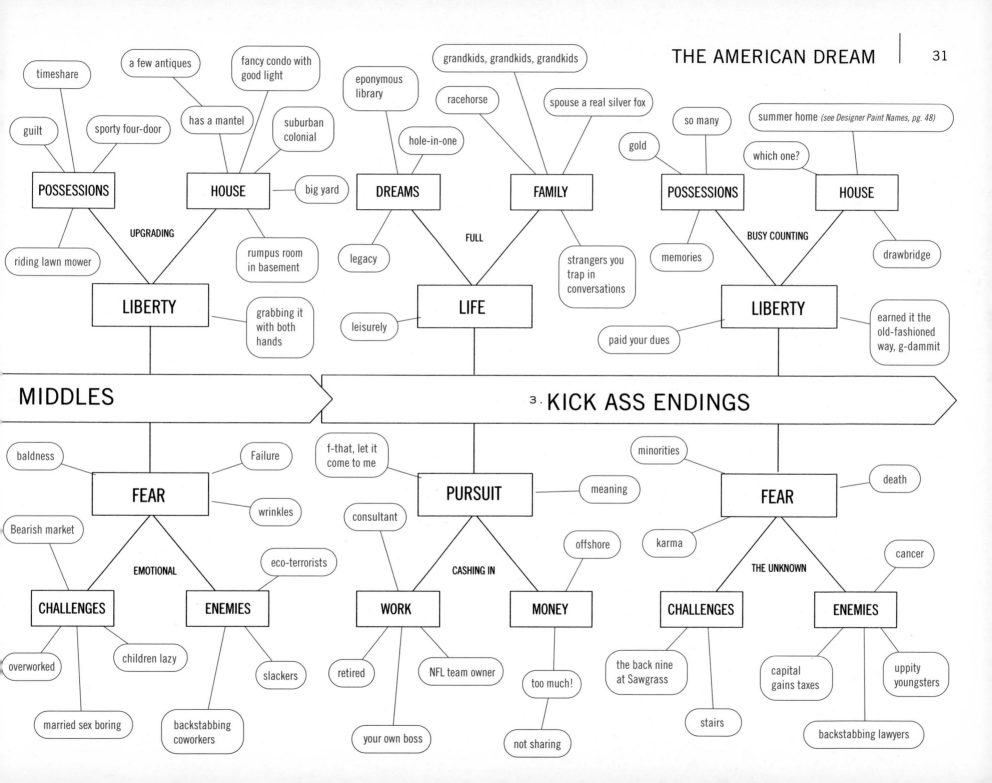

CHAIN RESTAURANTS

Maybe you've had this experience before: You're driving to Minnesota to buy a futon because you and your girlfriend broke up but still have to share the same apartment for the next six months, and she refuses to sleep in the same bed with you after what you did. You want to get a bite to eat, but you're driving through some provincial burg that doesn't have a McDonald's or any other fast food that you recognize. It's dark and raining. You haven't eaten anything since post pre-dinner (also known as dunch), almost two hours ago. You can feel your blood sugar dropping—the steering wheel swerves in your suddenly weak fingers, your eyes can't focus; the road doubles and trebles through your rain-streaked windshield. Is this how you'll die? For a futon? The old gypsy's warning suddenly makes sense. Then, a neon sign swims out of the darkness: Hamburgers. Uncle Jonnie's Hamburgers.

The inside of the hamburger joint is like a hall of mirrors. The employee isn't wearing a uniform, the decor is strange and unique, and the atmosphere is unsettlingly one-of-a-kind. You look at the menu, which might as well be written in Arabic. You ask if they have chicken McNuggets—they have chicken fingers. You ask if you can get a number two—their menu isn't numbered. You ask if they have Big Macs—they have Uncle J's Double Love Burger with Rattlesnake Sauce. You ask to speak to the manager, and instead of rolling his eyes at you, the cashier says, "I'm Uncle Jonnie. What can I do for you?" Falling to the floor, you curl up into a ball and repeat over and over, "I'm lovin' it, I'm lovin' it, I'm lovin' it . . ." but the teleportation spell doesn't work.

If the unknown is the only thing you fear more than being thin, then you probably don't care that chain restaurants contribute to the homogenization of America, the steady decline of hourly wages, the rising obesity epidemic, and whatever other crazy stuff Upton Sinclair says from beyond the grave. (*See Figure 1: Deadly Fast Food and its Equivalent Health Effects.*) But whether you like chain restaurants or not, you still eat at them, because if you're not at home and need to eat, you basically have no other choice except for windfall apples and lichen.

Although the defining characteristics of chain restaurants—a group of separate restaurants rendered identical by a coldly calculating, controlling hive mind like the Borg—are identical for both fast food and casual dining, consumer perception of the two groups diverges drastically.

Fast food at its worst is viewed as a necessary evil, and at its best a guilty pleasure—a mercenary industry we grudgingly support in the interest of convenience and economy.

The categories on the fast food side of the Chain Restaurants chart reflect the contemptuous way most consumers view fast food: here's the Mexican place; here's the place I eat when I only

FIGURE 1: DEADLY FAST FOOD AND ITS EQUIVALENT HEALTH EFFECTS

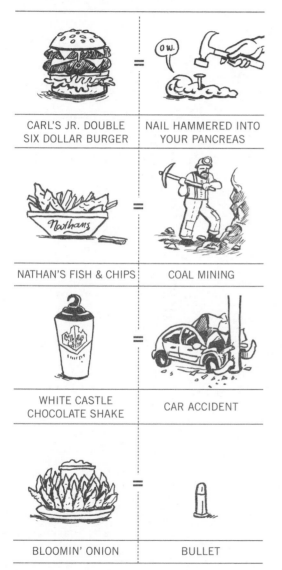

CARL'S JR. DOUBLE SIX DOLLAR BURGER	NAIL HAMMERED INTO YOUR PANCREAS
NATHAN'S FISH & CHIPS	COAL MINING
WHITE CASTLE CHOCOLATE SHAKE	CAR ACCIDENT
BLOOMIN' ONION	BULLET

have a dollar; here's the place I only eat at because I don't want to get off the turnpike.

Casual dining, on the other hand, occupies a more personal position in our lives, almost like family. While fast food is a necessity, like cleaning your ears or mowing the lawn, casual dining is a luxury—albeit a small one—like taking a bubble bath or masturbating at work. Casual dining is there for all the most important parts of lives, reflected in the three major categories: work, play, and love. You just got a promotion? Time for Margaritas at Chili's. The bar closed and you want waffles? Time for a triple stack at IHOP. You need to trick someone into thinking you're interesting and attractive? It's time for the Melting Pot.

Like a lover, casual dining often lies, but always for our benefit; they're white lies, intended to lift us from the dreariness of everyday reality. "Oh my god, look, we're in the Old West!" or "I'm your server and although we've never met, I'm super happy to see you! Here's a song I wrote about it!" Unlike a lover, casual dining will never say the hurtful lies that are sometimes spat in the heat of an argument. "I never really loved you," "I've had

better," or "Your charts are stupid, especially the one about salad dressing." *(See page 114.)*

Casual dining may lie, but it's a warm quilt of deceit, knitted to make us feel better and take all our money. Oh, wait, I forgot about that—chain restaurants are only nice to you because they want your money. So I suppose the whole "lover" metaphor doesn't work. I guess chain restaurants are really more like a hooker. Regardless, they're not a hooker that will make you drive to Minnesota to buy a futon. See how I tied the essay together at the end? It's just like *Finnegan's Wake!* [1]

----

(1) Can we speak frankly about James Joyce for a second? First swear you're not a secret member of the Literatti. Okay: Let me begin by saying that I love *Dubliners*, it's one of my favorite books—right up there with *I, the Jury* and *the Celery Stalks at Midnight*. *Ulysess* makes no sense but is still really cool. But does anyone else suspect *Finnegan's Wake* might just be an elaborate prank? Has anyone read that book and enjoyed it? Has anyone even simply read it? Did James Joyce ever read it? Probably not. Of course, he'd probably claim he couldn't read it because of he was almost blind by the time it was completed. *A likely excuse!*

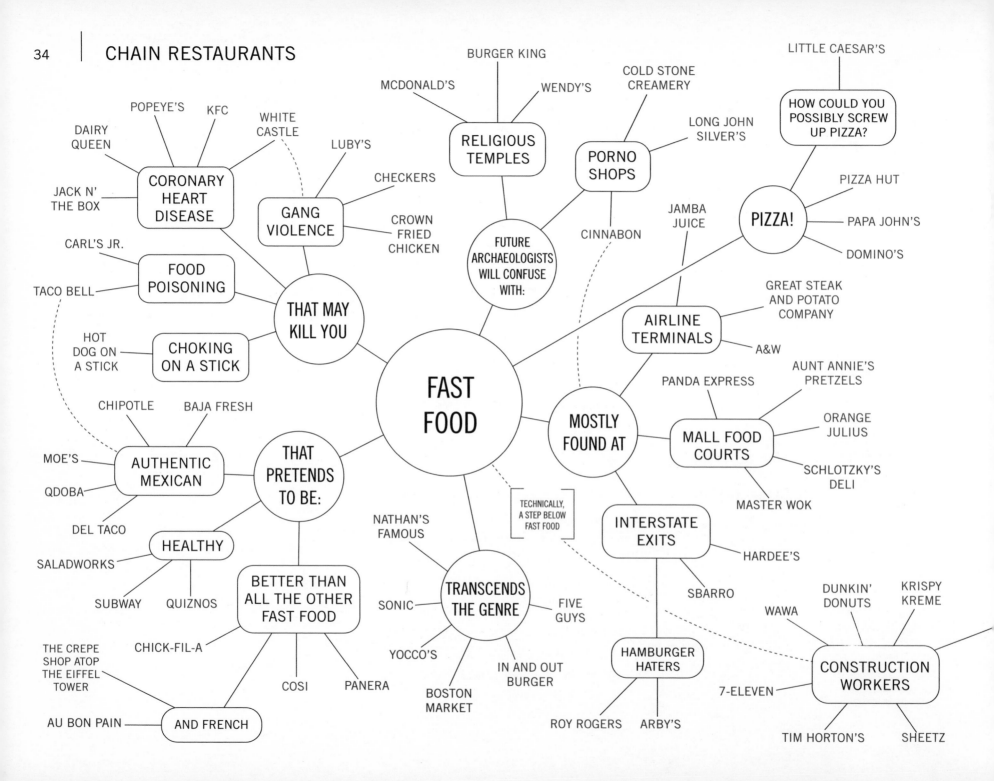

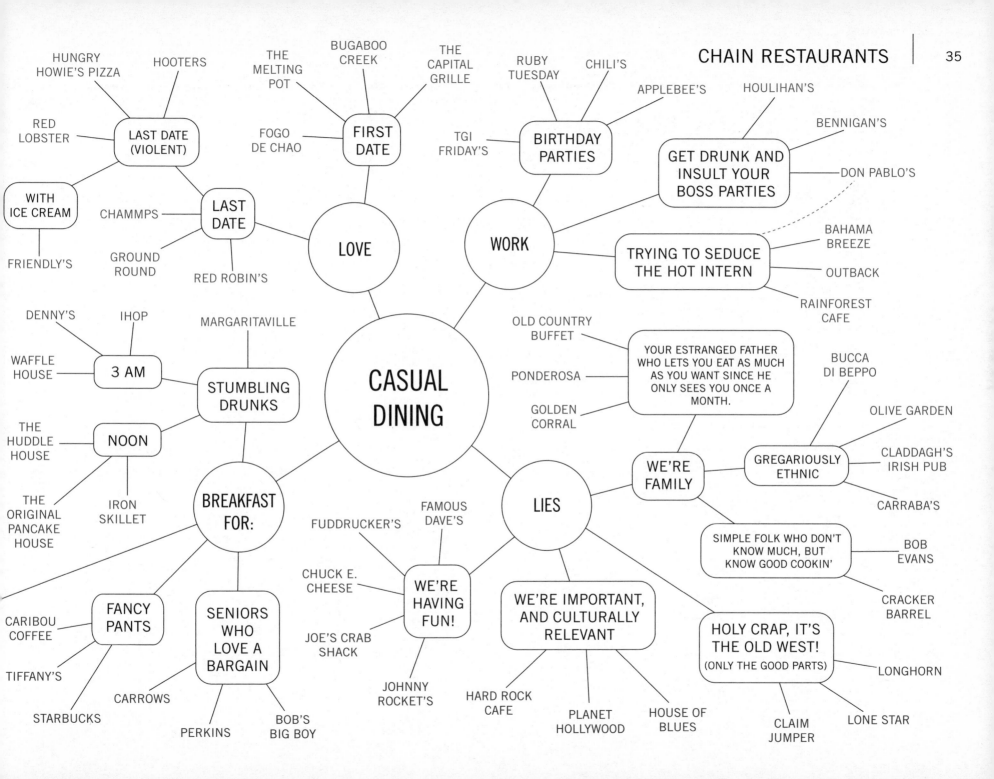

COLLEGE MAJORS

COLLEGE IS AN EXCITING TIME. There are no parents to tell you what to do, your future seems ripe with potential, and everything in your dorm room can be turned into a bong. *(See Figure 1: Improvised Bongs.)* It's easy to get distracted from the real purpose of college: creating a solid foundation for a career[1]. When graduates step

---

(1) Some people think knowledge has its own rewards that aren't reflected in dollar signs. These people are dangerous lunatics.

---

outside the protective campus grounds, they are like baby birds pushed from the nest for the first time: some of them will find their wings too wet, and plummet to their death; others will soar away and become vice-presidential district distribution managers. Before that harrowing moment of truth, one crucial question looms over entering freshmen, the answer to which will decide whether they ultimately fly or fall: what subject should they major in?

Should students major in a subject they love, or one that will lead to a lucrative career? The College Majors chart reflects this crucial quandary, and is therefore split into two major categories: useful and useless. In this capacity, usefulness is not defined by personal edification, or median salary of graduates. Usefulness refers to the likelihood of graduates obtaining a job in their field of study. *(See Figure 2: Match the College Major to the Job it Will Most Likely Lead to.)*

There are simply far more entry-level openings for salesmen than there are for philosophers . . . unless you can snag a job as a philosophy professor. This is the lone caveat for every single useless major: Like a smack addict selling drugs to support their habit, graduates can support themselves by teaching their same unmarketable skills to naive young people, with the bonus of having their summers free to add another hundred pages to that great novel they're still working on[2].

FIGURE 1: IMPROVISED BONGS

| PINEAPPLE + CARROT | DILDO | YODA FIGURINE | DRAGON + ESPRESSO MAKER + SNOW GLOBE + CLARINET |

FIGURE 2: MATCH THE COLLEGE MAJOR WITH THE JOB IT WILL MOST LIKELY LEAD TO

1. Marketing
2. Art Appreciation
3. Accounting
4. Painting
5. Data Processing
6. Philosophy

A. Coffee Barista
B. Marketing Manager
C. Part-time Barista
D. Data Processing Analyst
E. Senior Coffee Barista
F. Accountant

ANSWERS: 1,B / 2,A / 3,F / 4,E / 5,D / 6,C

The useful/useless duality extends throughout the secondary categories of the College Majors chart as well: fun and boring, altruistic and evil, easy and difficult. I know what you're thinking, "Well, I'll just pick a major on the useful side, under the fun category." Here's the catch: Fun is on the useless side! In fact, a major's usefulness quotient is in inverse proportion to how fun it is. *(See Figure 3:*

(2) The great novel I'm working on is about a blind Ukrainian groundskeeper who battles poison sumack and anti-Ukrainian racism in antebellum Mississippi. He also has a beautiful daughter who swims nude in the bayous at night. You can email my agent at gnarlyagent557@yahoo.com if you want to discuss publication. (Serious offers only, please.)

Fun and Usefulness Relationship for College Majors.) Almost all of the enticing sub-categories lay on the useless side. Herein lies the Catch-22 (English majors?), the cosmic joke of the College Majors chart—all majors have some drawback.

Want to major in a field that will lead to a lot of money? Your major will either be very difficult, or evil. Want to have fun and enjoy college? Your major will be useless. Want to get laid? Actually, if that's all you want, there are a couple majors that can accomplish that.

Yes, every college major has its drawbacks, and will probably lead to a job you'll hate. Ten years after graduation, sitting at a tiny desk in your gray cube while a superior belittles you in front of your spineless coworkers, you'll stare at the meaningless ones and zeros that fill your computer screen and think back to your halcyon college days: the parties, the pizza-fueled all-nighters, and the certain knowledge that you were destined for great things. You'll stand up and point your finger in your shocked boss's face and say, "I don't have to take this crap. I'm going back to college—for marine biology. I'm going to live on a boat, let

the sun bleach my hair blonde, and play with dolphins all day[3]." Perhaps the closest you'll get to your dream job will be cleaning tanks at Sea World, but you're guaranteed four great years until then.

FIGURE 3: FUN AND USEFULNESS RELATIONSHIP FOR COLLEGE MAJORS

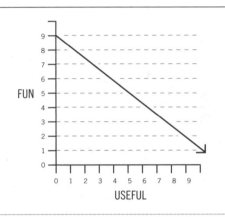

(3) LEARN TO SPEAK DOLPHIN

- I'm allergic to seaweed
  UUuukk EE-ee-EEEEeee-E (click, click)

- Although from the above-world, I still love your daughter!
  UUueeeeeEEEEEeeeeuuueeEEE

- The throne is not yours to take, Balfwain the slick!
  EEUuukkk Eeek Eeeek Uee, (click!)

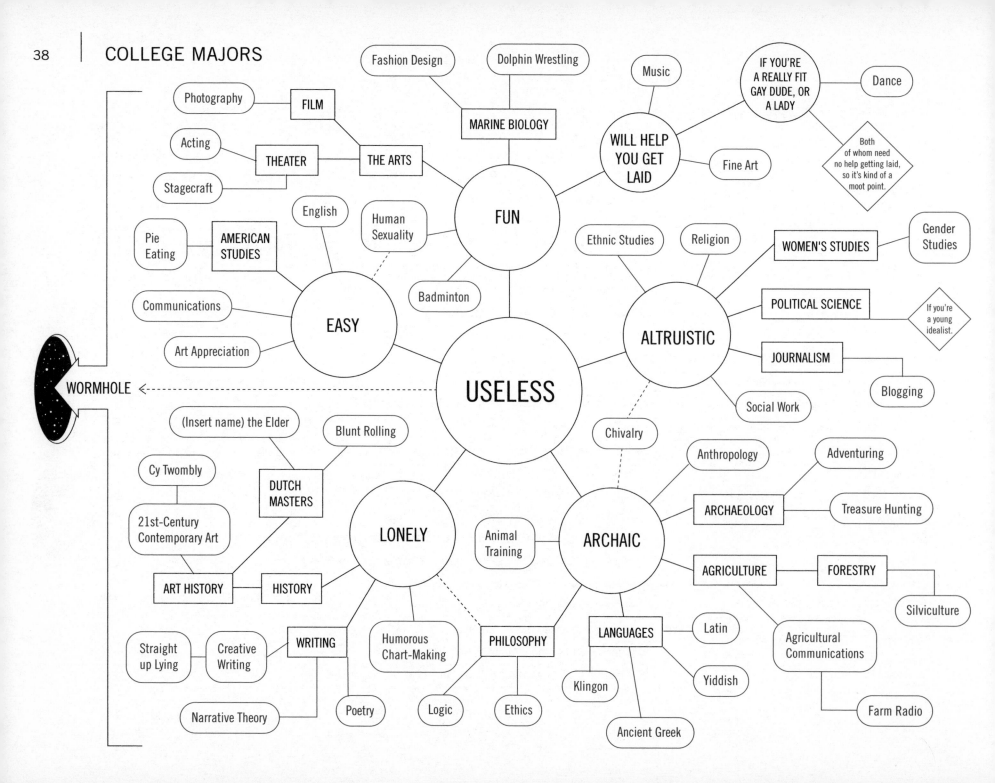

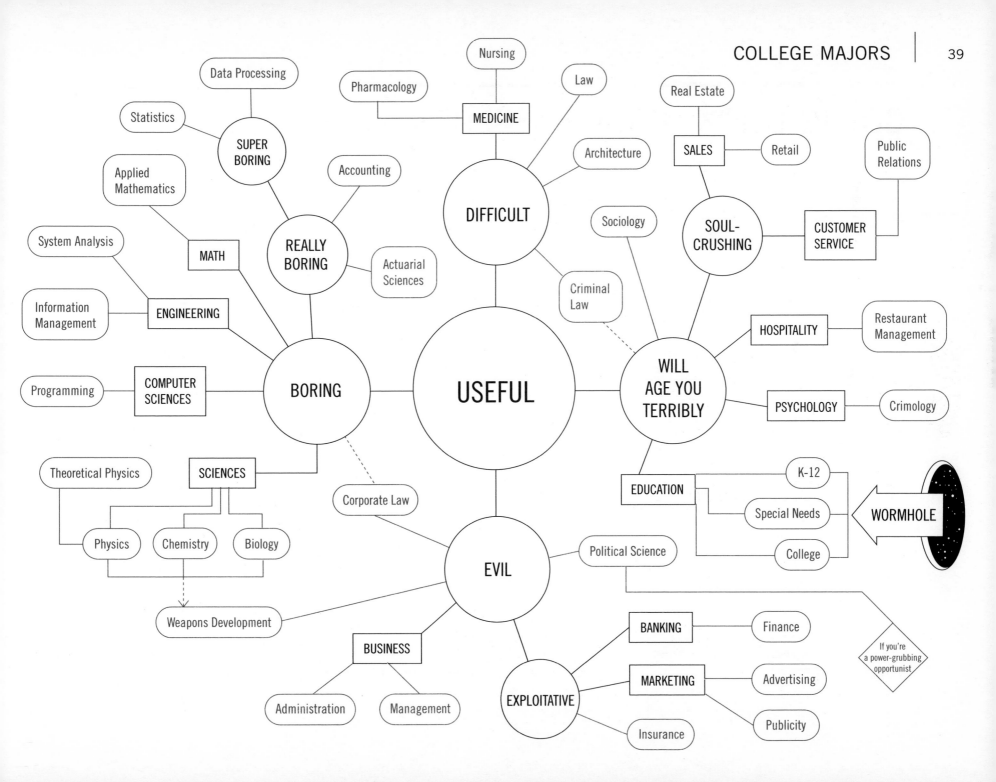

COMIC BOOK SOUND EFFECTS

COMIC BOOK SOUND EFFECTS—the floating words that accompany actions to simulate sound—are an elegant solution to the medium's technological limitations. Simple stacks of glossy paper held together with staples, comics have no video component, and must instead substitute small, primitive drawings in the place of high definition widescreen. They also, incredibly, lack an audio component—a feature even the lowly gramophone has—and must instead communicate the sound of Captain America's shield punching through an F-16's cockpit glass using large, cartoonishly distorted letters[1].

Comic book sound effects are a microcosm of the comic book medium as a whole. They are both a reaction to the medium's limitations and a celebration of its unique strengths. Like all microcosms, comic book sound effects reward

----

(1) A totally badass scene from Mark Millar's excellent comic mini-series *Civil War*.

scrutiny by providing insight into a related medium—in this case comics as a whole—that is otherwise too large to easily view.

Comic book sound effects make the actions they describe simultaneously more realistic—by simulating sound—and less realistic—because in the real world giant letters don't appear in the air when you do stuff. Comic books share a similar duality: they depict superpowers and massive battles that could never happen in the real world, but use these unrealistic scenarios to convey real human emotions with an intensity that wouldn't be possible using logical storylines. Bruce Wayne's grief over the death of his parents is given physical form in his crusade against crime, and we can feels its weight and darkness more palpably than if he behaved in a realistic way and just moped around his mansion drinking too much wine.

This concurrent increasing and decreasing of

reality has another effect when sound effects describe violence such as fighting, impact, or explosions. The increased reality makes the action more exciting, while the decreased reality makes the violence depicted more palatable by decreasing our empathy.

Some modern comics, in an attempt to be more realistic, have abandoned action sound effects. In addition to increasing the comic's verisimilitude, it also causes a higher degree of empathy with the characters. The reader imagines more realistic sounds, and all of sudden they're no longer watching a sterile, heroic ballet, they're watching a real person beating another real person to the brink of death with his fists.

When someone gets punched in the face in the real world, we don't hear the sound *BAM!* Instead we hear the sickening smack of bone against meat (*SMECK*) and the stifled cries of pain (*UGH! UHHHH*). Comic book sound effects insulate this violence while simultaneously amplifying it in a perfect manner to make the violence more palatable.

Alan Moore's seminal comic *Watchmen* doesn't have any action sound effects. In addition he places an unusual emphasis on human sounds that aren't dialogue: the distinctive *HURM* that Rorschach punctuates his speech with, the *NG NG NG* as the Comedian drains a bottle of whiskey, the *HUH HUH HUH* of two people having sex. Unlike action sound effects, these verbal sound effects add realism and emotional weight to the story. When the Comedian tries to rape Sally Jupiter, we're forced to read every *GUHH* and *GHUUCHH* she utters as he assaults her. It's an uncomfortable scene, and the violence is presented without the dampening benefits of any cartoonish *BIFFs* or *BOPs*. *(See Figure 1: Impact of Sound Effects on Violence Perception in Comics.)*

A testament to the flawless design of comic book sound effects is that even though they have no direct correlation in real life or other art forms, within the confines of the comic book page, they

seem completely normal. They're like a highly evolved, highly specialized animal that is completely at home in its own environment, but buffoonishly awkward in any other environment. Consider the penguin: It's a bird who can't fly, and who can barely even walk, but it can survive in one of the harshest environments on the planet. Your little toe is also similar: In the natural environment of your foot, surrounded by the other toes, it looks fine. But separate it from the others and place it out of context—hidden in the pages of a book, or perched on top of a sundae like a maraschino cherry—and you can suddenly see how ugly and odd the little bugger is. This demonstrates why comic book sound effects look silly in books and movies, and are so arresting when

viewed in an unexpected context, such as the fine art paintings of Roy Lichtenstein.

I don't want to give the impression that I think comics without action sound effects are superior to those with; both options should be available. Comics should not be forced to reside in the real world where every punch breaks the hero's knuckles, or every battle ends with the heart-wrenching sobs of victims' families. Comic books are a vital tool to help us safely explore our own conflicted feelings about conflict and violence, and if some training wheels are necessary to help us navigate that difficult road, so be it.

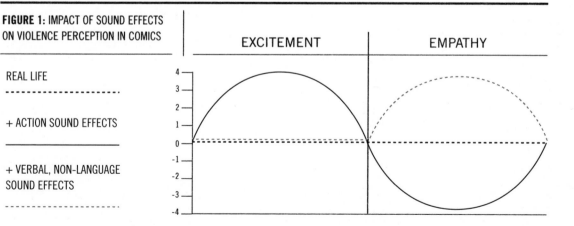

FIGURE 1: IMPACT OF SOUND EFFECTS ON VIOLENCE PERCEPTION IN COMICS

REAL LIFE

+ ACTION SOUND EFFECTS

+ VERBAL, NON-LANGUAGE SOUND EFFECTS

EXCITEMENT   EMPATHY

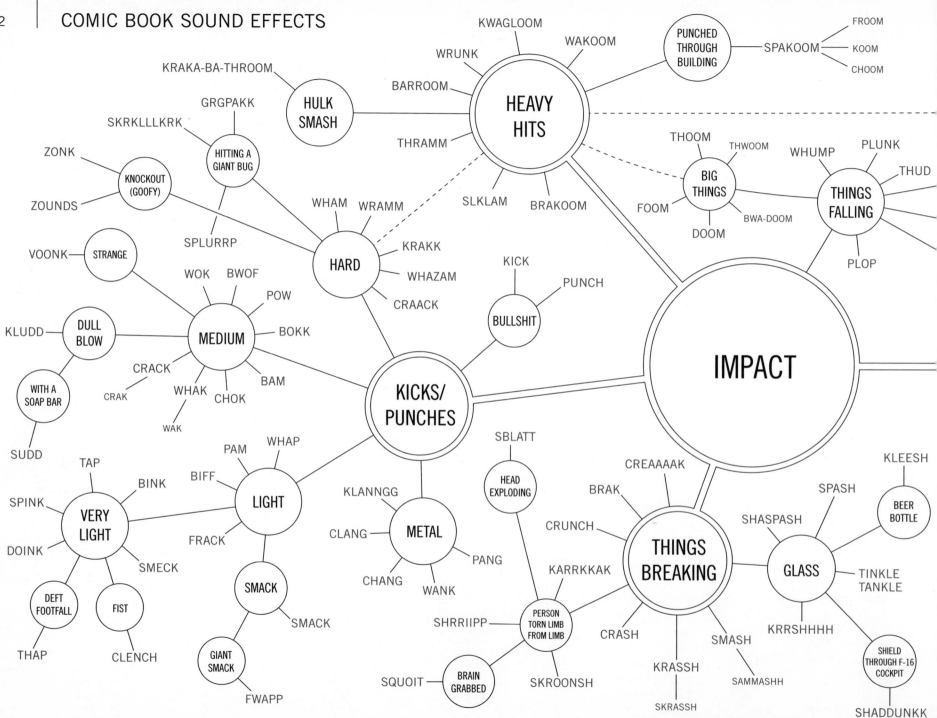

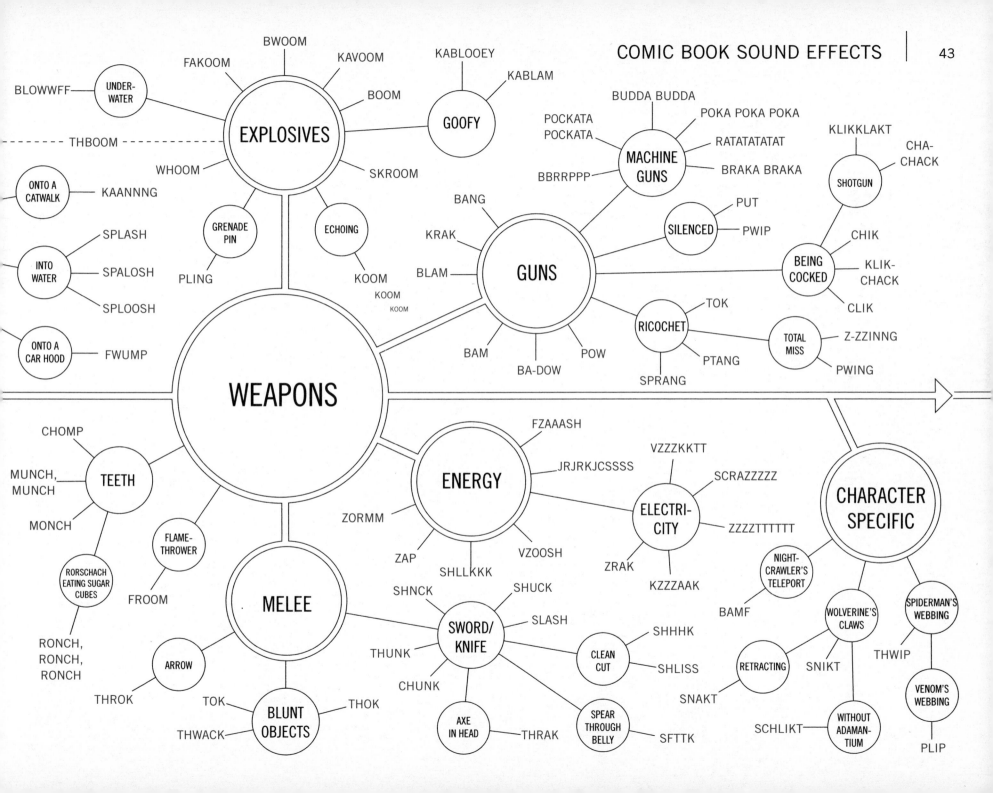

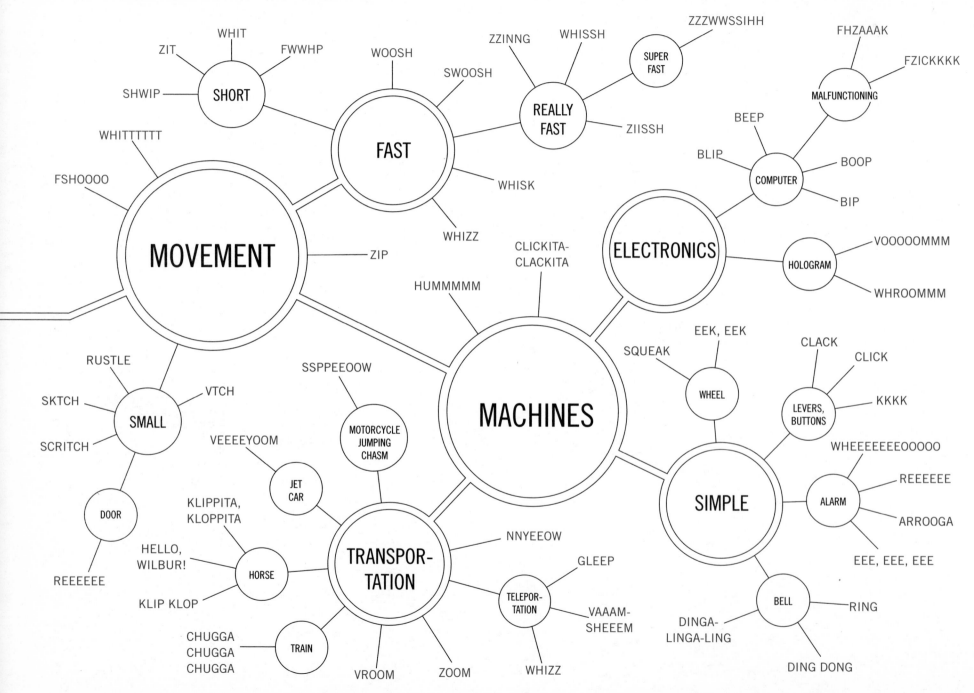

(continued from Comic Book Sound Effects, page 44)

SOUND EFFECTS FOR THE COMMON MAN

The majority of the onomatopoeia on the Comic Book Sound Effects chart *(see page 42)* are impractical for the average person to employ. Sure, *BRAKA BRAKA BRAKA!* is a great sound effect, but how often do you shoot a tommy gun? Not often enough! *POW*, *KRAKA-THOOM*, and *ZOUNDS!* are exciting but ultimately useless sounds in the lives of average, middle-class Americans—especially since at this point the "middle-class" is just a myth perpetuated by the upper class to keep the worker drones docile.

Therefore, illustrated here are sound effects non-superheroes can use to add a little drama to their lives. Enjoy them, Joe and Jane Average!

HURF!	BOOKA DOOK!	DWAK DWAK	OOOOHHM
EATING TOO MUCH CHOCOLATE	CHECKING FACEBOOK	PAYING BILLS	STARING INTO SPACE
ZOOV!	MIAARM	RINGA-NONO	DORP DORP
WATCHING TV	STEALING MP3S	IGNORING STUDENT LOANS	DOUBTING
ERP DERP	CLICK CLOG CLICK CLOG CLICK CLOG CLICK CLOG	ARR ERR	HRRRRMMM
FRETTING	BLOGGING	COMPROMISING	OBSERVING PASSIVELY
PFFFTT	DOOPILY DEE!	TEH DEH TEH DEH TEH DEH DEH TEH	GLURP
SITTING	DAYDREAMING	MAKING AWKWARD SMALL TALK	SWALLOWING PRIDE

DESIGNER PAINT NAMES

THE POETS HAVE FINALLY TAKEN OVER! They said they would do it, and they did. Remember back in 1970 when the famous beat generation poet Allen Ginsberg declared war against the United States of America live on the *Dick Cavett Show*? *(See Figure 1: Important Announcements Made on the* Dick Cavett Show.*)* A lot of people didn't recognize it as a declaration of war because of its vague, poetic phrasing—Ginsberg's exact words were "Carl Solomon! I'm with you in Rockland." But the code-breakers in Washington quickly recognized it as a secret message, and within hours delivered the deciphered declaration to President Nixon, which read "Moloch whose eyes are a thousand blind windows! Moloch! Moloch!" At first this seemed like a code too, but it wasn't, it was just the poets being weird. However their intentions were clear: the poets had declared war.

At first the poets attempted to get one of their own candidates into the White House, but their dreams were quickly shattered when Hunter S. Thompson (not quite a poet, but close enough) was unable to even win the election for Sheriff of Pitkin County, Colorado. After this full-frontal assault failed, they realized they would have to seize the reigns of power using more insidious methods.

Now, forty years later, the poets have finally infiltrated almost every square inch of our government, and are even in control of the White House; silently, secretly, our democracy has become a poetocracy. *(See Figure 2: The Secret Flag of the Poets.)*

FIGURE 2: THE SECRET FLAG OF THE POETS

(If you can figure out the symbolism behind this image, please let me know.)

FIGURE 1: IMPORTANT MOMENTS ON THE *DICK CAVETT SHOW*

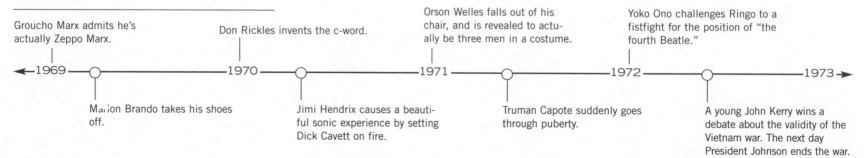

Groucho Marx admits he's actually Zeppo Marx.

Don Rickles invents the c-word.

Orson Welles falls out of his chair, and is revealed to actually be three men in a costume.

Yoko Ono challenges Ringo to a fistfight for the position of "the fourth Beatle."

←1969 — 1970 — 1971 — 1972 — 1973→

Marlon Brando takes his shoes off.

Jimi Hendrix causes a beautiful sonic experience by setting Dick Cavett on fire.

Truman Capote suddenly goes through puberty.

A young John Kerry wins a debate about the validity of the Vietnam war. The next day President Johnson ends the war.

How did the beatnik poets accomplish this bloodless revolution? (Dramatic pause.) *By planting their insidiously beautiful words inside paint names.* Forty years ago the oval office's walls were light tan with taupe accents; now they're sandy heather with approaching storm accents. The Cabinet Room used to be off-white; now it's Deauville. Just wait, in another ten years the White House will become the Bleached Linen House. The poets' replacement of non-poetic colors with their pleonastic pod people hues has allowed them to literally take control of every square inch of American housing, one remodeled living room at a time.

The hedonistic bohemians who started the Great Poetry War quickly discovered that they couldn't infiltrate the homes of average Americans without de-clawing their undomesticated poetry *(See Figure 3: Early Beat Poetry Paint Names.)* In order to subvert mainstream American culture, they had to first mimic it, in the same way that wild bears will dress like humans to get closer to picnic baskets. *(See Figure 4: Bear Disguises.)*

Designer paint names therefore use evocative language to tap into consumers' ideal domicile

FIGURE 3: EARLY BEAT POETRY PAINT NAMES

- Stunned Governments
- Endless Oil and Stone
- Angry fix
- Junky Yellow
- Hysterical Nudity Peach
- Peyote Solidities
- Ashcan Rantings
- Benzedrine Jitters
- Proletariat Pink
- Auburn in Gray
- Paradigm Subversion

- Freeland Limbo
- Crazy Young Negro Saxophone Player Who Wails and Wails like a Prince and the Sound explodes *Bang!* Like a Roman Candle and Everything is Beautiful and Alive and *Now*
- Factualist Bitch
- Black Meat

dreams. Yes, you may live in a dingy one-room apartment, but for the cost of a can of paint you can coat your walls in Crystal Chandelier, Amethyst Stone, or Shimmering Gold.

A lot of people, when they're looking to repaint a room, choose a color using the "eyeball method," where they will stare at various little swatches for hours upon hours, scrutinizing them under various lights, holding them against a couch, cocking their head and squinting. This method, while certainly appropriate in the pre-poetry days of paint names, is now as obsolete as the steam-powered cyborg. The best way to choose the

FIGURE 4: BEAR DISGUISES

PORKPIE HAT, TIE   CARPET

KILLER WHALE   LAMP

appropriate paint color is to use the Designer Paint Names chart on page 48. Begin by choosing your ideal domicile—Urban Loft, Country Cottage, Victorian Manor, or Island Bungalow—then follow the statements of personal philosophy that best match your own attitudes, and see what paint name they lead to.

DESIGNER PAINT NAMES

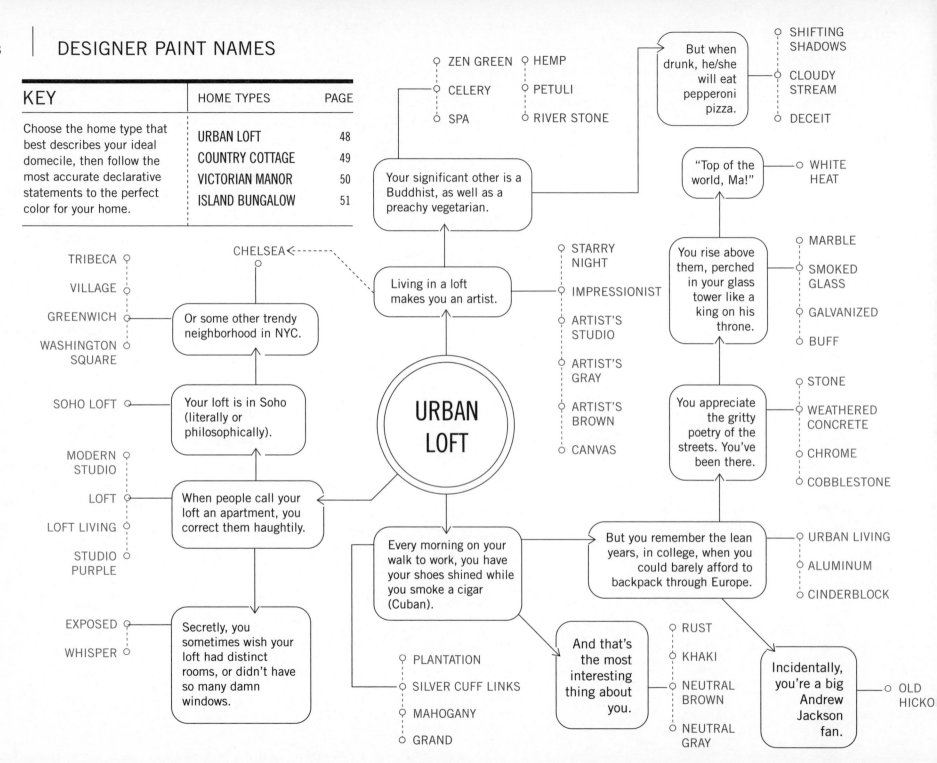

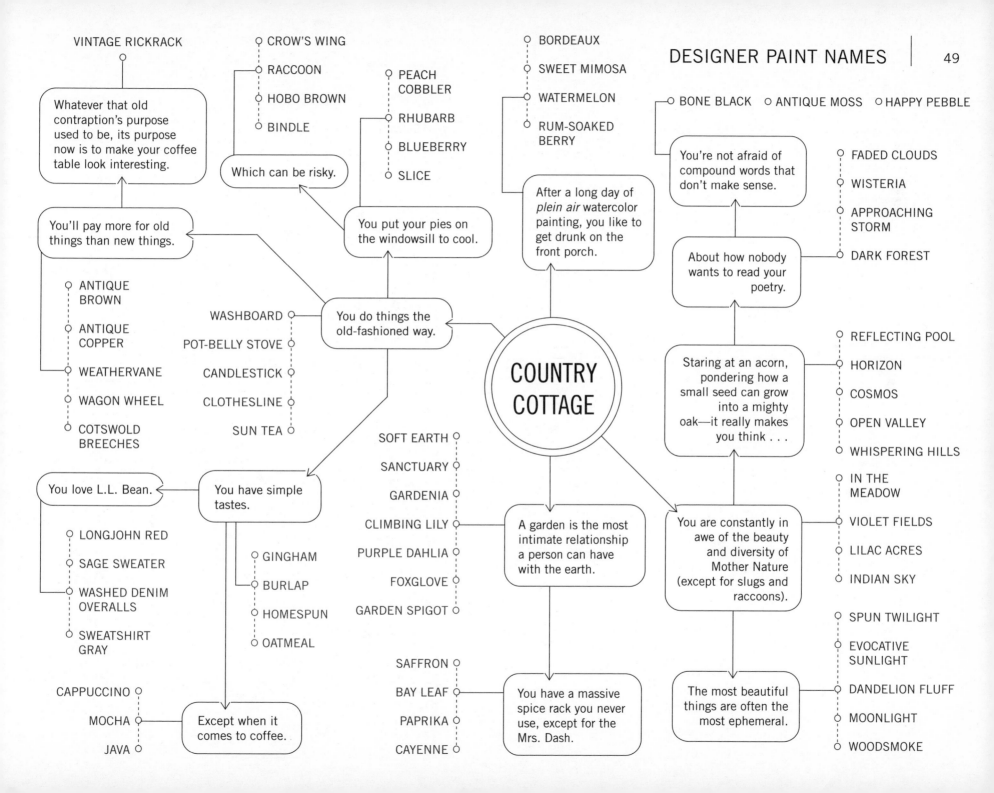

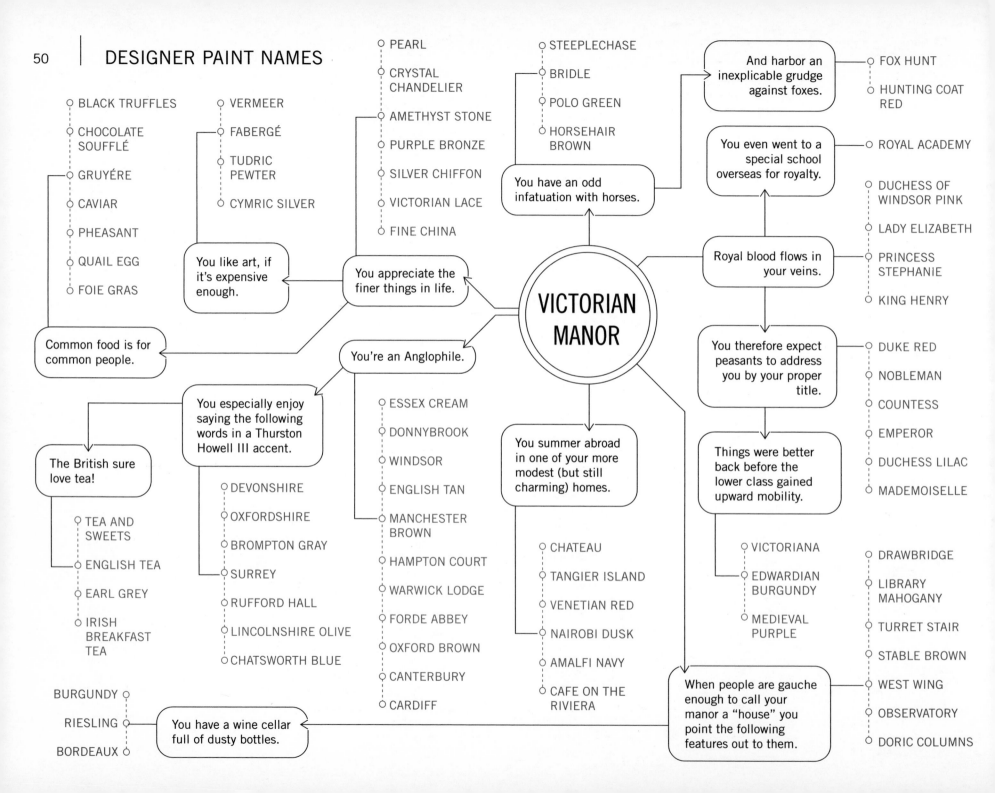

VICTORIAN MANOR

You appreciate the finer things in life.

- PEARL
- CRYSTAL CHANDELIER
- AMETHYST STONE
- PURPLE BRONZE
- SILVER CHIFFON
- VICTORIAN LACE
- FINE CHINA

You like art, if it's expensive enough.

- VERMEER
- FABERGÉ
- TUDRIC PEWTER
- CYMRIC SILVER

Common food is for common people.

- BLACK TRUFFLES
- CHOCOLATE SOUFFLÉ
- GRUYÉRE
- CAVIAR
- PHEASANT
- QUAIL EGG
- FOIE GRAS

You're an Anglophile.

You especially enjoy saying the following words in a Thurston Howell III accent.

- DEVONSHIRE
- OXFORDSHIRE
- BROMPTON GRAY
- SURREY
- RUFFORD HALL
- LINCOLNSHIRE OLIVE
- CHATSWORTH BLUE

- ESSEX CREAM
- DONNYBROOK
- WINDSOR
- ENGLISH TAN
- MANCHESTER BROWN
- HAMPTON COURT
- WARWICK LODGE
- FORDE ABBEY
- OXFORD BROWN
- CANTERBURY
- CARDIFF

The British sure love tea!

- TEA AND SWEETS
- ENGLISH TEA
- EARL GREY
- IRISH BREAKFAST TEA

You have an odd infatuation with horses.

- STEEPLECHASE
- BRIDLE
- POLO GREEN
- HORSEHAIR BROWN

And harbor an inexplicable grudge against foxes.

- FOX HUNT
- HUNTING COAT RED

You even went to a special school overseas for royalty.

- ROYAL ACADEMY

Royal blood flows in your veins.

- DUCHESS OF WINDSOR PINK
- LADY ELIZABETH
- PRINCESS STEPHANIE
- KING HENRY

You therefore expect peasants to address you by your proper title.

- DUKE RED
- NOBLEMAN
- COUNTESS
- EMPEROR
- DUCHESS LILAC
- MADEMOISELLE

Things were better back before the lower class gained upward mobility.

- VICTORIANA
- EDWARDIAN BURGUNDY
- MEDIEVAL PURPLE

You summer abroad in one of your more modest (but still charming) homes.

- CHATEAU
- TANGIER ISLAND
- VENETIAN RED
- NAIROBI DUSK
- AMALFI NAVY
- CAFE ON THE RIVIERA

When people are gauche enough to call your manor a "house" you point the following features out to them.

- DRAWBRIDGE
- LIBRARY MAHOGANY
- TURRET STAIR
- STABLE BROWN
- WEST WING
- OBSERVATORY
- DORIC COLUMNS

You have a wine cellar full of dusty bottles.

- BURGUNDY
- RIESLING
- BORDEAUX

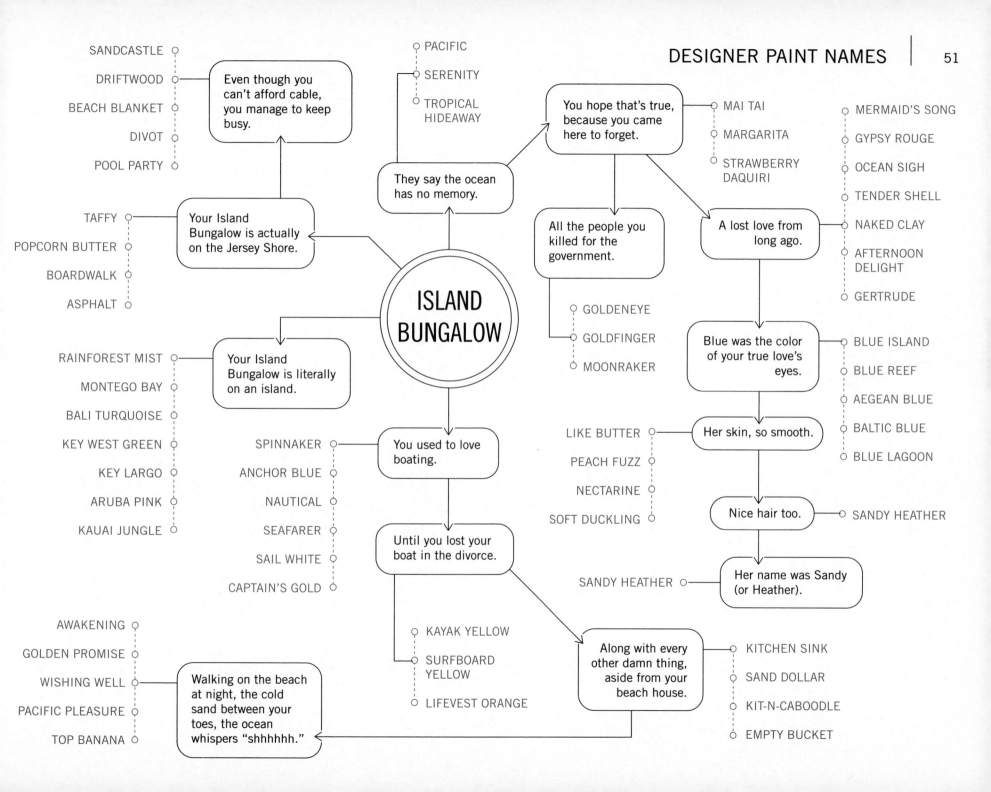

ISLAND BUNGALOW

They say the ocean has no memory.

Even though you can't afford cable, you manage to keep busy.
- SANDCASTLE
- DRIFTWOOD
- BEACH BLANKET
- DIVOT
- POOL PARTY

- PACIFIC
- SERENITY
- TROPICAL HIDEAWAY

Your Island Bungalow is actually on the Jersey Shore.
- TAFFY
- POPCORN BUTTER
- BOARDWALK
- ASPHALT

Your Island Bungalow is literally on an island.
- RAINFOREST MIST
- MONTEGO BAY
- BALI TURQUOISE
- KEY WEST GREEN
- KEY LARGO
- ARUBA PINK
- KAUAI JUNGLE

You used to love boating.
- SPINNAKER
- ANCHOR BLUE
- NAUTICAL
- SEAFARER
- SAIL WHITE
- CAPTAIN'S GOLD

Until you lost your boat in the divorce.
- KAYAK YELLOW
- SURFBOARD YELLOW
- LIFEVEST ORANGE

Walking on the beach at night, the cold sand between your toes, the ocean whispers "shhhhhh."
- AWAKENING
- GOLDEN PROMISE
- WISHING WELL
- PACIFIC PLEASURE
- TOP BANANA

You hope that's true, because you came here to forget.
- MAI TAI
- MARGARITA
- STRAWBERRY DAQUIRI

All the people you killed for the government.
- GOLDENEYE
- GOLDFINGER
- MOONRAKER

A lost love from long ago.
- MERMAID'S SONG
- GYPSY ROUGE
- OCEAN SIGH
- TENDER SHELL
- NAKED CLAY
- AFTERNOON DELIGHT
- GERTRUDE

Blue was the color of your true love's eyes.
- BLUE ISLAND
- BLUE REEF
- AEGEAN BLUE
- BALTIC BLUE
- BLUE LAGOON

Her skin, so smooth.
- LIKE BUTTER
- PEACH FUZZ
- NECTARINE
- SOFT DUCKLING

Nice hair too.
- SANDY HEATHER

Her name was Sandy (or Heather).
- SANDY HEATHER

Along with every other damn thing, aside from your beach house.
- KITCHEN SINK
- SAND DOLLAR
- KIT-N-CABOODLE
- EMPTY BUCKET

WHITE PAINT, DIFFERENT SHADES

LIGHT ↑

WHITE	Ultra white, Anthem white, Teacup, Design Studio White, White, Chalk White, Picket Fence white
VERY CLOSE TO WHITE	Del Coronado white, Lincoln white sash, Woodlawn bedroom white, Whitewash, Waning Moon
WHAT ANY REASONABLE PERSON WOULD CALL WHITE.	Pearly Violet, Naivete, Dove White, Sawyer White, Du Jour, Statuesque

ᵛ COOL WHITES ᵛ

KINDA' DIRTY WHITE	Pianissimo, Tempered Spring, Chartreuse Frost
WHITE AND A HINT OF SOME OTHER COLOR THAT MAY OR MAY NOT BE AN ILLUSION.	Italian Ice, Sea Cove, Frosted Shadow
OFF-WHITE	Betsy's Linen, New Monsoon, Bistro White, Homestead Resort Jefferson White
DIRTY WHITE	Morning Lake, Summer Eclipse, Light Moss, Blanched Pine, Parisian Mist, Sculpture White, Hotel St. Francis Clay Angel
FILTHY WHITE	Seashell Gray, Ivy Shadow, Blanched Pine, Promenade
LIGHT TAN	Pam's Lace, Pontoon White, Whitewashed Oak
JOY-SUCKING WHITE	Gray Opal, Fluffy Slippers, Homestead Resort Sky Blue, Bay Waves, Pelican, Paramount White

DARK ↓

GRAY OR TAN, IT'S HARD TO SAY.	Prudence, Blue Kiss, Lilac Muse, Polar Star, Filtered Shade, Ocean Buff, Totten's Inlet
DIRTY UNDIES, DUDE—THE WHITES.	Tempered Gray, Acropolis, Pale Linen, White Sash, Gray Shimmer
ZOMBIE GRAY	Dew Drop, Mineral Ash, Cool Gray, Hailstorm Gray, Summer Gray
SILVER-ISH	Modest Silver, White Pepper, Silver Dust
SILVER	Silver Leaf, Silver Splendor, Salute, Gray Palisade
DARKER GRAY-ISH	Emerald Ice, Subtle Canopy, Sweet Slumber, Gravity, Polished Silver, Seashore Fog, Oxygen White
I'D CALL THIS TAN, BUT THEY CALL IT WHITE	Angel Touch, Bleached Slate, Satin Snow, Lincoln White Sash, Hemingway
GREENISH OR BLUEISH WHITE, DEPENDING ON HOW HARD YOU SQUINT	Stillness, Neon Mint, Hotspring Green, Cool Elegance, Sweet Leaf
CLAY WHITE	Kabuki Clay, Tackroom White, Sailor's Knot, Montauk Driftwood, Arrowroot

LIGHT ↑

	ᵛ W A R M W H I T E S ᵛ
VERY LIGHT—CLOSE TO WHITE. PRETTY MUCH WHITE.	Lemon Edge, December Starlight, Sheepskin
KIND OF A WARM EGSHELL?	Polar White, Snow Cap, Del Coronado Tequila
IVORY	Veranda Ivory, Polished Ivory, Ivory Lace, Caribbean Walk, Frolick, Powder Soft, Jekyll Island Veranda Ivory
DIRTY IVORY	Thistle Seed, Romano, Barcelona White, Foxtrot, Antique Lace
SUN ON A WHITE WALL	Gilded Endive, Saffron Silk, Homestead Resort, Sunwash, Champagne Dance, Yellow Bliss, Oyster Bisque, Lemon Cream
CREAM	Lyndhurst Estate Cream, Kabuki Clay, Blush, Ancient Scroll, Cream Cake, Hazy Yellow
TANNISH CREAM	Muslin Wrap, Light Raffia, Cream in my Coffee, Linen Napkin
BRIGHT SUNLIGHT ON A WHITE DOG'S BACK	Spirited, Maize, Lemon Butter, Daisy Spell
KIND OF A SAD WHITE. BUT NOT BLUEISH.	Lilac Intuition, Cinema Screen, Ballroom Belle, Crushed Out
NOT WHAT I'D CALL PINK, BUT AGAIN, I WASN'T CONSULTED.	Heirloom Pink, Sugarcane Pink, Pink Breeze
HAPPY WHITE	Lemon Sorbet, Cosmic Cream, Sweet Almond, Peach Kiss, Peach Gala

DISTURBINGLY FLESH-LIKE	Apricot Ice, Whipped Peach, Orange Sparkle, Apricot Fluff, Tangerine Dream
BLUSH	Noble Blush, Exaltation, Fair Maiden, Perfection, Adobe Blush
SORT OF AN EFFEMINATE WHITE. HARD TO EXPLAIN.	Lilac Muse, Soft Silk, Winter Dawn, Woodlawn Dewkist, Virtue, Dress Rehearsal
DIRTY TAN	A True Antique, Drumskin, Unforgettable, Malted Milk
DUSTY PINKISH WHITE	Sheer Light, Gray Sky, Sandstone Gray, Tsunami Gray
LIGHT TAUPE	Parlor Taupe, Copper Melon, Cobblestone Walk

FIGURE 1: WHITES CONSPICUOUSLY ABSENT FROM THIS LIST

| SKULL WHITE | MYSTERY CREAM | ALBINO MONK EGSHELL | GREAT WHITE |

DARK ↓

DETHRONED OR DISGRACED BEAUTY QUEENS

EVERY COUPLE YEARS a beauty queen does something awful, and the whole country holds its collective breath to watch the gruesome drama unfold like a herd of buffalo stampeding off a cliff in slow motion. What compels these pure, beautiful creatures to plummet to their doom and, more significantly, why do we watch with rapt fascination?

Beauty pageants are not as popular as they used to be. They were embraced during the 50s and 60s, and even as late as the 1980s the pageant continued to draw high television ratings. But since then the American public has inexplicably grown weary of watching pretty ladies prance around like show ponies. *(See Figure 1: Why Aren't we Watching Beauty Pageants?)*

Hardly anybody watches beauty pageants anymore, but everybody watches beauty pageant scandal coverage. Indeed, the only pageant winners the general public is familiar with are the

FIGURE 1: WHY AREN'T WE WATCHING BEAUTY PAGEANTS?

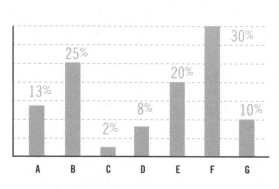

A. NOT ENOUGH NUDITY
B. JEALOUS
C. DON'T LIKE BEAUTY
D. TOO BUSY WORKING THREE JOBS AND RAISING FIVE CHILDREN ALONE SINCE OUR HUSBAND LEFT . . . BECAUSE WE WEREN'T PRETTY ENOUGH
E. SHARK WEEK
F. DON'T LIKE THE "INTERVIEW" PART
G. BUSY WRITING OUR DOCTORAL THESIS ON WOMEN'S STUDIES

dethroned and disgraced ones, even though disgraced beauty queens constitute a minute percentage of the total pageant winners. *(See Figure 2: Distribution of Beauty Queen Scandal.)* If this trend continues, it could lead to a future in which beauty pageants merge with *Mad Max Beyond Thunderdome*, and become a crucible whose *sole* purpose is to yield beautifully unstable psychopaths who must be kept in electric shackles, lest they run amock and try to assassinate the president.[1]

The public likes to see beautiful people do ugly things, because it reassures us that our lives aren't so horrible. So much media exposure is beautiful people doing beautiful things, and while it's pleasant to vicariously share in the glamorous lives of movie stars, it also throws into sharp perspective the un-glamorousness of our own lives. But seeing a candid shot of a celebrity looking haggard and wrinkly, dressed in a pair of dirty sweatpants as she stumbles to the 7-Eleven,

(1) Actually the plot of a sci-fi novel I'm working on called *Beautiful Beauty Queen Psycopath Assassin.*

FIGURE 2: DISTRIBUTION OF BEAUTY QUEEN SCANDAL

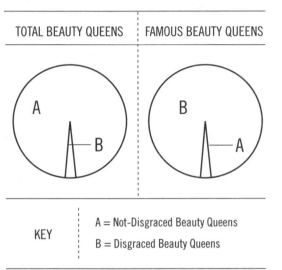

TOTAL BEAUTY QUEENS | FAMOUS BEAUTY QUEENS

KEY

A = Not-Disgraced Beauty Queens

B = Disgraced Beauty Queens

evens the equation back out again. We can literally have it both ways, tearing down our altars to fame even as we build new ones.

Some people claim that beauty pageants such as Miss Universe are uniquely misogynistic, and have no counterpart in the male world—that there is no *Mr.* Universe competition. These people have never heard of the Mr. Universe competition, and also have neglected to notice that the U.S. Presidency has also evolved into a beauty pageant of its own kind, complete with its own disgraced

queens (I'm looking at you, Clinton and Nixon). In the entire history of our country there has only been one truly ugly president (John Quincy Adams—what a face!) and one fat president (Taft, who, despite his weight, was handsome and a spiffy dresser). There have been a few rather plain presidents (Woodrow Wilson, George H.W. Bush) but no straight up goofy-looking galoots[1] (although Carter came close) and certainly nobody who looked un-Presidential. Hell, Warren G. Harding and Ronald Reagan were elected *primarily* because of their Presidential bearing. That is the key: to *be* President, you have to *look* like a president. In our media-saturated society, where almost all our information arrives secondhand, perception is reality. The election of Barack Obama was a historical milestone on the road to racial equality, but ask yourself this—would we have elected him if he had a lazy eye?[2]

(1) I know some people think Lincoln was ugly, but I say the proof is in the pudding: Look at all the portraits of him people have hanging on their walls. Nobody hangs up pictures of ugly people, no matter how many Unions they've preserved.

(2) No. We also would not have elected him if he had a mustache.

FIGURE 3: REFER TO THIS KEY TO DECIPHER THE ICONS ON THE CHART ON PAGES 56-57

KEY

Refer to this key to decode the icons above each of the beauty queens on pages 56-57

ICON	SCANDALOUS BEHAVIOR
ℂ	VIOLATED CONTRACT
📷	NUDE OR SEMI-NUDE PHOTOS
⛓	ARRESTED
🍸	ALLEGED DRINKING PROBLEM
💉	ALLEGED DRUG PROBLEM
♛	ALLOWED TO RETAIN CROWN

MARY LEONA GAGE

TITLE
Miss USA 1957

SCANDAL
Lied about marital status and age. Was actually only 18, and was married with two kids.

STATS	1	2	3	4	5
HOTNESS					
SCANDALOUSNESS					
SCANDAL FAME					
POST-SCANDAL FAME					

FUN FACT: Mary was Miss USA for only one day.

MARJORIE WALLACE

TITLE
Miss World 1973

SCANDAL
Engaged in numerous high-profile relationships. Failed to perform duties.

STATS	1	2	3	4	5
HOTNESS					
SCANDALOUSNESS					
SCANDAL FAME					
POST-SCANDAL FAME					

FUN FACT: Allegedly slept with Tom Jones.

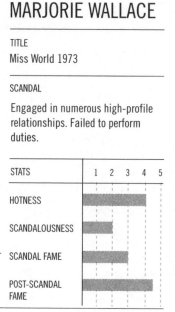

VANESSA WILLIAMS

TITLE
Miss America 1984

SCANDAL
Posed for nude photos in *Penthouse*.

STATS	1	2	3	4	5
HOTNESS					
SCANDALOUSNESS					
SCANDAL FAME					
POST-SCANDAL FAME					

FUN FACT: Resigned, but was allowed to officially retain title.

OXANA FEDOROVA

TITLE
Miss Universe 2002

SCANDAL
Gained weight. Neglected to perform the duties of her title. Was offended by Howard Stern.

STATS	1	2	3	4	5
HOTNESS					
SCANDALOUSNESS					
SCANDAL FAME					
POST-SCANDAL FAME					

FUN FACT: Oxana is also a police officer with the rank of major.

KUMARI FULBRIGHT

TITLE
Miss Arizona 2005

SCANDAL
Kidnapped, robbed, and tortured her ex-boyfriend. Reportedly bit him several times.

STATS	1	2	3	4	5
HOTNESS					
SCANDALOUSNESS					
SCANDAL FAME					
POST-SCANDAL FAME					

FUN FACT: Kumari is also a law student.

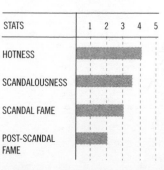

TARA CONNER

TITLE
Miss USA 2006

SCANDAL
Reported underage drinking and cocaine use. Also made out with Miss Teen USA Katie Blair.

STATS	1	2	3	4	5
HOTNESS					
SCANDALOUSNESS					
SCANDAL FAME					
POST-SCANDAL FAME					

FUN FACT: Tara was allowed to keep her crown.

KATIE REES

TITLE

Miss Nevada 2007

SCANDAL

Posed for semi-nude photos of her making out with other girls. Assaulted a police officer.

STATS	1	2	3	4	5
HOTNESS	▓▓				
SCANDALOUSNESS	▓▓▓▓				
SCANDAL FAME	▓▓				
POST-SCANDAL FAME	▓				

FUN FACT: Rees bites another girl's nipple in one of the photos.

LINDSEY EVANS

TITLE

Miss Louisiana Teen USA 2008

SCANDAL

Skipped out on a diner bill, but left her purse behind, which had marijuana in it.

STATS	1	2	3	4	5
HOTNESS	▓				
SCANDALOUSNESS	▓				
SCANDAL FAME	▓				
POST-SCANDAL FAME	▓				

FUN FACT: *Playboy*'s playmate of the month for October 2009.

KEISHLA RIVERA

TITLE

Miss Petite Puerto Rico 2009

SCANDAL

Made death threats and assaulted competition organizers. Unauthorized product endorsement.

STATS	1	2	3	4	5
HOTNESS	▓▓▓▓▓				
SCANDALOUSNESS	▓▓				
SCANDAL FAME	▓				
POST-SCANDAL FAME	▓				

FUN FACT: Keishla is only 5' 2".

CARRIE PREJEAN

TITLE

Miss California 2009

SCANDAL

Made controversial remarks about gay marriage. Posed for semi-nude photos. Didn't repay boob-job loan.

STATS	1	2	3	4	5
HOTNESS	▓▓				
SCANDALOUSNESS	▓▓				
SCANDAL FAME	▓▓▓				
POST-SCANDAL FAME	▓▓▓				

FUN FACT: After her dethroning, a sex tape also allegedly surfaced.

LAURA ZUNIGA

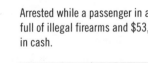

TITLE

Miss Mexico International 2009

SCANDAL

Arrested while a passenger in a car full of illegal firearms and $53,000 in cash.

STATS	1	2	3	4	5
HOTNESS	▓▓▓▓				
SCANDALOUSNESS	▓▓▓				
SCANDAL FAME	▓				
POST-SCANDAL FAME	▓				

FUN FACT: A judge declared Laura not guilty of any crimes.

RIS LOW

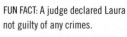

TITLE

Miss Singapore World 2009

SCANDAL

Credit card fraud.

STATS	1	2	3	4	5
HOTNESS	▓				
SCANDALOUSNESS	▓▓				
SCANDAL FAME	▓▓▓				
POST-SCANDAL FAME	▓▓▓▓				

FUN FACT: Known for her inspiring malapropisms, such as BOOMZ!

DOOMSDAY SCENARIOS

I HAVE GOOD NEWS and bad news. The bad news is that the world is going to end—maybe today or maybe a million years from now, but its destruction is inevitable. The end may come without warning; everything you know, including your cat, could be obliterated at any moment. "Oh no," you think, "armageddon won't happen to me." You know who else thought that? *(See Figure 1: This Guy.)*

That's the bad news, and I realize it's depressing. However, remember, I have good news as well: the

FIGURE 1: THIS GUY

good news is that, odds are, the end of the world is going to be awesome. Like a gut-shot gunslinger in an old western, the human race will fling itself over the balcony railing, screaming melodramatically as it falls.

For instance, theoretically, there are one-dimensional cracks in the fabric of space called cosmic string. Although only a proton thin, they run the length of the universe and have incredible density. We're not sure whether or not they exist, but they might, and if they do, and if one were to touch the earth, the earth would be torn apart in a matter of seconds. The whole earth, reduced to cosmic rubble by invisible space string. How cool is that?[1]

Or, there's a chance that, if a large enough meteor hits the earth (it's happened before) it could trigger simultaneous underwater volcanic

(1) Cooler than nuclear winter, which is another completely plausible doomsday scenario.

FIGURE 2: NOT THE END OF THE WORLD

- *Everybody Loves Raymond* no longer in syndication
- Last week of summer camp
- Misplacing your baby
- Having your parents embarrass you in front of friends
- Zit on prom night
- Bad haircut
- Locking your keys in the car
- Everyone leaving the party before you get there
- Losing the Best Supporting Actress Oscar to Marisa Tomei in *My Cousin Vinny*

eruptions that would make the oceans boil, spawning giant hurricanes that merge and form a hypercane, a giant storm the size of North America. Not to mention the volcanic ash and dust that would blot out the sun. Whoah.

Tidal waves, biblical plagues, alien invasion, hell reaching its maximum capacity and forcing the dead to rise from their graves—they're all exciting doomsday scenarios. There are, however, a few boring doomsday scenarios: dwindling natural resources, a global pandemic, pollution, and global warming are all steady, gradual problems that could ultimately destroy the human race, but probably not before they bore us to death. Nobody wants to spend their afterlife telling other spirits "How did I die? Well, the earth's temperature climbed half a degree every year for twenty years, which doesn't seem like much, but that increase significantly increased the amount of algae in the oceans, which upset the foodchain and blabbity-blab blab boring scientific stuff." The biggest reason to fight global warming is so we can obliterate ourselves in a flashier way, like by creating a miniature black hole or zombie plague.

This brings up a frequently asked question: are humans stupid enough to end the world? This is a facetious question, because causing doomsday is anything but easy. Look at dodo birds—the dummies—they came nowhere near obliterating themselves. Rats, pigs—and yes, *humans*—had to do it for them. In a way, completely destroying our planet would be an impressive accomplishment, the crowning capstone to our pyramid of self-destructive behavior.

FIGURE 3: WHO WILL INHERIT THE EARTH?

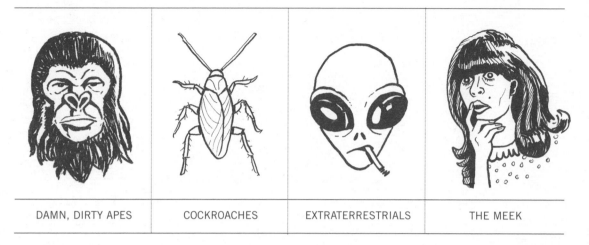

| DAMN, DIRTY APES | COCKROACHES | EXTRATERRESTRIALS | THE MEEK |

However, "doomsday" in the sense I'm charting here doesn't require global demolition, merely the extinction of the human species (or permanent enslavement by another race, such as the "Alien Zoo" or "Planet of the Apes" scenarios). The earth is a 4.5 billion-year-old ball of rock that is much harder to destroy than the human race, and the majority of doomsday scenarios would leave the earth intact enough to support other life forms. *(See Figure 3: Who Will Inherit the Earth?)*

Even if we avoid the many natural or unnatural catastrophes that could end the world, in a billion years our sun's steady increase in brightness will evaporate all the oceans, which means there will be no place to vacation and the Earth will consequently be unlivable. Ultimately the universe will either continue expanding and tear itself apart at the seams, or reverse course and contract, ending in a cataclysmic reversal of the big bang.

And while it would suck to be in the middle of one of those apocalyptic situations, you have to admit that the end of the world is far more exciting than anything else you've ever done, except for that time you made out with the high school chemistry student teacher and then smoked grass in the back of his van.

DOOMSDAY SCENARIOS

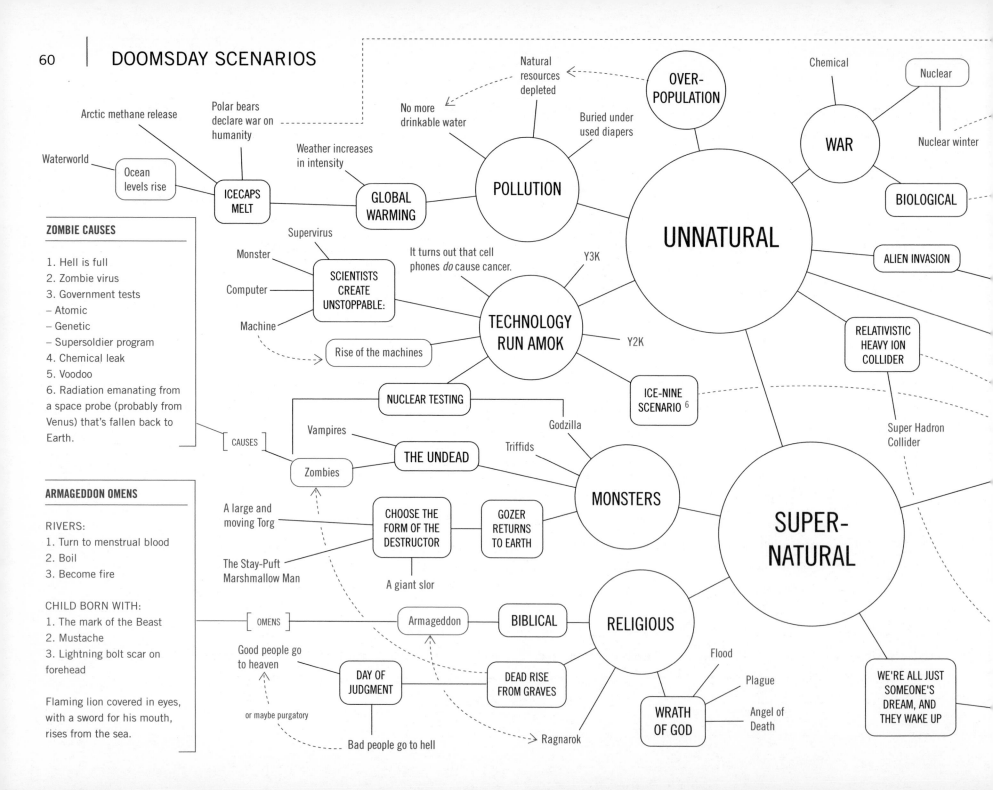

OVER-POPULATION
- Natural resources depleted
- No more drinkable water
- Buried under used diapers

WAR
- Chemical
- Nuclear
- Nuclear winter
- BIOLOGICAL

POLLUTION
- Weather increases in intensity

GLOBAL WARMING
- Arctic methane release
- Polar bears declare war on humanity

ICECAPS MELT
- Waterworld
- Ocean levels rise

UNNATURAL
- ALIEN INVASION
- RELATIVISTIC HEAVY ION COLLIDER
- Super Hadron Collider

TECHNOLOGY RUN AMOK
- It turns out that cell phones *do* cause cancer.
- Y3K
- Y2K
- ICE-NINE SCENARIO [6]

SCIENTISTS CREATE UNSTOPPABLE:
- Supervirus
- Monster
- Computer
- Machine
- Rise of the machines

NUCLEAR TESTING

Godzilla

Triffids

THE UNDEAD
- Vampires
- Zombies

MONSTERS

CHOOSE THE FORM OF THE DESTRUCTOR
- A large and moving Torg
- The Stay-Puft Marshmallow Man
- A giant slor

GOZER RETURNS TO EARTH

SUPER-NATURAL

RELIGIOUS

BIBLICAL
- Armageddon
- DEAD RISE FROM GRAVES

DAY OF JUDGMENT
- Good people go to heaven
- or maybe purgatory
- Bad people go to hell

Ragnarok

WRATH OF GOD
- Flood
- Plague
- Angel of Death

WE'RE ALL JUST SOMEONE'S DREAM, AND THEY WAKE UP

[CAUSES]

[OMENS]

ZOMBIE CAUSES

1. Hell is full
2. Zombie virus
3. Government tests
– Atomic
– Genetic
– Supersoldier program
4. Chemical leak
5. Voodoo
6. Radiation emanating from a space probe (probably from Venus) that's fallen back to Earth.

ARMAGEDDON OMENS

RIVERS:
1. Turn to menstrual blood
2. Boil
3. Become fire

CHILD BORN WITH:
1. The mark of the Beast
2. Mustache
3. Lightning bolt scar on forehead

Flaming lion covered in eyes, with a sword for his mouth, rises from the sea.

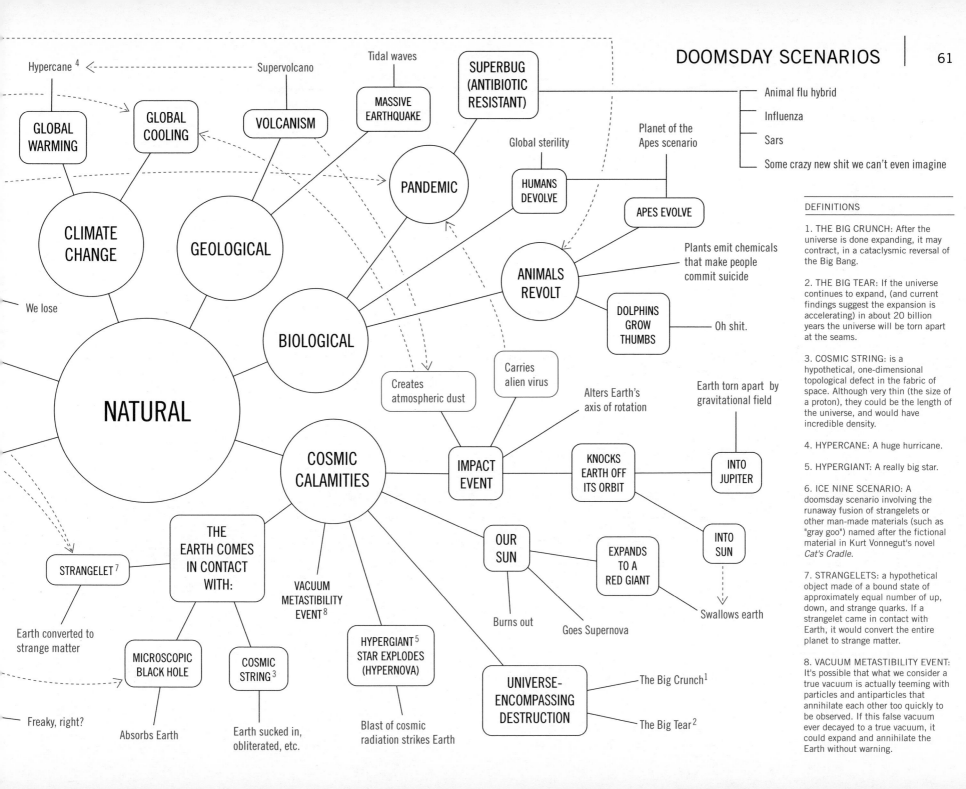

Natural (central node) branches:

- **CLIMATE CHANGE**
  - GLOBAL WARMING → Hypercane [4]
  - GLOBAL COOLING
  - We lose
- **GEOLOGICAL**
  - VOLCANISM → Supervolcano
  - MASSIVE EARTHQUAKE → Tidal waves
- **BIOLOGICAL**
  - PANDEMIC
  - SUPERBUG (ANTIBIOTIC RESISTANT)
    - Animal flu hybrid
    - Influenza
    - Sars
    - Some crazy new shit we can't even imagine
  - HUMANS DEVOLVE — Global sterility
  - APES EVOLVE — Planet of the Apes scenario
  - ANIMALS REVOLT
    - Plants emit chemicals that make people commit suicide
    - DOLPHINS GROW THUMBS — Oh shit.
- **COSMIC CALAMITIES**
  - IMPACT EVENT
    - Creates atmospheric dust
    - Carries alien virus
    - Alters Earth's axis of rotation
    - KNOCKS EARTH OFF ITS ORBIT
      - INTO JUPITER — Earth torn apart by gravitational field
      - INTO SUN — Swallows earth
  - OUR SUN
    - Burns out
    - Goes Supernova
    - EXPANDS TO A RED GIANT
  - THE EARTH COMES IN CONTACT WITH:
    - STRANGELET [7] — Earth converted to strange matter
    - MICROSCOPIC BLACK HOLE — Absorbs Earth
    - COSMIC STRING [3] — Earth sucked in, obliterated, etc.
  - Freaky, right?
  - VACUUM METASTABILITY EVENT [8]
  - HYPERGIANT [5] STAR EXPLODES (HYPERNOVA) — Blast of cosmic radiation strikes Earth
  - UNIVERSE-ENCOMPASSING DESTRUCTION
    - The Big Crunch [1]
    - The Big Tear [2]

DEFINITIONS

1. THE BIG CRUNCH: After the universe is done expanding, it may contract, in a cataclysmic reversal of the Big Bang.

2. THE BIG TEAR: If the universe continues to expand, (and current findings suggest the expansion is accelerating) in about 20 billion years the universe will be torn apart at the seams.

3. COSMIC STRING: is a hypothetical, one-dimensional topological defect in the fabric of space. Although very thin (the size of a proton), they could be the length of the universe, and would have incredible density.

4. HYPERCANE: A huge hurricane.

5. HYPERGIANT: A really big star.

6. ICE NINE SCENARIO: A doomsday scenario involving the runaway fusion of strangelets or other man-made materials (such as "gray goo") named after the fictional material in Kurt Vonnegut's novel *Cat's Cradle*.

7. STRANGELETS: a hypothetical object made of a bound state of approximately equal number of up, down, and strange quarks. If a strangelet came in contact with Earth, it would convert the entire planet to strange matter.

8. VACUUM METASTABILITY EVENT: It's possible that what we consider a true vacuum is actually teeming with particles and antiparticles that annihilate each other too quickly to be observed. If this false vacuum ever decayed to a true vacuum, it could expand and annihilate the Earth without warning.

DRINKS ONLY COLLEGE STUDENTS ORDER

OF ALL THE VALUABLE LESSONS you learn at college, none is as important as how to drink until you almost die—unless you're one of those nerds who doesn't drink, and instead spends their evenings studying and anticipating with relish the inevitable day when all the jocks who used to mock them have to come crawling to the door of their lucrative software company, begging for a job. *(See Figure 1: How Are the Nerds Getting Revenge?)*

I never went to college, because I learned everything I needed to know on the streets—in the grimy back alleys and darkened juke joints; the smoky nightclubs and dead-end avenues; the crazy criss-crossing maze of forgotten roads and grimy tenements that I grew to know like the veins on the back of my work-hardened hands—you prissy, pampered, ivy league fop. Actually, I didn't learn *everything* on the streets, I also learned quite a few things on an Alaskan crabbing boat. And there was this old WWII vet who had half his face burned off, and when I was a kid I'd play chess

with him—learned a lot of stuff from that guy. And I learned massage therapy from the University of Phoenix Online.

One thing I definitely didn't learn on the streets was how to drink like a college student. So when I began research on this chart, I had no idea what sort of drink names I would find. Had I known, I might've charted something less disturbing, like war crimes or Victorian medical oddities. *(See Figure 2: Less Disturbing Than the Drink Names You're About to Read.)*

The names of drinks only college students order provide a revealing snapshot into the minds of young adults at a pivotal age—and that snapshot is the scariest photo I've ever seen. It's like that blurry photo of Bigfoot, if Bigfoot was staring right at you, had a massive erect penis, and was wearing a *Who Farted?* T-shirt. That startling mélange of mystery, smut, and innocence is at the black, beating heart of drinks only college

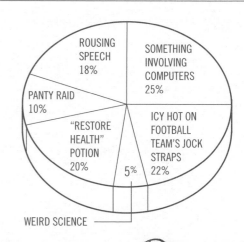

FIGURE 1: HOW ARE THE NERDS GETTING REVENGE?

ROUSING SPEECH 18%

SOMETHING INVOLVING COMPUTERS 25%

PANTY RAID 10%

"RESTORE HEALTH" POTION 20%

ICY HOT ON FOOTBALL TEAM'S JOCK STRAPS 22%

5%

WEIRD SCIENCE

FIGURE 2: LESS DISTURBING THAN THE DRINK NAMES YOU'RE ABOUT TO READ

students order. They are simultaneously jaded and juvenile, appetizing and disgusting, innocent and profane. Witness the sophomoric sacrilege of the Dragon Dick, Vampire's Woo Woo, Spunk Guzzler, and Fuck My Bum Crack.

The profane names and scandalous nature of most of these drinks are an embarrassingly inept attempt for college students to assert their adulthood. "I can shittin' swear if I dick-suckin' want to, Mom! Pass the smurf-fuckin' potatoes!" The desire to shock often supplants all other considerations, including plausibility (e.g., the Bear Fucker), desirability (e.g., the Sweaty Shit), and acknowledgment of cosmic irony (e.g., the Call an Ambulance).

No exploration of college drinking habits would be complete without mentioning that other uniquely collegiate tradition—drinking games. *(See Figure 3: Fun Drinking Games!)* You can't just unceremoniously suck down a drink like the Lick My Banana—it deserves pageantry, pomp, a special sacred process not unlike the changing of the guard at Buckingham Palace, or that crazy dance lizards do before they have sex. *(See Figure 4: Lizard Mating Dance.)*

FIGURE 3: FUN DRINKING GAMES!

QUARTERS: Take a stack of a hundred quarters and hide each quarter in a different spot all over the city. Then go into a bar and get shit-faced. When the bill comes, leave a treasure map detailing the locations of each and every quarter in lieu of payment.

BULLSHIT: Get a deck of cards and a bottle of alcohol. After shuffling the deck, place it facedown in the center of the table. Drink the bottle of alcohol. Think about how everything is such bullshit. Mutter the word "bullshit" over and over again between drinks. When the bottle is empty scatter the cards all over the room.

DEATH IN THE AFTERNOON: Go to Spain and drink wine until you become a truly great author. Write very truly and very fully, standing as you bang out your stories on an old Smith-Corona. See a bullfight or two. Lay in a big bed with a plump-thighed woman and drink cold sweating glasses of beer naked under the crisp white sheets and the spinning palm frond fan. Forty years later blow your brains out with a shotgun.

WHY ARE WE DOING THIS?: Have everyone stand in a circle. Turn to the person on your left and ask, "Why are we doing this?" Then they turn to the person on their left and say the same thing. This continues until someone decides to say, "Human interaction frightens me." This reverses the order of play, and the person on their right now has to say, "Alcohol numbs my fear." Anytime someone screws up or says the wrong thing, they have to drink. Anyone who tries to break free from the circle should be tackled, dragged into the center of the circle and forced to make small talk with the least attractive person at the party.

FIGURE 4: LIZARD MATING DANCE

DRINKS ONLY COLLEGE STUDENTS ORDER

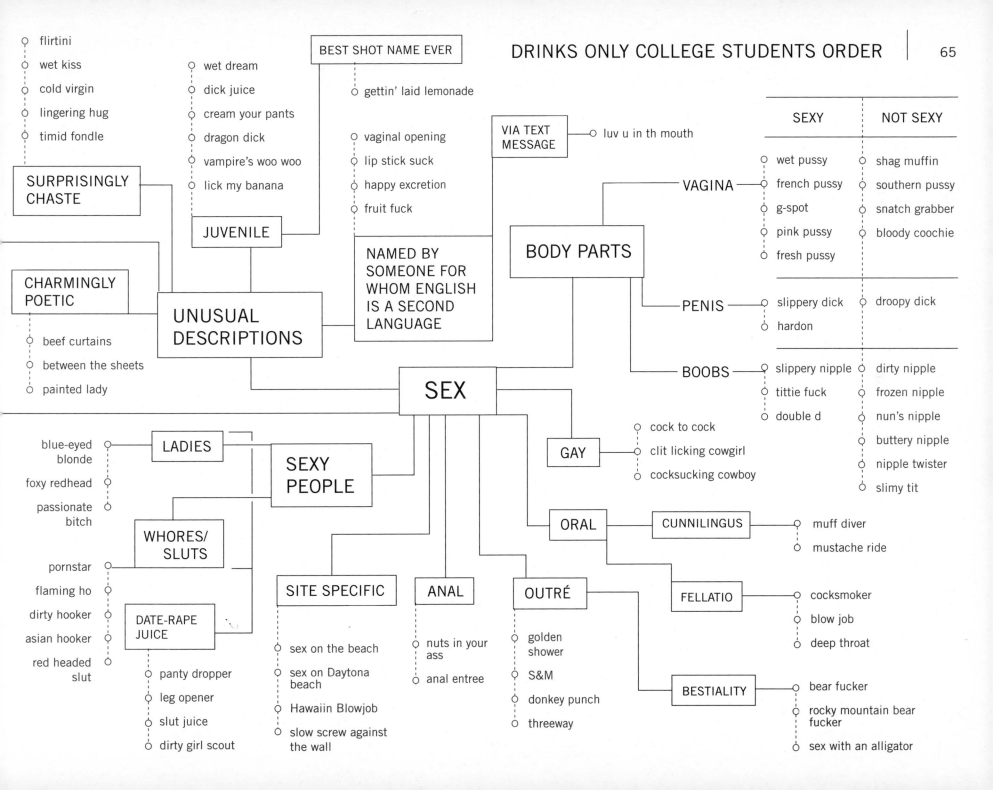

flirtini
wet kiss
cold virgin
lingering hug
timid fondle

SURPRISINGLY CHASTE

wet dream
dick juice
cream your pants
dragon dick
vampire's woo woo
lick my banana

JUVENILE

BEST SHOT NAME EVER

gettin' laid lemonade

vaginal opening
lip stick suck
happy excretion
fruit fuck

VIA TEXT MESSAGE

luv u in th mouth

NAMED BY SOMEONE FOR WHOM ENGLISH IS A SECOND LANGUAGE

BODY PARTS

CHARMINGLY POETIC

beef curtains
between the sheets
painted lady

UNUSUAL DESCRIPTIONS

VAGINA

SEXY	NOT SEXY
wet pussy	shag muffin
french pussy	southern pussy
g-spot	snatch grabber
pink pussy	bloody coochie
fresh pussy	

PENIS

slippery dick
hardon

droopy dick

BOOBS

slippery nipple
tittie fuck
double d

dirty nipple
frozen nipple
nun's nipple
buttery nipple
nipple twister
slimy tit

SEX

LADIES

blue-eyed blonde
foxy redhead
passionate bitch

SEXY PEOPLE

GAY

cock to cock
clit licking cowgirl
cocksucking cowboy

WHORES/ SLUTS

pornstar
flaming ho
dirty hooker
asian hooker
red headed slut

DATE-RAPE JUICE

panty dropper
leg opener
slut juice
dirty girl scout

SITE SPECIFIC

sex on the beach
sex on Daytona beach
Hawaiin Blowjob
slow screw against the wall

ANAL

nuts in your ass
anal entree

OUTRÉ

golden shower
S&M
donkey punch
threeway

ORAL

CUNNILINGUS

muff diver
mustache ride

FELLATIO

cocksmoker
blow job
deep throat

BESTIALITY

bear fucker
rocky mountain bear fucker
sex with an alligator

SMURFS
- papa smurf
- flaming smurf
- smurf poo

BALLS
- monkey balls
- dog balls
- dolphin nutsack

FARTING
- duck fart
- gorilla fart

REAL
- hairy buffalo
- blue dolphin
- texas rattlesnake
- cockroach
- polar bear

IMAGINARY
- angry dragon
- leprechaun orgasm
- brass monkey
- flying yak

ANIMALS

COMIC BOOKS
- Incredible Hulk
- Kryptonite
- Green Lantern

TV & MOVIES
- cookie monster
- Freddie Kruger
- Iceman
- ecto cooler
- Marge Simpson

POP CULTURE

SCI-FI
- Romulan ale
- mind meld
- jedi mind trick

ANIMAL CRUELTY
- squashed frog
- squashed black alley cat
- goat's blood
- lambs to the slaughter

POSSIBLE, BUT UNCOMMON
- pitbull on crack
- 3-headed parrot
- electric monkey

If you want to order a drink that tastes like gumballs, but don't want all your frat brothers to mock you, then order the drink using its alternate, tough name.

TOUGH VERSION	SISSY VERSION
original sin	caramel apple
gay farmer	jolly rancher
rainbow rocks	skittles
dubble cum	bubble gum
gummy rattlesnake	gummy worm
urine drop	lemon drop
cavity tabs	pez
swedish lesbian fish	swedish fish
midget turd	tootsie roll
Roy Roger	Shirley Temple

FOOD

CANDY

BAKED GOODS
- chocolate cake
- apple pie
- blueberry pancake
- strawberry cheesecake

PRESIDENTS
- the great emancipator
- the Van Burinator
- Polk You in the Pooper
- J.F.U.C.K. U UP
- magic bullet
- Teddy's twisted tea

- Hussein in the membrane
- scotch on Baracks
- Obamatini

OBAMA
- Obama mama
- Obamma slamma'
- Baracardi and lime
- rum and hope

(Continued from Fun Drinking Games!, page 63.)

ADVANCED DRINKING GAMES: ASSHOLE

This is a great game to play if you like to create mircocosms of the natural social inequities that maintain the ever-widening gap between the have and have-nots. *(See The American Dream, page 28.)* Any number of people can play, but you need at least four people for the following roles (in order of descending authority): President, Vice-President, Vice-Asshole, and Asshole. Each player has total authority over the players below them, and can command them to drink or perform various degrading tasks.

DETERMINING ROLES:

The most popular or feared person at the party is automatically elected President. The shorter guy that agrees with everything he says becomes the Vice-President. The awkward introvert who's too shy to admit he doesn't want to play the game is the Vice-Asshole, and the social pariah who is so desperate for acceptance he'll do absolutely anything is branded the asshole. (I have included handy icons you can sew onto patches and make each person wear, or, if the President deems it nec-essary, can literally be branded into the players' flesh (if you don't have a brand, try a curling iron).

HOW TO BEGIN:

Each round begins with each of the players ful-filling their role's prescribed duties.

President: Remember all the times you've disappointed your father. Visualize everyone as tiny pawns you move on a chessboard. Cruelly demean people based on whims. Dole out miniscule por-tions of kindness and bask in the resultant fawning gratitude. Wonder why homeless people don't just get a job.

Vice-President: Turn your fear of being demoted to Vice-Asshole into fuel that stokes your white-hot furnace of cruelty. Kiss the President's ass. Visualize your fear of failure and social rejection as a scarecrow. Now put the Asshole's face on that scarecrow; treat the scarecrow accordingly.

Vice-Asshole: Take comfort in the fact that no matter how bad you have it, you have it better than the Asshole. Prove to everyone you're not the Asshole by being crueler to the asshole than anyone else. Do not touch the Asshole, for fear that his bad luck might rub off on you.

Asshole: Reflect on the irony that you're the only person who's actually *not* behaving like an ass-hole. Wonder why you're playing this game, and then remember that even negative attention is better than being ignored. Pray to the god of your choice for deliverance/vengeance.

ALTERNATE VERSION 1:

Add a deck of cards to the mix; move them around the table in meaningless patterns while everyone berates the Asshole.

ALTERNATE VERSION 2:

The Asshole refuses to play the game, but every-one calls him an asshole anyway. He leaves the party, but continues to play the game for the rest of his life.

EVIL TWINS

ARE YOU FAMILIAR WITH Isaac Newton's third law of motion? I'm sure you are, everybody knows it. Summarized in plain English, the law states that "for every action there is an equal and opposite reaction." *(See Figure 3: Newton's Third Law Summarized into Various Vernaculars.)* Newton's laws of motion form the basis of classical mechanics, and explain innumerable natural phenomena: the recoil of a gun, the orbit of the moon, and—most famously—the presence of an evil twin for every person on the planet.

Newton formulated the third law of motion after discovering his own twin, the German philosopher, mathematician, and polymath Gottfried Wilhelm Leibniz. *(See Figure 1: Separated at Birth?)* Like Newton, Leibniz was a brilliant polymath who made significant discoveries in a wide range of fields. This in itself was not conclusively twinny, but when Leibniz invented infinitesimal calculus simultaneously and independently of Newton, their twin connection became undeni-

able. Newton took immediate action to discredit and ruin Leibniz, thereby exposing himself as the evil twin and demonstrating the Second Law of Twins: the evil twin will always try to kill the good twin. Although there was ample evidence that Leibniz had achieved his discoveries independently, Newton succeeded in discrediting Leibniz, who died in relative obscurity for a scientist of his eminence. (FUN FACT: Leibniz invented the binary system, the system of 1s and 0s that helped *The Matrix* look cool.)

If you still don't believe that Leibniz was the good twin, then examine his work in philosophy, where he invented Théodicée optimism, the idea that the world we live in is the best of all possible worlds. Conversely, Newton's personal coat of arms was crossed shinbones on a black background. *(See Figure 2: Newton's Personal Coat of Arms. I'm Not Even Making This Up.)* Newton was *literally waving a flag* that declared how evil he was. "Look at me, I'm a pirate!"

FIGURE 1: SEPARATED AT BIRTH?

| ISAAC NEWTON | GOTTFRIED LEIBNIZ |

FIGURE 2: NEWTON'S PERSONAL COAT OF ARMS. I'M NOT EVEN MAKING THIS UP.

If only Leibniz had been aware of the Twin Nature of the Universe and understood its laws, he could've anticipated Newton's attacks. If Abel

FIGURE 3: NEWTON THIRD'S LAW SUMMARIZED FROM THE ORIGINAL LATIN INTO VARIOUS VERNACULARS

Plain English: For every action, there is an equal and opposite reaction.

LOLcats: OH HAI! I'M IN UR GALAXY, GETTIN FUZZBALLS ALL OVR UR PHYSIKS!! =(^.^)=

Orwellian Newspeak: All thing also make unthing

Late '90's hip hop: Mo' money mo' problems

Inspirational quote: When God closes a door, Satan opens a window.

Sitcom character catchphrase: You smack my ass, I'll SIT. ON. YOUR. FAAAACE!

Movie tagline: They Started This. He'll Finish it.

Old-timey radio serial cliffhanger: Havok! Luthor has swept up and taken Lois Lane to his evil lair in the center of the Earth! *What will Superman do?*

Bodice-ripper: Two bodies working against each other in perfect motion. He THRUSTS his turgid manhood into her waiting loveliness and she takes him in, accepting, moving with him in response.

had understood the symbolic significance of Cain's jet black goatee, he might not have turned his back on his murderous brother. The question you should ask is not "Do I have a twin?" but rather "Which twin am I?" It's helpful to know whether you're the good or evil twin for a couple of reasons:

1. The evil twin always tries to kill the good twin. So, if you're the good twin, you'll want to watch your back. And if you're the evil twin, and you've always felt adrift and unfulfilled in life, now you know why: go kill your goody-two-shoes twin and trick his spouse into bearing your child.

2. There are sub-categories of twins within the main groups of good and evil, and each of them has different needs. For instance, if you're an evil twin created by the good twin's nemesis as a living weapon, you might want to kill your creator as well as the good twin.

3. If you're the evil twin, and don't want your good twin to know, it's smart to shave your goatee off. Similarly, a good twin can pur-

chase a false goatee at a costume store to confuse his evil counterpart.

You might think to yourself, "I'd certainly know if I was the evil twin," but you'd be surprised. The evil twin almost never realizes they're not the good one, just as people who wear sunglasses indoors don't realize they're not the cool one, and my girlfriend doesn't realize she's not the one who can force me to cut off my ponytail [1].

FIGURE 4: BOTH THESE GUYS THINK THEY'RE THE GOOD TWIN, BUT ACTUALLY, ONLY ONE IS

Correct answer: A

(1) She tried to talk me out of it by saying ponytails are for girls, so I showed her a picture of Steven Seagal and said, "Does this look like a girl to you?"

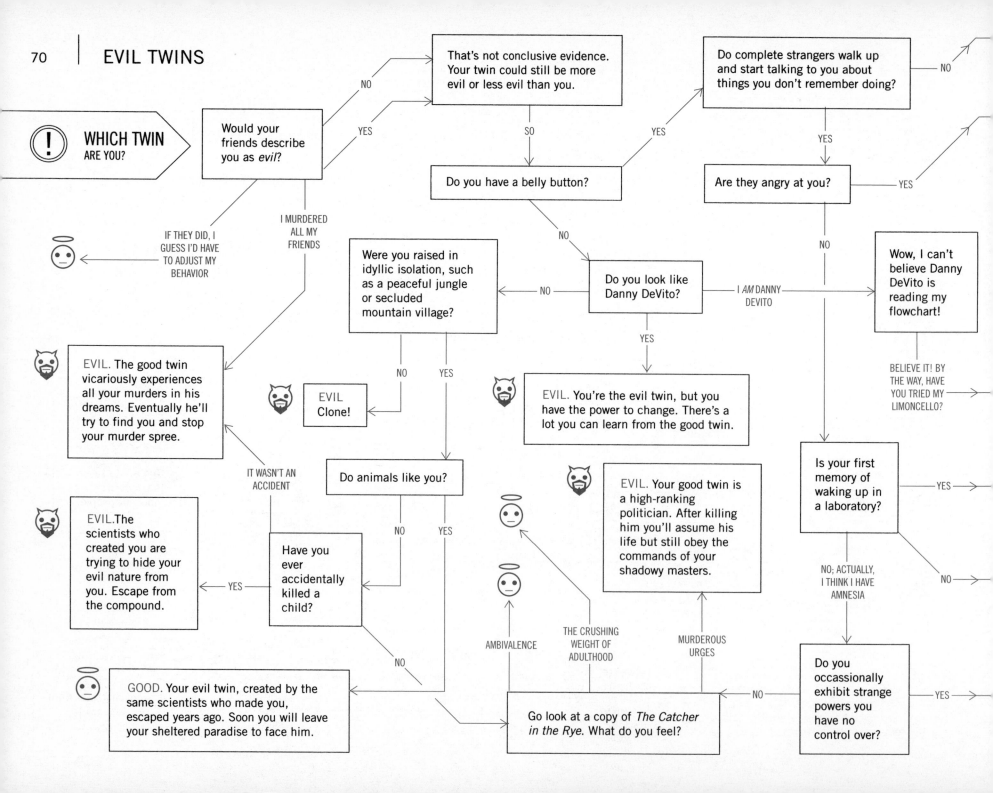

WHICH TWIN ARE YOU?

Would your friends describe you as *evil*?

NO → That's not conclusive evidence. Your twin could still be more evil or less evil than you.

YES → I MURDERED ALL MY FRIENDS

IF THEY DID, I GUESS I'D HAVE TO ADJUST MY BEHAVIOR

SO → Do you have a belly button?

Do complete strangers walk up and start talking to you about things you don't remember doing?

NO

YES → Are they angry at you?

YES

Were you raised in idyllic isolation, such as a peaceful jungle or secluded mountain village?

NO → Do you look like Danny DeVito?

I AM DANNY DEVITO → Wow, I can't believe Danny DeVito is reading my flowchart!

BELIEVE IT! BY THE WAY, HAVE YOU TRIED MY LIMONCELLO?

EVIL. The good twin vicariously experiences all your murders in his dreams. Eventually he'll try to find you and stop your murder spree.

EVIL Clone!

YES ↓ / NO

EVIL. You're the evil twin, but you have the power to change. There's a lot you can learn from the good twin.

Do animals like you?

IT WASN'T AN ACCIDENT

EVIL. The scientists who created you are trying to hide your evil nature from you. Escape from the compound.

YES ← Have you ever accidentally killed a child?

EVIL. Your good twin is a high-ranking politician. After killing him you'll assume his life but still obey the commands of your shadowy masters.

Is your first memory of waking up in a laboratory?

YES → / NO →

NO; ACTUALLY, I THINK I HAVE AMNESIA

AMBIVALENCE / THE CRUSHING WEIGHT OF ADULTHOOD / MURDEROUS URGES

GOOD. Your evil twin, created by the same scientists who made you, escaped years ago. Soon you will leave your sheltered paradise to face him.

NO → Go look at a copy of *The Catcher in the Rye*. What do you feel?

NO ← Do you occasionally exhibit strange powers you have no control over?

YES →

Do you have large gaps in your memory, after which you wake up exhausted to find your shoes covered in mud and blood spattered all over your clothes?

— NO → GOOD. Soon you'll be arrested for a crime you never commited, but also have no alibi for. You'll escape from police custody and become a noble fugitive whose sole mission is to clear his name.

YES ↓

Have you ever been bitten by a large wolf?

— YES → You're a werewolf. However, that doesn't prove whether you're the good or evil twin.

— NO → EVIL & GOOD. The evil twin is inside you. Eventually the gaps in your memory will grow larger and larger as your dark half exerts its control.

Does your body sometimes lose its tangibility, so you can see through it?

— NO →

— YES →

SO → Rolling Stones or Beatles?

BEATLES →

STONES →

No. You have a limoncello? Like, the lemon dessert liqueur?

YEAH, IT'S CALLED DANNY DEVITO'S LIMONCELLO. IT'S NOT JUST FOR DESSERT, YOU CAN DRINK IT ANY TIME. → GOOD. You're the good Danny DeVito.

Your good twin will kill you.

You'll fight your good twin, but in the end redeem yourself by spontaneously sacrificing your own life to save the lives of innocent people.

Was a scientist there who showed you a photo of someone who looked very similar to you, and who he claimed was your evil twin?

— YES → EVIL. He lied. You're the evil twin, created by the scientist to destory his nemesis. *(See Supervillain Schemes, page 126.)*

NO, THE LABORATORY WAS ON FIRE → EVIL. You're a failed experiment. You'll waste years searching for your creator, trying to find some answers.

Is your face hideously disfigured?

— NO →

— YES →

Do you have a goatee?

— NO → GOOD. You're so boring, you must be the good twin.

— YES →

Here, have a shot of Danny DeVito's Limoncello.

You're a shape-shifting alien whose spaceship crashed on earth. The crash impact gave you amnesia. Stumbling from the wreckage, you reflexively took the form of the first person you saw.

I REMEMBER NOW! BY THE WAY, DO YOU KNOW WHY MY SPACESHIP CRASHED? → I do. Are you ready to have your mind blown?

NO →

— YES → GOOD. Your evil twin sabotaged the warp drive.

EVIL. Your good twin is an artist, and you're a character from one of his stories come to life.

FEARS

FEAR IS ONE OF THE MOST primal human emotions, and a vital survival mechanism. Its primary purpose is to keep people alive by preventing them from engaging in life-threatening behaviors like taunting bears, dating Greeks, and jumping Snake River Canyon on an X-1 Skycycle. *(See Figure 1: Evel Knievel's Greatest Fears.)* But if fear is only there to keep people away from lethal situations, then why are so many of us scared of innocuous things like mice, peeing in public, and Indian food?

The answer is simple: out of all the human emotions, fear is the second dumbest (which is saying something). None of the emotions are particularly smart, but fear is a real dumbbell, scoring even lower than love—whose blindness and ignorance is perennially memorialized in song—and not coming anywhere near the most intelligent of the emotions, Anger, which is able to bide its time and fashion elaborate traps from bamboo. *(See Figure 2: Intelligence Ranking of Emotions.)*

How dumb is fear? It can't tell the difference between a tiger and a pop quiz. If I showed you a tiger and a pop quiz in algebra, would you be able to tell the difference?[1] You would think so.

----

(1) One easy way to tell the difference between a test and a tiger is that you can write on a test in pen or pencil, but only write on a tiger in pen.

FIGURE 1: EVEL KNIEVEL'S GREATEST FEARS

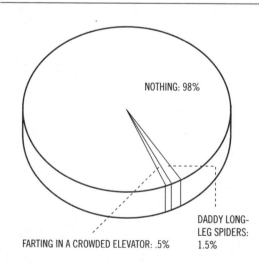

NOTHING: 98%

DADDY LONG-LEG SPIDERS: 1.5%

FARTING IN A CROWDED ELEVATOR: .5%

FIGURE 2: INTELLIGENCE RANKING OF EMOTIONS

#	EMOTION	QUALITIES
1	Anger	Patient, cunning
2	Curiosity	Good at puzzle solving
3	Acceptance	Mature
4	Boredom	Gifted but mercurial
5	Hope	Good verbal skills
6	Disgust	Confident
7	Compassion	Good judge of character
8	Guilt	Excellent memory
9	Happiness	Easily fooled
10	Sadness	Bad at math
11	Embarrassment	Irrational
12	Anxiety	Short attention span
13	Apathy	One trick pony
14	Frustration	Basically bad at everything
15	Regret	Pointless
16	Surprise	Illiterate
17	Love	Illogical, blind
18	Desire	Blind, deaf, and no taste
19	Fear	Super stupid
20	Hysteria	Beyond stupid

But if either one of them was actually placed in front of you in the real world, they would both trigger an identical physiological fear response—increased heart rate, dilated pupils, and tightened muscles primed with oxygen.[2]

Considering the fact that fear's sole purpose is to protect people from life-threatening situations, it's surprising how poor it is at accurately recognizing lethal situations. For instance, when asked to rank their greatest fears, people routinely list public speaking above death, which is so funny that Jerry Seinfeld even wrote a joke about it (*I'm Telling You for the Last Time*, 1998; if you're afraid to die laughing, don't buy it!). The late 90s supernatural drama *Buffy the Vampire Slayer*, about a female high-school student who's also a vampire hunter, succinctly portrayed our fear mechanisms' inability to distinguish between actually lethal and merely stressful situations. In a typical episode Buffy had to prevent an ancient vampire from killing thou-

sands of people by opening a portal to a demonic dimension, but was simultaneously terribly worried about whether or not she was going to make the cheerleading squad (spoiler alert: she doesn't make the cheerleading squad, but in Season 7 they finally seal the Hellmouth).

The crucial factor in deciding whether a fear is rational or irrational is its severity and the circum-

stances surrounding it. For instance, if you see a clown on TV and get scared, that fear is irrational. However, if you see a clown sitting quietly in a Windsor armchair in your darkened living room—only the softly glowing cherry of the cigarette in his mouth illuminating his face whenever he inhales—then any fear you feel in that situation is perfectly rational. *(See Figure 3: Rationality of Fears Based on Location and Situation.)*

FIGURE 3: RATIONALITY OF FEARS BASED ON LOCATION AND SITUATION

FEARS	RATIONAL FEAR	POSSIBLY RATIONAL FEAR	IRRATIONAL FEAR
HEIGHTS	Skydiving	Climbing a ladder	Wearing high heels
PUBLIC HUMILIATION	Starring on a reality television show	Giving a best man speech	Opening presents on Christmas morning
COMMITMENT	Getting married	Purchasing a cell phone plan	Buying a goldfish
MACHINES	Dystopian future where machines rule	Working in a woodshop	Watching a Roomba commercial
SPIDERS	Exploring the Amazon jungle	Lifting a rotten log	Trying on underwear
FAILURE	Fiddling contest with the Devil	Spelling bee	Solitaire

---

(2) After the first couple seconds though, pop quizzes and tigers cause vastly different physical changes, especially if you're allergic to either cat hair or having your face chewed on.

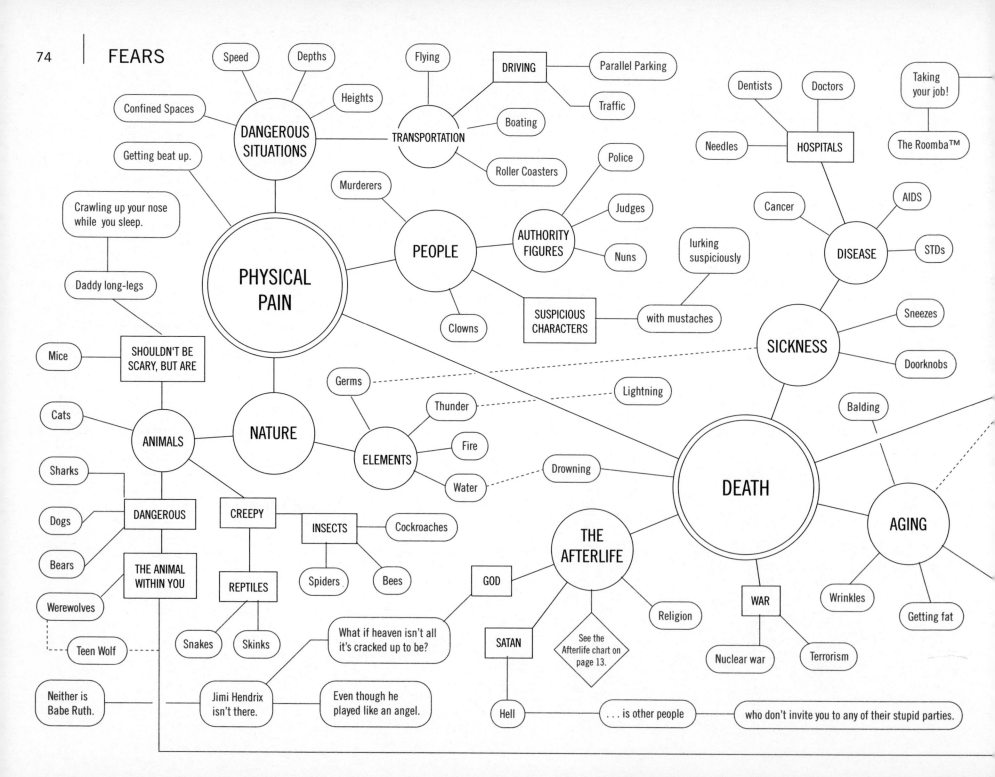

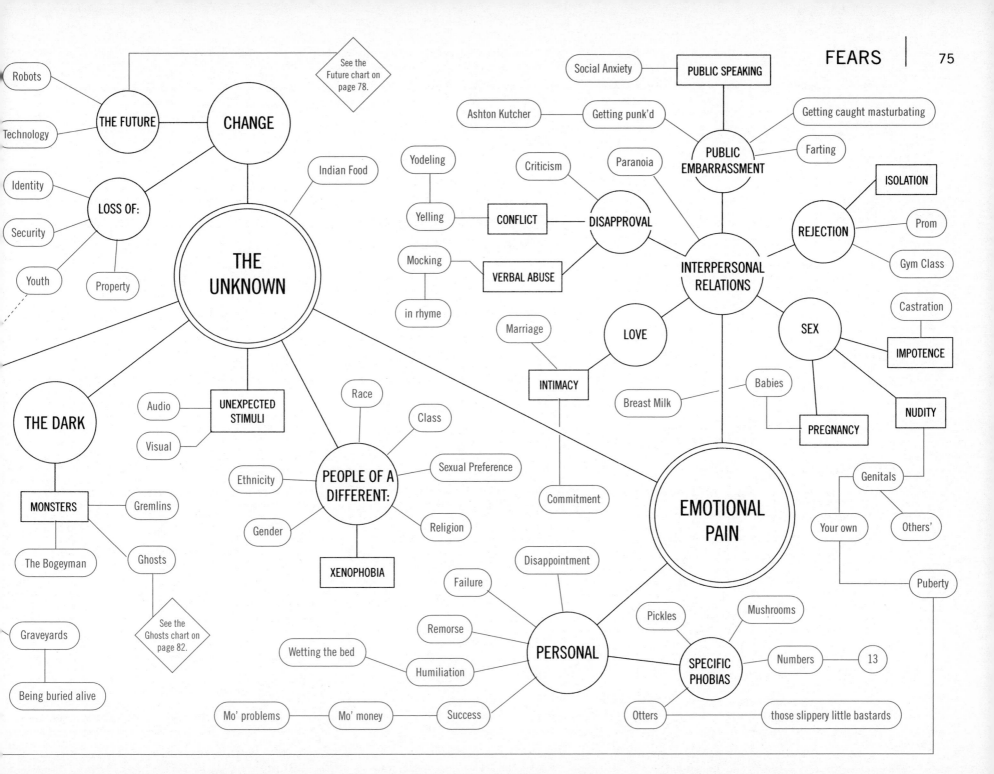

THE FUTURE

"GREETINGS, MY FRIEND. We are all interested in the future, for that is where you and I are going to spend the rest of our lives. And remember my friend, future events such as these will affect you in the future. You are interested in the unknown . . . the mysterious. The unexplainable. That is why you are here."

—*The Great Criswell*

This quote is an excerpt from the monologue at the beginning of Ed Wood's seminal film *Plan 9 From Outer Space*; the Great Criswell, a prophet sent to warn humanity about its apocalyptic future, stares into the camera and speaks directly to the audience. I'd like to direct your attention to the second sentence: "We are all interested in the future, for that is where you and I are going to spend the rest of our lives." This sentence is true, and it also looks nice when engraved in a chiseled serif font on a glowing radium plaque, which makes it the best kind of truth—the kind

that can easily be viewed on the dark side of the moon, where the remnants of the human race will mount their rebellion against the machines in the year 2025.

You are interested in the unknown, that is why you are here. *(See Figure 1: What You Want to Know About the Future.)* Unfortunately, we won't have time machines for another twenty years (some scientists say twenty-three), and by then the

---

FIGURE 1: WHAT YOU WANT TO KNOW ABOUT THE FUTURE

---

1. Will Papa's Mustache win the third race?
2. When can I replace my girlfriend with a Robo-Gal?*
3. Is this as good as it gets?
4. Should I buy an alpaca farm?
5. When will the Rastafari overthrow Babylon and reach Zion?
6. Is this an awkward phase that I'll eventually grow out of? Please say yes.

---

*Don't bother. With the constant malfunctions, they're just as much trouble as the old-fashioned kind.

future will already be here. However, I have something even better than a time machine: *educated guesses*. And when I say *educated*, what I mean is "four years of art school," and when I say *guesses* what I mean is "absolute certainties."

Before you accuse me of sorcery, let me assure you that none of the predictions on the Future chart were attained through the use of occult methods[1]. They are predictions, not prophecies, and

---

(1) Although I didn't use sorcery to make my predictions about the future, I probably could've, because my girlfriend is a witch, and I bet she'd help me see into the future if I asked her to—but that would open up a whole can of worms, because then *she'd* ask *me* to design a logo for her coven, or chart positive witch role models in popular culture, or something like that. Sometimes I think she's not really a witch, she just likes to wear black. But after I think that I'll get really bad acne for a week, or I'll flick on the lights in the bathroom the next morning to find a spider sitting on my toothbrush, just staring at me. So she's probably a witch.

as such most of them were realized through relatively pedestrian methods. *(See Figure 2: How Were These Predictions Made?)* It doesn't take a Nostradamus to figure out that lasers will replace flyswatters, cheese graters, and reasoned debate, or that herds of teacup pigs will replace dogs as household pets.

I can tell by the pink hue of your mood ring that you're still skeptical about the validity of these predictions. Well, it doesn't matter, because by the time any of these predictions could possibly be disproved, this book will be long out of print and my writing legacy overshadowed by my career as a holovision product endorsement spokesperson for my line of home-cooking conveniences. *(See Figure 3: Inventions in the Horner Line of Home Cooking Convenience Products.)*

However, if my predictions *do* turn out to be true (they will), and twenty years from now you discover yourself searching for some small way to thank me, here is what you can do: Visit the Ed Wood Memorial on the dark side of the moon and—when Orion's belt aligns with Mars—whisper my name into the windless, eternal night. Then please break me out of whatever robot-controlled radon mine I'm toiling in, assuming the machines haven't already wiped my mind or turned me into a living battery, in which case just kill me.

FIGURE 3: INVENTIONS IN THE HORNER LINE OF HOME COOKING CONVENIENCE PRODUCTS

- The Horner Tub-Style Mechanical Chicken Plucker
- The Horner EZPZ Swine Sizzler
- In the Shell Egg Yolk Teleporter
- The Horner Lazer Flavr HD Tongue Dazzler
- The Horner Hand-Held Peppercorn Incinerator
- The Dial-A-Genetically-Modified-Crime-Against-God-Frankenfood
- Smokeless Sandwich Crust Disintegrator

DIGITAL WIRELESS MINI COMPUTER SPOON

FIGURE 2: HOW WERE THESE PREDICTIONS MADE?

A. Common Sense
B. Uncommon Sense
C. Read about it in a Philip K. Dick novel
D. Calculus
E. Hairdresser told me
F. Magic 8-Ball
G. Using the Farmer's Almanac
H. With a graphing calculator
I. Found beneath a loose flagstone in an ivy-covered corner of the garden
J. Careful observation of sunspot activity
K. Gut feeling
L. Not using sorcery, I can tell you that
M. Tip from a guy whose cousin is a bookie
N. 12 hours of meditation in a Hopi sweat lodge

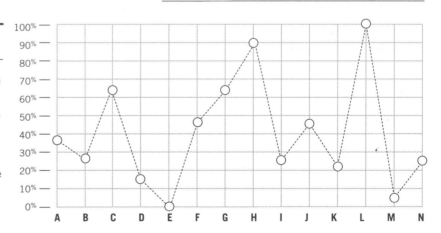

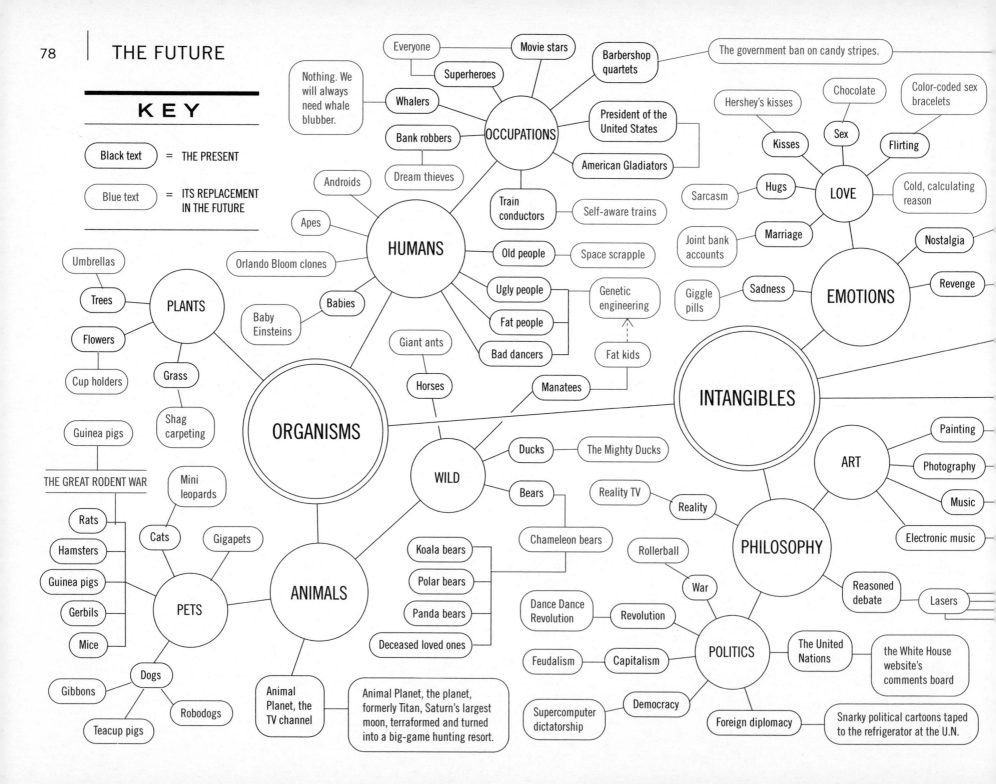

KEY

Black text = THE PRESENT

Blue text = ITS REPLACEMENT IN THE FUTURE

HUMANS

OCCUPATIONS
- Everyone → Movie stars
- Superheroes
- Whalers → Nothing. We will always need whale blubber.
- Barbershop quartets → The government ban on candy stripes.
- Bank robbers
- Dream thieves
- President of the United States
- American Gladiators
- Train conductors → Self-aware trains

- Androids
- Apes
- Orlando Bloom clones
- Babies
- Old people → Space scrapple
- Ugly people
- Fat people
- Bad dancers
- Genetic engineering
- Fat kids

LOVE
- Hershey's kisses
- Chocolate
- Color-coded sex bracelets
- Kisses
- Sex
- Flirting
- Sarcasm → Hugs
- Cold, calculating reason
- Joint bank accounts → Marriage

EMOTIONS
- Nostalgia
- Revenge
- Giggle pills → Sadness
- Manatees

PLANTS
- Umbrellas → Trees
- Flowers → Cup holders
- Grass → Shag carpeting

- Baby Einsteins

ORGANISMS

Giant ants
Horses

INTANGIBLES

ART
- Painting
- Photography
- Music
- Electronic music

WILD
- Ducks → The Mighty Ducks
- Bears → Chameleon bears
- Koala bears
- Polar bears
- Panda bears
- Deceased loved ones

PHILOSOPHY
- Reality TV → Reality
- Reasoned debate → Lasers

PETS
- Guinea pigs
- THE GREAT RODENT WAR
- Rats
- Hamsters
- Guinea pigs
- Gerbils
- Mice
- Mini leopards
- Cats
- Gigapets
- Dogs → Robodogs
- Gibbons
- Teacup pigs

ANIMALS
- Animal Planet, the TV channel → Animal Planet, the planet, formerly Titan, Saturn's largest moon, terraformed and turned into a big-game hunting resort.

POLITICS
- Rollerball → War
- Dance Dance Revolution → Revolution
- Feudalism → Capitalism
- Supercomputer dictatorship → Democracy
- Foreign diplomacy
- The United Nations → the White House website's comments board
- Snarky political cartoons taped to the refrigerator at the U.N.

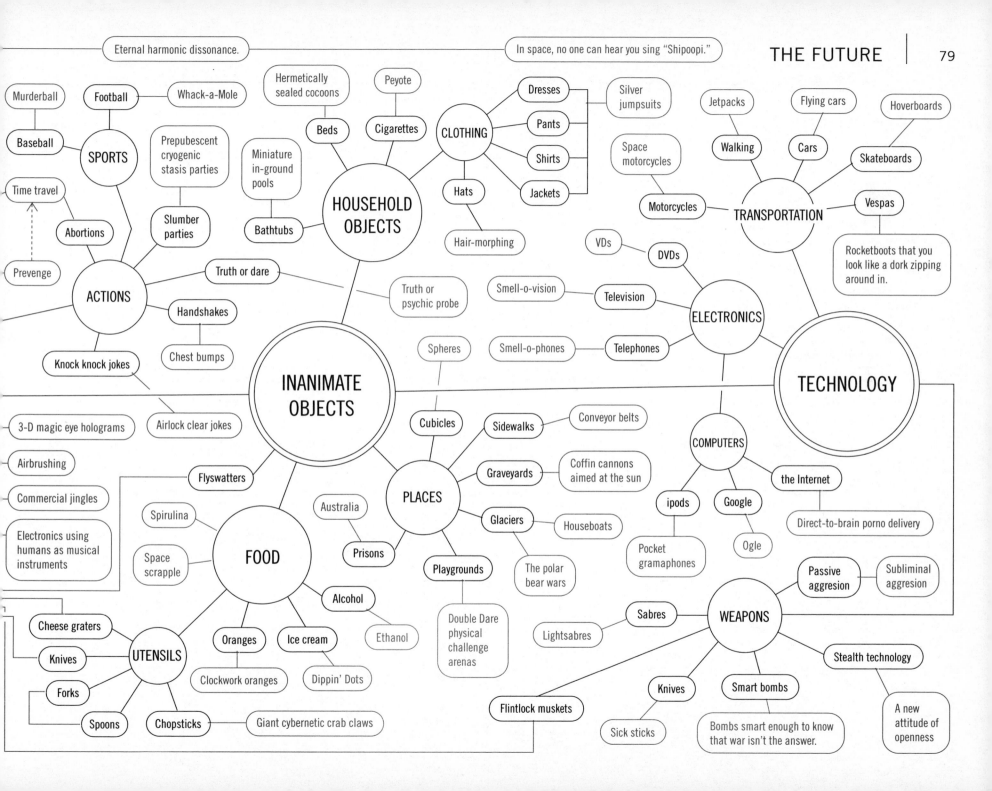

GHOSTS

GHOSTS ARE AWESOME when they're on TV guarding pirate treasure, in a movie trying to solve their own murder, or in a play scaring the crap out of crazy old Hamlet. But when ghosts are in your house, pushing pennies up the wall and spinning picture frames, they are scary. Which is why, when dealing with ghosts, it's important to make informed decisions.

Here's a hypothetical situation: You're driving past a hairpin turn late at night and see a shoeless woman in white trying to hitch a ride. Do you:

A. Pick her up
B. Try to hit her with your car
C. Yell "Get a room!" as you speed past

The correct answer is A; it's cool, you can pick her up. She's a benevolent ghost. Or, more specifically, a harmless localized ghost, haunting the site of her death. So actually you could probably go with B or C as well and not suffer any reper-cussions, although I don't know why you'd yell "get a room!" at someone who's by themselves; you usually yell it at couples who are kissing, or a mother who's breastfeeding.

Here's another hypothetical situation: You're at a big party a king is throwing. A green knight wearing green armor rides in on a green horse; he challenges you to a fight. He hands you a big axe (guess what color it is), and says that you can have the first hit, but he's allowed to return the blow one year and one day from now. Do you:

A. Think you're super clever and chop his head off
B. Take this as a sign you've drank too much meade and walk home, singing loudly
C. Politely decline his offer and try to steer the conversation in a different direction

This hypothetical situation is actually the open-ing scene of the famous 14th-century story of *Sir Gaiwan and the Green Knight*. In the story, Sir Gaiwan chooses option A and lops the Green Knight's head clean off, because he's the kind of person who thinks that kind of behavior is appro-priate at a party, and is always looking for some-thing melodramatic and scandalous to do. However the Green Knight simply picks up his decapitated head and tells Sir Gaiwan that he'll see him in a year and a day. And then everyone at the party slowly swivels their head to stare at Sir Gaiwan, and quietly goes "Ooooooooo," like he just dropped his tray in the cafeteria.

Heed my words, people: Know your ghosts. *(See Figure 1: Ghost Identification Chart.)* Some of them are friendly, some are mean, and some are just here to ruin Christmas by showing you how miserly and sad your life has been up to that point. But considering how tragedy-prone Christmas always is, if you escape the season with only a lit-tle haunting, you're getting off easy. *(See Figure 2: Christmas Tragedies.)*

FIGURE 1: GHOST IDENTIFICATION CHART

THE GREEN KNIGHT*	LOW BUDGET	SCOOBY-DOO VILLAIN	CREEPY KID
FRIENDLY	LARGE MARGE†	TORMENTED	GHOST RIDERS

* From *Sir Gaiwan and the Green Knight*.

† From *Pee-Wee's Big Adventure*.

FIGURE 2: CHRISTMAS TRAGEDIES

1. Grandma run over by reindeer
2. Christmas goose too silly for consumption
3. Rendition of *Jingle Bell Rock* doesn't rock the way a song with the word "rock" in its title should
4. Nakatomi Towers taken over by terrorists
5. Global warming turns out to not be a liberal media scam; Santa's operation at the North Pole melts and sinks beneath the Arctic Ocean's icy waves.
6. Elves unionize
7. Born Jewish
8. Rabid squirrel in Christmas tree
9. Christmas bonus actually just a ham
10. Father dresses as Santa: falls off roof; gets stuck in chimney; kisses Mommy
11. Mogwai gets wet
12. Left at home while family goes on trip to Paris; forced to fight burglars
13. Ghost of your former business partner drops by and gives you a hard time for being a humbug
14. You have four different Christmases to go to in ONE SINGLE DAY!
15. You shoot your eye out
16. Caught under mistletoe with lecherous stepparent, and your eyes lock for one second too long
17. Father leaves to buy cigarettes, never returns
18. That *sweater* you're wearing is the *real* tragedy!
19. You discover that the true meaning of Christmas is soulless capitalism
20. All the Christmas presents and decorations are stolen from your tiny village . . . or is it a tragedy after all?

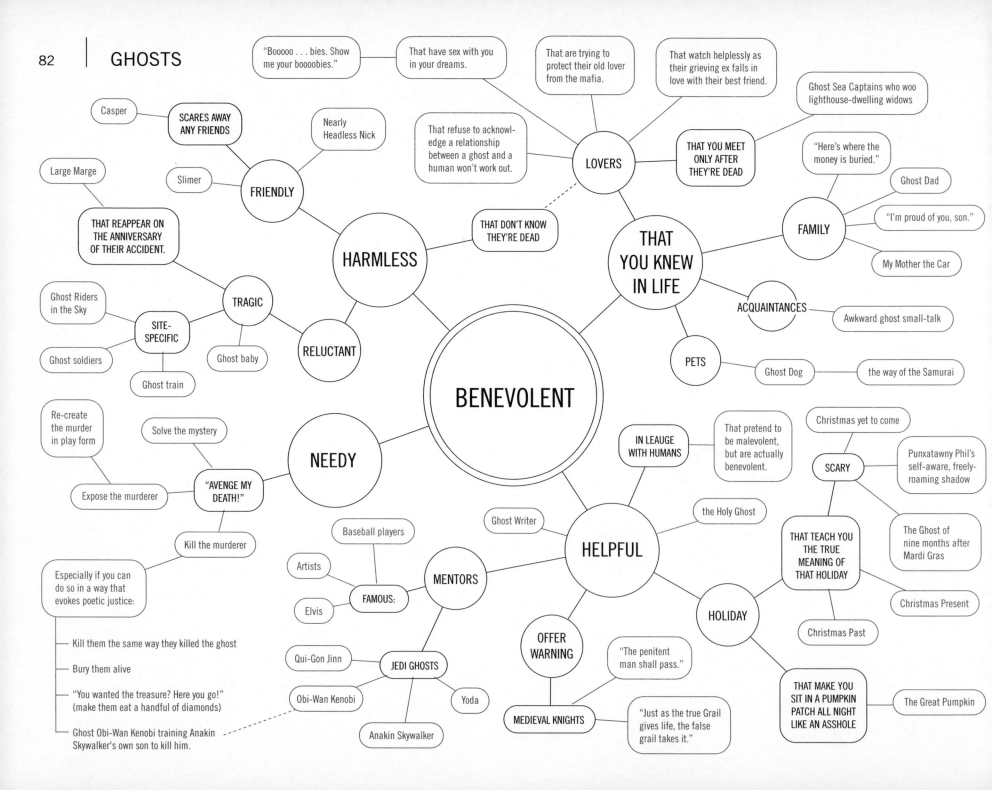

"Booooo . . . bies. Show me your boooobies."

That have sex with you in your dreams.

That are trying to protect their old lover from the mafia.

That watch helplessly as their grieving ex falls in love with their best friend.

Ghost Sea Captains who woo lighthouse-dwelling widows

Casper

SCARES AWAY ANY FRIENDS

Nearly Headless Nick

That refuse to acknowledge a relationship between a ghost and a human won't work out.

LOVERS

THAT YOU MEET ONLY AFTER THEY'RE DEAD

"Here's where the money is buried."

Large Marge

Slimer

FRIENDLY

THAT YOU KNEW IN LIFE

FAMILY

Ghost Dad

"I'm proud of you, son."

THAT REAPPEAR ON THE ANNIVERSARY OF THEIR ACCIDENT.

THAT DON'T KNOW THEY'RE DEAD

My Mother the Car

HARMLESS

Ghost Riders in the Sky

TRAGIC

ACQUAINTANCES

Awkward ghost small-talk

Ghost soldiers

SITE-SPECIFIC

Ghost baby

RELUCTANT

BENEVOLENT

PETS

Ghost Dog

the way of the Samurai

Ghost train

Re-create the murder in play form

Solve the mystery

IN LEAUGE WITH HUMANS

That pretend to be malevolent, but are actually benevolent.

Christmas yet to come

NEEDY

Expose the murderer

"AVENGE MY DEATH!"

SCARY

Punxatawny Phil's self-aware, freely-roaming shadow

Kill the murderer

the Holy Ghost

THAT TEACH YOU THE TRUE MEANING OF THAT HOLIDAY

The Ghost of nine months after Mardi Gras

Especially if you can do so in a way that evokes poetic justice:

Ghost Writer

HELPFUL

— Kill them the same way they killed the ghost

Baseball players

Christmas Present

— Bury them alive

Artists

FAMOUS:

MENTORS

Christmas Past

— "You wanted the treasure? Here you go!" (make them eat a handful of diamonds)

Elvis

HOLIDAY

— Ghost Obi-Wan Kenobi training Anakin Skywalker's own son to kill him.

OFFER WARNING

"The penitent man shall pass."

THAT MAKE YOU SIT IN A PUMPKIN PATCH ALL NIGHT LIKE AN ASSHOLE

The Great Pumpkin

Qui-Gon Jinn

JEDI GHOSTS

Obi-Wan Kenobi

Yoda

MEDIEVAL KNIGHTS

"Just as the true Grail gives life, the false grail takes it."

Anakin Skywalker

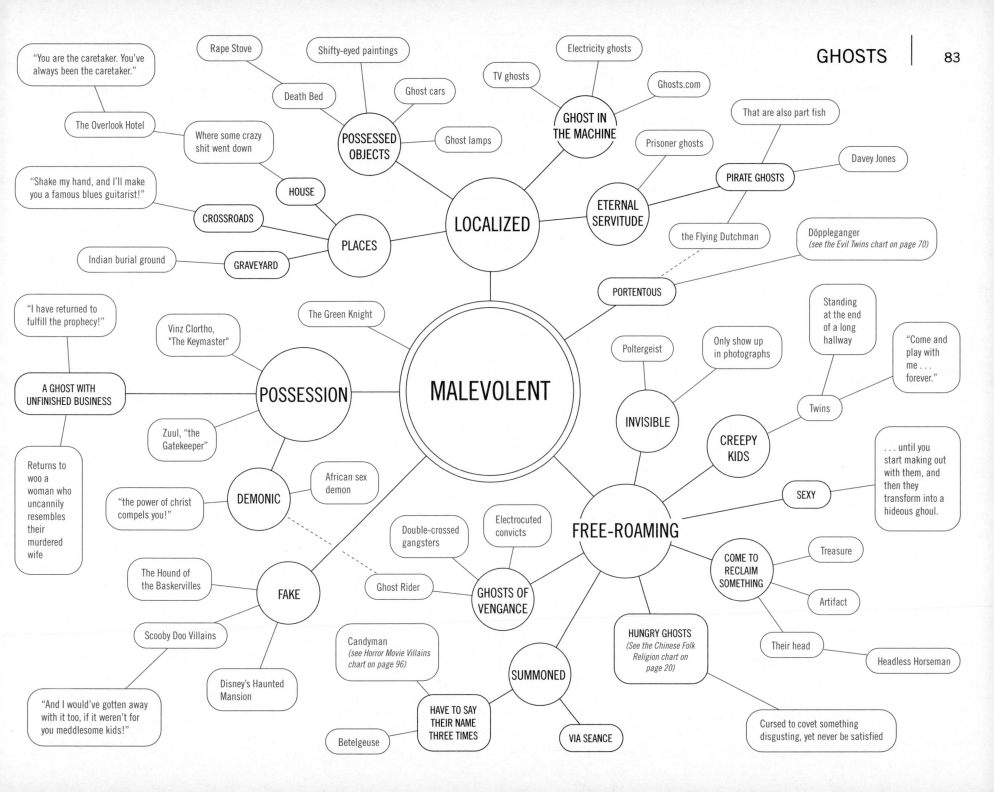

HEAVY METAL BAND NAMES

HEAVY METAL IS A GENRE OF ROCK distinctive for its loudness, machismo, and theatricality. So it's no wonder that heavy metal band names are similarly theatrical. What is perhaps unexpected is their universally pessimistic slant. You would think being in a heavy metal band is fun: rocking out, hanging with the guys, scoring groupies. Yet most heavy metal names focus on the negative: death, darkness, and rampant misspelling.

Of all the band name charts I've drawn[1], heavy metal band names are the most homogenous in their philosophical worldview. Blackness and darkness are the prevailing themes of heavy metal band

----

(1) A cappella, Acid jazz, Adai-adai, Ambient, Anti-folk, Appalachia, Bamboo band, Bob Marley tribute bands, Calypso, Celtic Reggae, Delta Blues, Doo wop, Dubtronica, Emo, Ethereal Wave, Futurepop, Garage Bands, Gypsy funk, Hard bop, High School Marching Bands, Jam Bands, Jug bands, Kabuki, Mambo, Muzak, Naked funk, Nerdcore, Nintendocore, Polka, Progressive trance, Quadrille, Raggamuffin, Ramvong, Sacred harp, Sea shanties, Tropicalia, Weird Al, and Zydeco.

names. Heavy metal bands view this darkness as complete and inescapable. Not only do they talk about the darkness in everyday life—Venom, Poison, Anthrax, Anal Apocalypse—they go on to assure viewers that there is no light in the afterlife.

A large percentage of heavy metal band names are open criticisms of modern culture (*see Figure 1: What is Heavy Metal Rebelling Against?*), but their favorite thing to rebel against is definitely organized religion, because it accomplishes multiple goals.

1. It's easy to make fun of God, because ever since the New Testament, he usually turns the other cheek.

2. Biblical words—sabbath, ragnarok, stigmata, testament—sound badass, and are closely related to three secondary heavy metal band name categories: arcane words, death, and medieval.

FIGURE 1: WHAT IS HEAVY METAL REBELLING AGAINST?

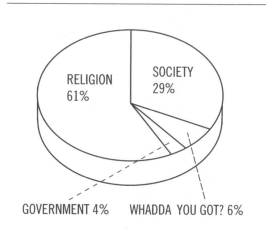

RELIGION 61%

SOCIETY 29%

GOVERNMENT 4%   WHADDA YOU GOT? 6%

3. You gotta rebel against something. Why not religion?

Religious oxymorons like Black Sabbath and Shotgun Messiah create especially memorable names. Their popularity suggest that heavy metal bands are attracted to the hardcore cache of the badass, vengeful God of the Old Testament while simultaneously repelled by the loving Jesus of the New Testament.

I often see interesting shapes emerge when I'm charting a subject, but even I was shocked when, during my work on this chart, a flaming pentagram appeared in the middle of the page. It emerged suddenly, accompanied by a clap of thunder that shook my house and stopped all the clocks at midnight. Just as suddenly as it appeared, it disappeared, leaving nothing but the stench of sulfur and a burn mark on my Ikea coffee table (its name is Ölm—note the umlaut). The debate that raged in the 1980s about the link between heavy metal and Satan worshipping can now be put to rest: heavy metal is the Devil's music. This explains the popularity of the sign of the horns as a heavy metal gesture, and the comparative obscurity of the unicorn horn gesture. (*See Figure 2: Know Your Horns.*) This does not, however, mean that listening to metal automatically makes you a Satan worshipper, it simply means you and Satan have one more thing in common besides enjoying porn.

An interesting aspect of heavy metal band names is the large percentage of arcane, foreign, misspelled, or completely made up words: Queensryche, Pantera, Motley Crue, Megadeth, Agathodaimon, Ratt. Their usage seems to be a band's way of saying "We don't belong to this world, we don't speak your language . . . now get out of my room."

Of the foreign words heavy metal bands appropriate, most are German or Scandinavian. A few are Spanish, and none are French. (*See Figure 3: Badass Ranking of Foreign Languages.*) Germanic languages are an obvious choice because of their universally menacing tones and bitchin' umlauts (even my coffee table's name sounds tough). As an added bonus, the blackletter fonts associated with Germany look great on T-shirts and album covers, and can make any word look badass. (*See Figure 4: Logo for the Death Metal Band Bunny Hug.*) Just because a band name isn't German, that doesn't mean it can't have an umlaut or three. Why? *Why not.* The answer is bold in its simplicity, and typifies the heavy metal band's disregard for rules both societal and grammatical.

FIGURE 2: KNOW YOUR HORNS

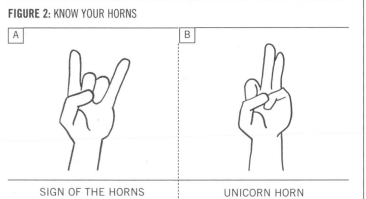

SIGN OF THE HORNS   UNICORN HORN

FIGURE 3: BADASS RANKING OF FOREIGN LANGUAGES

1. German
2. Russian
3. Spanish
4. Cockney English
5. Japanese
6. Italian
7. American
8. French
9. British
10. Indian
11. Chinese

FIGURE 4: LOGO FOR THE DEATH METAL BAND BUNNY HUG

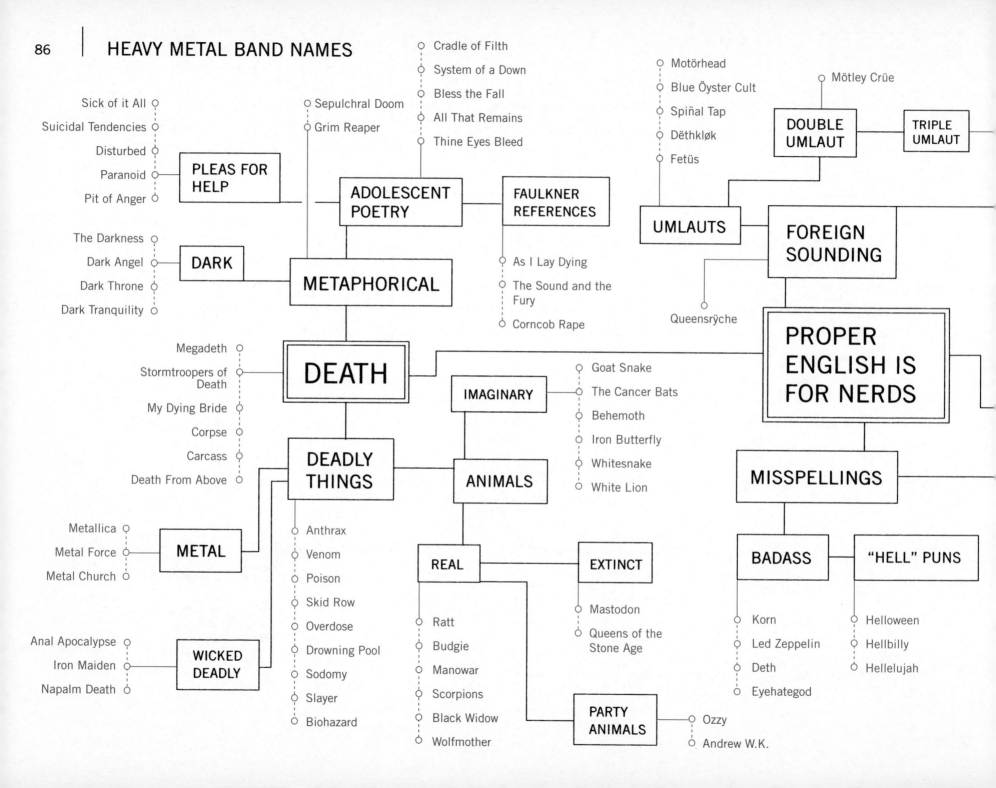

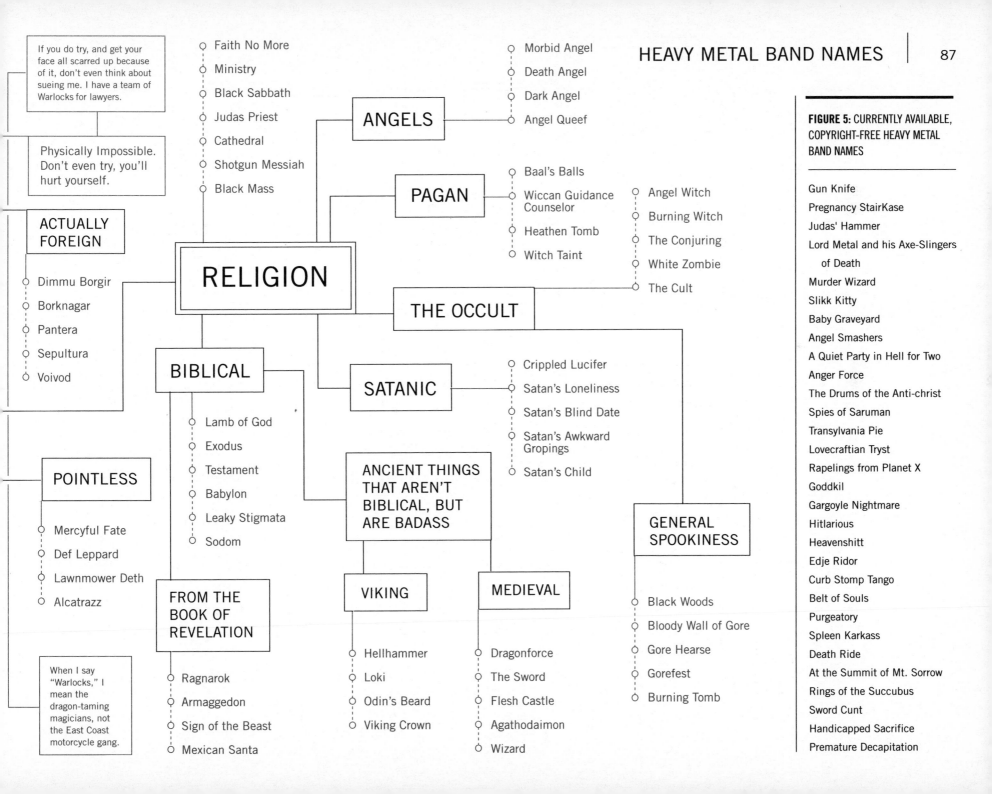

If you do try, and get your face all scarred up because of it, don't even think about sueing me. I have a team of Warlocks for lawyers.

Physically Impossible. Don't even try, you'll hurt yourself.

Faith No More
Ministry
Black Sabbath
Judas Priest
Cathedral
Shotgun Messiah
Black Mass

ANGELS
Morbid Angel
Death Angel
Dark Angel
Angel Queef

ACTUALLY FOREIGN
Dimmu Borgir
Borknagar
Pantera
Sepultura
Voivod

RELIGION

PAGAN
Baal's Balls
Wiccan Guidance Counselor
Heathen Tomb
Witch Taint

Angel Witch
Burning Witch
The Conjuring
White Zombie
The Cult

THE OCCULT

BIBLICAL
Lamb of God
Exodus
Testament
Babylon
Leaky Stigmata
Sodom

SATANIC
Crippled Lucifer
Satan's Loneliness
Satan's Blind Date
Satan's Awkward Gropings
Satan's Child

POINTLESS
Mercyful Fate
Def Leppard
Lawnmower Deth
Alcatrazz

ANCIENT THINGS THAT AREN'T BIBLICAL, BUT ARE BADASS

FROM THE BOOK OF REVELATION
Ragnarok
Armaggedon
Sign of the Beast
Mexican Santa

VIKING
Hellhammer
Loki
Odin's Beard
Viking Crown

MEDIEVAL
Dragonforce
The Sword
Flesh Castle
Agathodaimon
Wizard

GENERAL SPOOKINESS
Black Woods
Bloody Wall of Gore
Gore Hearse
Gorefest
Burning Tomb

When I say "Warlocks," I mean the dragon-taming magicians, not the East Coast motorcycle gang.

FIGURE 5: CURRENTLY AVAILABLE, COPYRIGHT-FREE HEAVY METAL BAND NAMES

Gun Knife
Pregnancy StairKase
Judas' Hammer
Lord Metal and his Axe-Slingers of Death
Murder Wizard
Slikk Kitty
Baby Graveyard
Angel Smashers
A Quiet Party in Hell for Two
Anger Force
The Drums of the Anti-christ
Spies of Saruman
Transylvania Pie
Lovecraftian Tryst
Rapelings from Planet X
Goddkil
Gargoyle Nightmare
Hitlarious
Heavenshitt
Edje Ridor
Curb Stomp Tango
Belt of Souls
Purgeatory
Spleen Karkass
Death Ride
At the Summit of Mt. Sorrow
Rings of the Succubus
Sword Cunt
Handicapped Sacrifice
Premature Decapitation

HEROES AND VILLAINS

IF YOU WATCH OLD WESTERN MOVIES, you can immediately distinguish the heroes from the villains. The villains look and act like bad guys: they kill indiscriminately, five-o-clock shadow peppers their perpetually sneering faces, and they kick dogs. The hero is equally recognizable: handsome and dapper, he rides a white horse and only kills as an absolute last resort—usually after he's already gallantly given the villain a chance to live, which the villain inevitably exploits by trying to shoot the hero in the back. However, action heroes have evolved rapidly since Douglas Fairbanks first put on Zorro's mask, and one consequence is that the line separating heroes from villains has become thinner and thinner. Indeed, one goal of sophisticated modern films is the avoidance of one-dimensional characters; the result is that contemporary heroes and villains have more similarities than differences, and the antihero has become a popular contemporary archetype.

Nowhere are the film archetypes of hero and villain portrayed more clearly than in the genres of action and horror. Action movies and horror movies have many similarities: a single, compelling character drives the story, there is a high level of action and violence, which is of equal or greater importance than the plot, and the prevailing theme is the struggle between good and evil. However, a significant difference between action and horror is that when we watch action movies our favorite character is the hero, and when we watch horror movies our favorite character is the villain.

Even when a hero is on the deep end of the anti-hero scale—such as Popeye Doyle in *The French Connection* or Snake Plissken in *Escape From New York*—we recognize them as the hero because the film is told through their eyes; they're the protagonist. The vital distinction that quarantines villains in the antagonist role is that we (rarely) see the film from their point of view.

Although the audience isn't *supposed* to like the villain, they are nevertheless our favorite part of horror movies. The only reason we even care about the protagonist in a horror movie is because we want to see how the villain will try to kill him. In many horror films with a lengthy franchise, such as *Friday the 13th* or *A Nightmare on Elm Street*, the audience comes to regard the villain with less fear than fondness.

Aside from the narrative roles of protagonist and antagonist, what behaviors distinguish contemporary action heroes from horror villains? The two defining characteristics we've assigned to heroes both hinge on the morality of killing:

1. Action heroes don't kill people: This used to be true in the majority of action films, and some heroes (Batman) don't kill people, but the majority are at least *willing* to kill. Many action heroes who we think of as non-lethal have actually amassed respectable body counts; Indiana Jones is a good

example. When I started this chart the only people I could remember Indiana Jones killing were the Cairo Swordsman and the Nazi pugilist that Indy neglects to warn about the spinning propeller that is right behind him. However, rewatching the Indiana Jones films and counting all the kills, I was shocked at how many henchmen Indy actually disposes of—46 by my count, across the four films. The thing is, he kills them so casually, it's not the focus of the film: Indy's in a coal cart, careening through the mines, and after a struggle he throws a Thuggee henchman out of the speeding cart; well, that guy's dead now. But we don't care. You know who does care? That Thuggee's pet cat, who's at home alone and now is going to slowly starve to death.

This brings us to the second distinction:

2. Action heroes only kill bad people: As we've already begun to discuss, I think this distinction is spurious. Are all the nameless henchmen that action heroes flippantly mow down with machine gun fire or casually toss over bridges evil? Most of them just stand around doing their job—flanking a doorway in matching black turtlenecks and sunglasses, or flipping big switches while wearing a hazmat suit. I bet many of them have families to support, and are henching (industry term) on weekends just to make ends meet, or because it's the only way they can receive healthcare. But heroes don't stop to administer morality tests to every rank-and-file henchman before blowing up a volcano fortress or Alpine stronghold.

Herein lies another important distinction between the portrayal of violence in action and horror movies. In action movies violence fuels the action, but the consequences of the violence are incidental, and the emotion it elicits in the viewer is excitement; in horror movies the violence is the primary focus of the movie, and by treating its consequences with importance it elicits fear in the viewer. Viewed thusly horror movies are actually less immoral than action movies, because they acknowledge the reality of violence that action movies so glibly gloss over.

I counted all the people each of the heroes and villains on this chart killed and was not surprised to discover that the heroes have killed more peo-ple. When Chuck Norris opens fire on the enemy's POW camp in *Missing In Action*, he can casually mow down dozens of enemy combatants per second—*braka, braka, braka!* But every time Jason Voorhees kills someone, it's important; the camera is forced to linger—it just takes longer for villains to kill people.

Godzilla is a unique character because he started as villain but turned into a hero over the course of his lengthy film franchise. Godzilla was originally created as a metaphor for the atomic bombing of Japan during WWII, so I made his body count the estimated number of casualties from Nagasaki and Hiroshima. As a cipher for the unspeakable violence of war, Godzilla is the ultimate villain, conjured to help an entire country comprehend and mourn its grave losses. The original *Gojira* is an incredibly moving, slow funeral dirge; the camera lingers on each building Godzilla crushes, forcing you to consider each life squashed by his rampage. He stands apart from and above all the other characters on this chart so much that I haven't placed him into either group, and instead depicted him in the chart's key.

K E Y

TYPE OF VILLAIN OR HERO

VILLAINS	ARCHETYPE
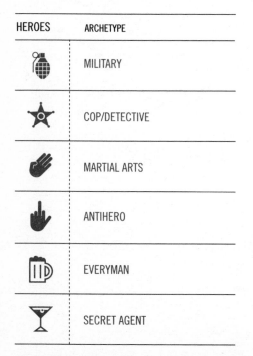	MONSTER
	DEMONIC/MAGIC
	SLASHER*

*Although villains like Jason Voorhees and Michael Meyers may technically be magic, their m.o. is still more slasher than demonic/magic, so I've classified them as slashers.

HEROES	ARCHETYPE
	MILITARY
	COP/DETECTIVE
	MARTIAL ARTS
	ANTIHERO
	EVERYMAN
	SECRET AGENT

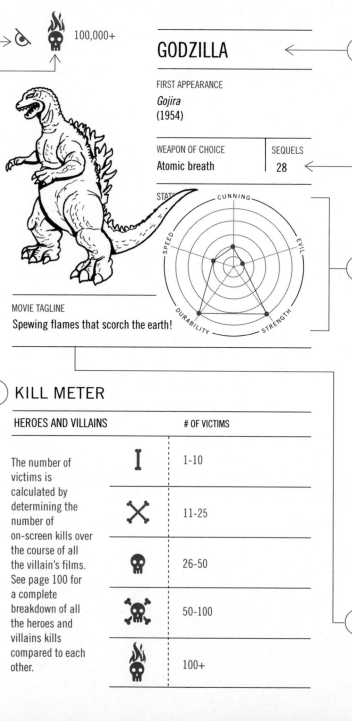

(1)

100,000+

MOVIE TAGLINE
Spewing flames that scorch the earth!

GODZILLA

(3) CHARACTER NAME

FIRST APPEARANCE

Gojira
(1954)

WEAPON OF CHOICE	SEQUELS
Atomic breath	28

STAT

Black numbers indicate sequels starring the original actor; a plus sign and numbers in blue indicate sequels that star the main character portrayed by a different actor (unless the character is masked).

See the next page for clarification of the numbers' meanings.

(4) **STRENGTHS AND WEAKNESSES**

The farther the dots are from the center, the higher their corresponding number.

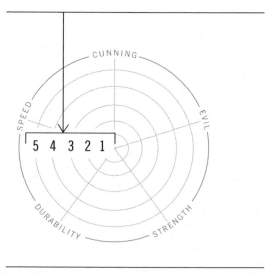

(2) **KILL METER**

HEROES AND VILLAINS	# OF VICTIMS
The number of victims is calculated by determining the number of on-screen kills over the course of all the villain's films. See page 100 for a complete breakdown of all the heroes and villains kills compared to each other.	
I	1-10
X	11-25
💀	26-50
☠	50-100
🔥	100+

(5) QUOTE

In the case of nonspeaking horror movie villains, the quote is replaced with either their movie tagline or a brief description of their best kill.

> (4B)

	CUNNING	EVIL	STRENGTH	DURABILITY	SPEED
1	Basic animal intelligence	Will kill if threatened or to satisfy basic animal needs.	Below average human strength	Easy to kill	Can't move faster than a walk. Clumsy.
2	Smart enough to operate a chainsaw.	Only kills certain people; kills with a rationale. Capable of remorse.	Average human strength	Average human durability	Average human speed and dexterity
3	Knows to look for you under the bed.	Kills indiscriminately; enjoys killing, but is capable of mercy.	Stronger than you are.	Can be killed with conventional weapons, but it won't be easy	Faster than you are; dexterous and graceful.
4	Sets elaborate traps, always one step ahead of you.	Enjoys killing, incapable of mercy or remorse.	Strong enough to crush your head with its hands.	Can only be killed with heavy weapons or under special circumstances.	Creepy quick—one second they're not there, and the next, there they are.
5	Always waiting in the backseat as you frantically rev the car engine.	Pure evil	Strong enough to crush buildings with its hands.	Basically indestructible	Way faster than that crappy 2-door you're trying to outrun them with.

	INTELLIGENCE	ACTING	CHARISMA	FIGHTING SKILL	HUMOR
1	Just shoots and hits stuff.	Walking prop.	Not likeable. Strangely off-putting.	Just shoots a gun, usually from the hip	Totally serious
2	Average intelligence.	Can effectively portray one emotion (probably *stoicism*).	Seems like an okay guy	Can throw a punch that looks like it really hurts.	Able to deliver unfunny puns with the affectation of a robot.
3	Utilizes their intelligence as a weapon to outwit the enemy, but mostly during fights.	Able to convincingly convey a wide range of emotions.	You like this person. They have a certain something.	Can kick higher than their waist and utilizes creative throws or improvised weapons.	Funny like the funny guy in your office, who's actually pretty funny.
4	Able to figure out the villain's true motives and strategize.	Able to imbue the dialogue with added meaning, subtle shades of emotion between the lines.	Exudes a strong aura of intensity that makes you want to watch them.	Bitchin' jump kicks and punches that break bones.	*Witty*, which is a level above *funny*, because it's natural and casual, not forced.
5	Smarter than the audience.	Makes you forget you're watching an actor.	An unforgettable and unique presence that no other actor can mimic.	Pulls fighting moves that you didn't know were fighting moves.	Laughs in the face of danger! Has a humorous demeanor in addition to funny dialogue.

LEE

25

FIRST APPEARANCE
Enter the Dragon
(1973)

PORTRAYED BY	SEQUELS
Bruce Lee	0

STATS

INTELLIGENCE · ACTING · CHARISMA · STRENGTH · FIGHTING SKILL · HUMOR

QUOTE
"Hooooooooooooaaa . . . YAH!"

JAMES BRADDOCK

177

FIRST APPEARANCE
Missing in Action
(1984)

PORTRAYED BY	SEQUELS
Chuck Norris	2

STATS

INTELLIGENCE · ACTING · CHARISMA · STRENGTH · FIGHTING SKILL · HUMOR

QUOTE
"I don't need a weapon, I am one."

INDIANA JONES

46

FIRST APPEARANCE
Raiders of the Lost Ark
(1981)

PORTRAYED BY	SEQUELS
Harrison Ford	3

STATS

INTELLIGENCE · ACTING · CHARISMA · STRENGTH · FIGHTING SKILL · HUMOR

QUOTE
"Snakes. Why'd it have to be snakes?"

JOHN MATRIX

81

FIRST APPEARANCE
Commando
(1985)

PORTRAYED BY	SEQUELS
Arnold Schwarzenegger	0

STATS

INTELLIGENCE · ACTING · CHARISMA · STRENGTH · FIGHTING SKILL · HUMOR

QUOTE
"You're a funny man . . . that's why
I'm going to kill you last."

JOHN McCLANE

57

FIRST APPEARANCE
Die Hard
(1988)

PORTRAYED BY	SEQUELS
Bruce Willis	3

STATS

INTELLIGENCE · ACTING · CHARISMA · STRENGTH · FIGHTING SKILL · HUMOR

QUOTE
"Yippee-ki-yay, motherfucker."

JACK RYAN

3

FIRST APPEARANCE
Patriot Games
(1992)

PORTRAYED BY	SEQUELS
Harrison Ford	1 +2

STATS

INTELLIGENCE · ACTING · CHARISMA · STRENGTH · FIGHTING SKILL · HUMOR

QUOTE
"Where's my family?!"

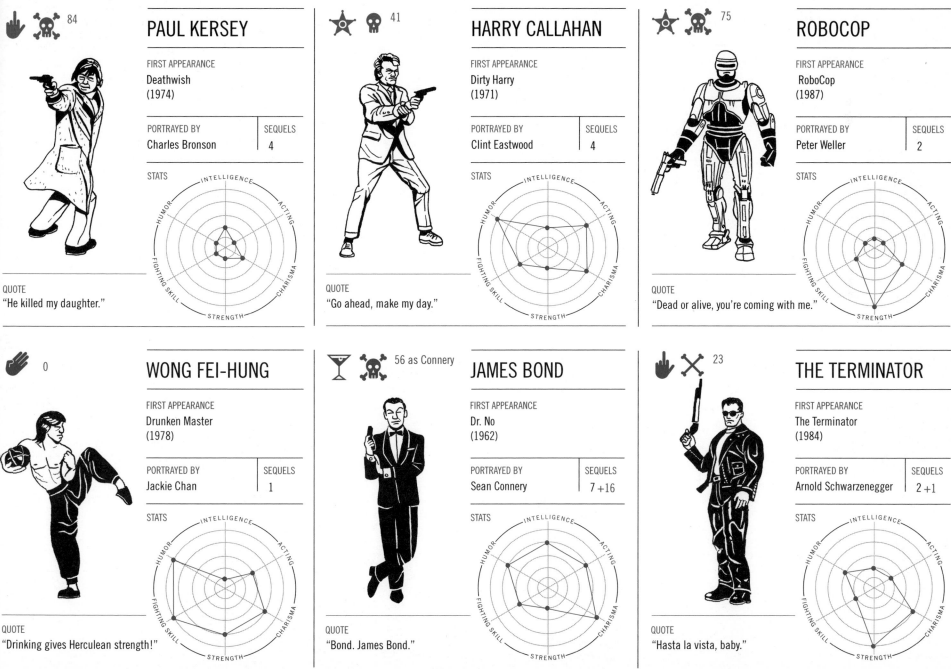

PAUL KERSEY

84

FIRST APPEARANCE
Deathwish
(1974)

PORTRAYED BY	SEQUELS
Charles Bronson	4

STATS

QUOTE
"He killed my daughter."

HARRY CALLAHAN

41

FIRST APPEARANCE
Dirty Harry
(1971)

PORTRAYED BY	SEQUELS
Clint Eastwood	4

STATS

QUOTE
"Go ahead, make my day."

ROBOCOP

75

FIRST APPEARANCE
RoboCop
(1987)

PORTRAYED BY	SEQUELS
Peter Weller	2

STATS

QUOTE
"Dead or alive, you're coming with me."

WONG FEI-HUNG

0

FIRST APPEARANCE
Drunken Master
(1978)

PORTRAYED BY	SEQUELS
Jackie Chan	1

STATS

QUOTE
"Drinking gives Herculean strength!"

JAMES BOND

56 as Connery

FIRST APPEARANCE
Dr. No
(1962)

PORTRAYED BY	SEQUELS
Sean Connery	7 +16

STATS

QUOTE
"Bond. James Bond."

THE TERMINATOR

23

FIRST APPEARANCE
The Terminator
(1984)

PORTRAYED BY	SEQUELS
Arnold Schwarzenegger	2 +1

STATS

QUOTE
"Hasta la vista, baby."

CASEY RYBACK

59

FIRST APPEARANCE
Under Siege
(1992)

PORTRAYED BY	SEQUELS
Steven Seagal	1

STATS

INTELLIGENCE · ACTING · CHARISMA · STRENGTH · FIGHTING SKILL · HUMOR

QUOTE
"(I'm) just a lowly, lowly, cook."

FRANK DUX

0

FIRST APPEARANCE
Bloodsport
(1988)

PORTRAYED BY	SEQUELS
Jean-Claude Van Damme	0 + 3

STATS

INTELLIGENCE · ACTING · CHARISMA · STRENGTH · FIGHTING SKILL · HUMOR

QUOTE
"Aren't you a little old for videogames?"

SNAKE PLISSKEN

35

FIRST APPEARANCE
Escape From New York
(1981)

PORTRAYED BY	SEQUELS
Kurt Russell	1

STATS

INTELLIGENCE · ACTING · CHARISMA · STRENGTH · FIGHTING SKILL · HUMOR

QUOTE
"I don't give a fuck about your war."

NEO

29

FIRST APPEARANCE
The Matrix
(1999)

PORTRAYED BY	SEQUELS
Keanu Reeves	2

STATS

INTELLIGENCE · ACTING · CHARISMA · STRENGTH · FIGHTING SKILL · HUMOR

QUOTE
"I know kung fu."

MAX ROCKATANSKY

18

FIRST APPEARANCE
Mad Max
(1979)

PORTRAYED BY	SEQUELS
Mel Gibson	2 +1

STATS

INTELLIGENCE · ACTING · CHARISMA · STRENGTH · FIGHTING SKILL · HUMOR

QUOTE
"Any longer out on that road and I'm one of them."

THE BRIDE

77

FIRST APPEARANCE
Kill Bill
(2003)

PORTRAYED BY	SEQUELS
Uma Thurman	1

STATS

INTELLIGENCE · ACTING · CHARISMA · STRENGTH · FIGHTING SKILL · HUMOR

QUOTE
"Wiggle your big toe."

ELLEN RIPLEY

🍺 ✖ 18

FIRST APPEARANCE
Alien
(1979)

PORTRAYED BY	SEQUELS
Sigourney Weaver	3

STATS

QUOTE
"Get away from her, you bitch."

JASON BOURNE

🍸 🦴 10

FIRST APPEARANCE
The Bourne Identity
(2002)

PORTRAYED BY	SEQUELS
Matt Damon	2

STATS

QUOTE
"Everything I found out, I wanna forget."

JOHN SHAFT

🖕 💀 48

FIRST APPEARANCE
Shaft
(1971)

PORTRAYED BY	SEQUELS
Richard Roundtree	2

STATS

QUOTE
"You are one wise Caucasian, Vic."

RIGGS & MURTAUGH

⭐ 💀 50

FIRST APPEARANCE
Lethal Weapon
(1987)

PORTRAYED BY	SEQUELS
Danny Glover, Mel Gibson	3

STATS

QUOTE
"I'm getting too old for this shit!"

JOHN RAMBO

💣 💀🔥 220

FIRST APPEARANCE
Rambo: First Blood
(1982)

PORTRAYED BY	SEQUELS
Sylvester Stallone	3

STATS

QUOTE
"They drew first blood, not me."

ETHAN HUNT

🍸 💀 43

FIRST APPEARANCE
Mission: Impossible
(1996)

PORTRAYED BY	SEQUELS
Tom Cruise	2

STATS

QUOTE
". . . you've never *seen* me very upset."

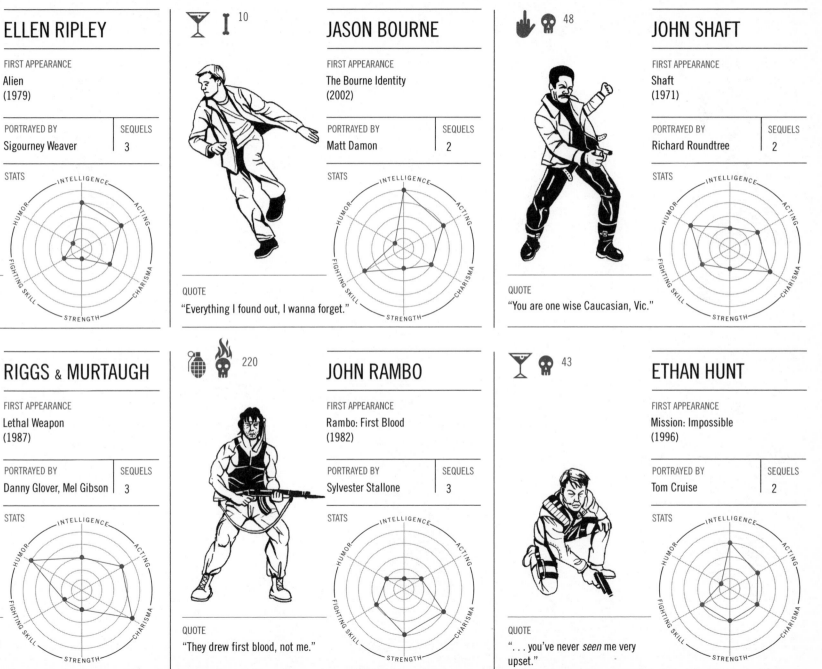

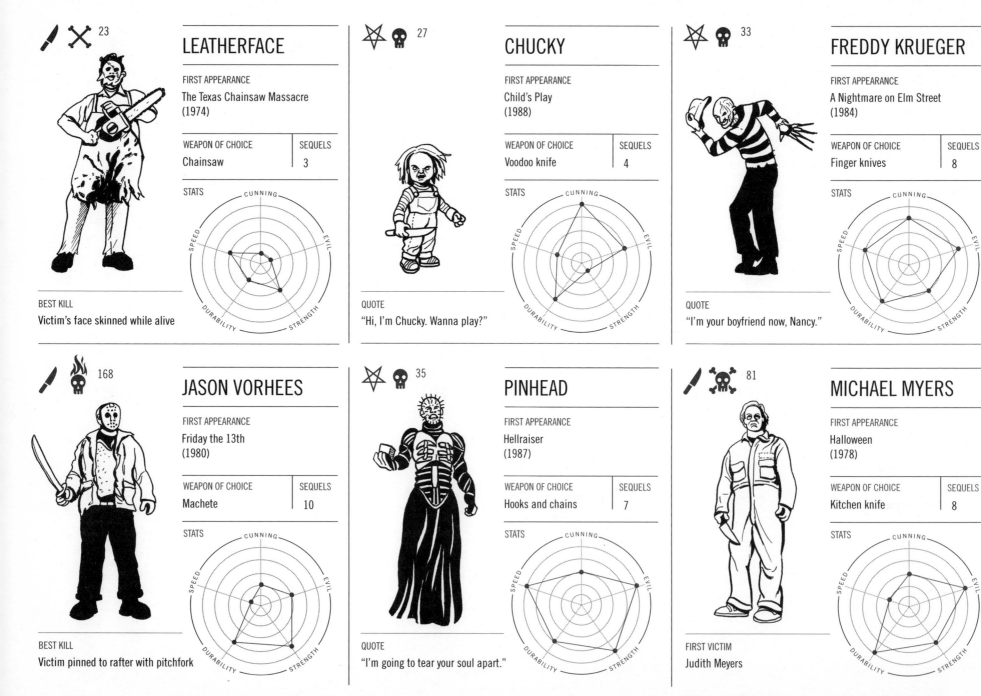

LEATHERFACE

FIRST APPEARANCE
The Texas Chainsaw Massacre
(1974)

WEAPON OF CHOICE	SEQUELS
Chainsaw	3

STATS

BEST KILL
Victim's face skinned while alive

CHUCKY

FIRST APPEARANCE
Child's Play
(1988)

WEAPON OF CHOICE	SEQUELS
Voodoo knife	4

STATS

QUOTE
"Hi, I'm Chucky. Wanna play?"

FREDDY KRUEGER

FIRST APPEARANCE
A Nightmare on Elm Street
(1984)

WEAPON OF CHOICE	SEQUELS
Finger knives	8

STATS

QUOTE
"I'm your boyfriend now, Nancy."

JASON VORHEES

FIRST APPEARANCE
Friday the 13th
(1980)

WEAPON OF CHOICE	SEQUELS
Machete	10

STATS

BEST KILL
Victim pinned to rafter with pitchfork

PINHEAD

FIRST APPEARANCE
Hellraiser
(1987)

WEAPON OF CHOICE	SEQUELS
Hooks and chains	7

STATS

QUOTE
"I'm going to tear your soul apart."

MICHAEL MYERS

FIRST APPEARANCE
Halloween
(1978)

WEAPON OF CHOICE	SEQUELS
Kitchen knife	8

STATS

FIRST VICTIM
Judith Meyers

THE TALL MAN

79

FIRST APPEARANCE
Phantasm
(1979)

WEAPON OF CHOICE	SEQUELS
Flying silver orb	3

STATS

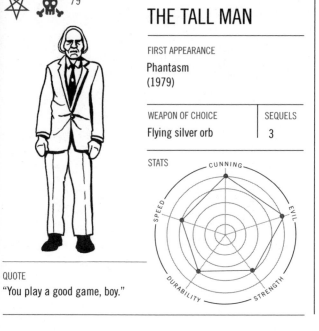

QUOTE
"You play a good game, boy."

PUMPKINHEAD

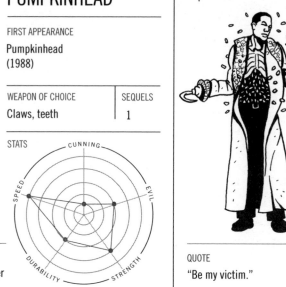

7

FIRST APPEARANCE
Pumpkinhead
(1988)

WEAPON OF CHOICE	SEQUELS
Claws, teeth	1

STATS

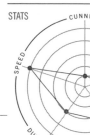

WEAKNESS
Physical link to human summoner

CANDYMAN

28

FIRST APPEARANCE
Candyman
(1992)

WEAPON OF CHOICE	SEQUELS
Hook hand	2

STATS

QUOTE
"Be my victim."

LEPRECHAUN

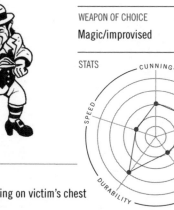

27

FIRST APPEARANCE
Leprechaun
(1993)

WEAPON OF CHOICE	SEQUELS
Magic/improvised	5

STATS

BEST KILL
Pogo stick jumping on victim's chest

NORMAN BATES

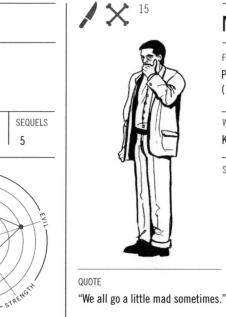

15

FIRST APPEARANCE
Psycho
(1960)

WEAPON OF CHOICE	SEQUELS
Kitchen knife	3

STATS

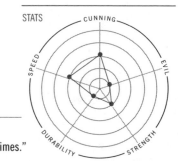

QUOTE
"We all go a little mad sometimes."

PENNYWISE

5

FIRST APPEARANCE
It
(1990)

WEAPON OF CHOICE	SEQUELS
Teeth, deadlights	0

STATS

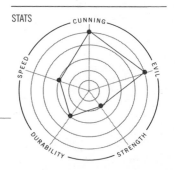

QUOTE
"They all float down here."

DAMIEN THORN

62

FIRST APPEARANCE
The Omen
(1976)

WEAPON OF CHOICE	SEQUELS
Unlikely accidents	3

STATS

BEST KILL
Victim impaled on church spire

THE BLOB

51

FIRST APPEARANCE
The Blob
(1958)

WEAPON OF CHOICE	SEQUELS
Lethal absorption	1

STATS

MOVIE TAGLINE
Beware the blob!

THE DJINN

47

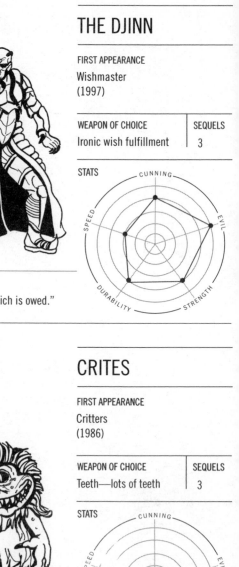

FIRST APPEARANCE
Wishmaster
(1997)

WEAPON OF CHOICE	SEQUELS
Ironic wish fulfillment	3

STATS

QUOTE
"I claim that which is owed."

HANNIBAL LECTER

21

FIRST APPEARANCE
Manhunter
(1986)

WEAPON OF CHOICE	SEQUELS
Teeth	4

STATS

QUOTE
"I ate his liver with some fava beans and a nice Chianti."

GHOSTFACE

27

FIRST APPEARANCE
Scream
(1996)

WEAPON OF CHOICE	SEQUELS
Bowie knife	3

STATS

QUOTE
"Do you like scary movies?"

CRITES

18

FIRST APPEARANCE
Critters
(1986)

WEAPON OF CHOICE	SEQUELS
Teeth—lots of teeth	3

STATS

MOVIE TAGLINE
The original tasty entree!

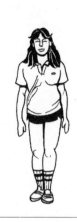 45

ANGELA BAKER

FIRST APPEARANCE
Sleepaway Camp
(1983)

WEAPON OF CHOICE	SEQUELS
Improvised	2

STATS

BEST KILL
Curling iron up the hoo-ha

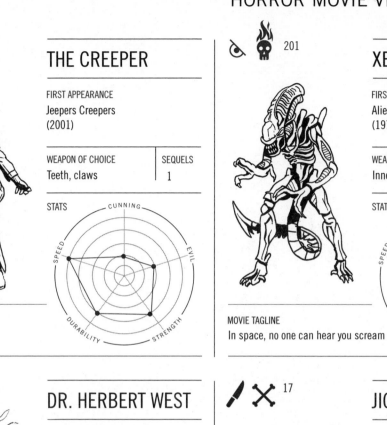 19

THE CREEPER

FIRST APPEARANCE
Jeepers Creepers
(2001)

WEAPON OF CHOICE	SEQUELS
Teeth, claws	1

STATS

MOVIE TAGLINE
What's Eating You?

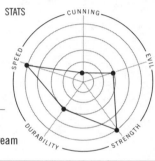 201

XENOMORPHS

FIRST APPEARANCE
Alien
(1979)

WEAPON OF CHOICE	SEQUELS
Inner maw	5

STATS

MOVIE TAGLINE
In space, no one can hear you scream

 17

JAWS

FIRST APPEARANCE
Jaws
(1975)

WEAPON OF CHOICE	SEQUELS
Teeth	3

STATS

MOVIE TAGLINE
Don't go in the water

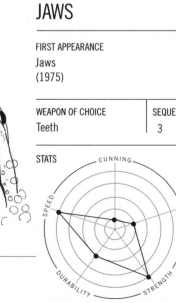 14

DR. HERBERT WEST

FIRST APPEARANCE
Re-Animator
(1985)

WEAPON OF CHOICE	SEQUELS
Re-animate syrum	2

STATS

QUOTE
"Who's going to believe a talking head?"

 17

JIGSAW

FIRST APPEARANCE
SAW
(2004)

WEAPON OF CHOICE	SEQUELS
Elaborate traps	5

STATS

QUOTE
"Live or die, make your choice."

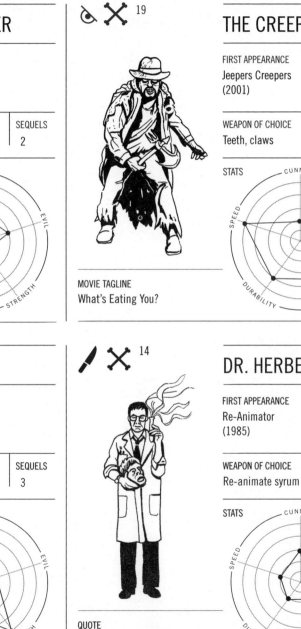

1,000 x 100
GODZILLA

To get an accurate perception of Godzilla's
body count, multiply this circle's size by 1000.

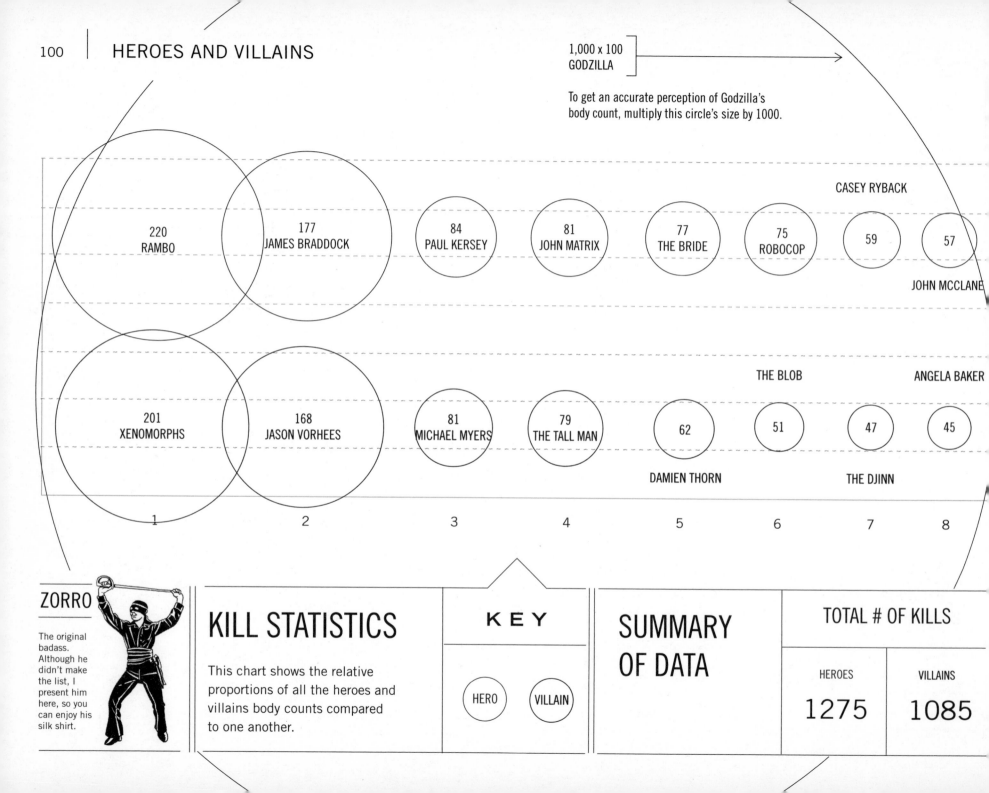

220
RAMBO

177
JAMES BRADDOCK

84
PAUL KERSEY

81
JOHN MATRIX

77
THE BRIDE

75
ROBOCOP

CASEY RYBACK

59

57

JOHN MCCLANE

201
XENOMORPHS

168
JASON VORHEES

81
MICHAEL MYERS

79
THE TALL MAN

THE BLOB

62

51

ANGELA BAKER

47

45

DAMIEN THORN

THE DJINN

1   2   3   4   5   6   7   8

ZORRO

The original
badass. Although he
didn't make
the list, I
present him
here, so you
can enjoy his
silk shirt.

KILL STATISTICS

This chart shows the relative
proportions of all the heroes and
villains body counts compared
to one another.

K E Y

HERO   VILLAIN

SUMMARY
OF DATA

TOTAL # OF KILLS

HEROES	VILLAINS
1275	1085

CHARACTER ARCHETYPE	💣	⭐	✋	☝	🍺	🍸		👁	⛤	🔪
% OF TOTAL CHARACTERS	16	16	16	21	16	13		25	37	38
% OF TOTAL KILLS	42	17.4	8	16.3	7.5	8.5		28.8	31.6	39.6

Highest numbers in blue

JAMES BOND 56
JOHN SHAFT 50
ETHAN HUNT 48
SNAKE PLISSKEN 46
LEE 43
ELLEN RIPLEY 18 — 41
JASON BOURNE 10 — 35
WONG FEI HUNG 0 — 29
25

RIGGS AND MURTAUGH
INDIANA JONES
HARRY CALLAHAN
NEO
THE TERMINATOR 23
MAX ROCKATANSKY 18
JACK RYAN 3
FRANK DUX 0

FREDDY KRUEGER 35
CHUCKY 27 — 33
GHOSTFACE 27 — 28
HANNIBAL LECTER 21
CRITES 18
JIGSAW 17
DR. HERBERT WEST 14
PENNYWISE 5

PINHEAD
CANDYMAN
LEPRECHAUN 27
LEATHERFACE 23
THE CREEPER 19
JAWS 17
NORMAN BATES 15
PUMPKINHEAD 7

9 10 11 12 13 14 15 16 17 18 19 20 21 22 23 24

AVERAGE # OF KILLS

PER FILM		PER CHARACTER	
HEROES	VILLAINS	HEROES	VILLAINS
25	12.3	51	45

TOTAL # OF SEQUELS

HEROES	VILLAINS
51	88

AVERAGE # OF SEQUELS

PER CHARACTER	
HEROES	VILLAINS
2.125	3.6

KILLS, GRAND TOTAL
2360

FILMS, GRAND TOTAL
187

HOW TO WIN AN ARGUMENT

TRUTH IS AN ILLUSION, a mirage in a desert of uncertainty. People spend their entire lives searching for it, companies make millions of dollar selling it, and leaders control billions of people by claiming to understand the truth, but in reality they're all just guessing. Nobody can verify the truth of any statement one-hundred-percent, nobody can say anything that can't be thrown into doubt through the application of shrewd questioning.

History offers innumerable examples of fallacies that were once widely accepted facts: We used to think Earth was the center of the universe; we used to think bloodletting was good for your health; we used to think tap-dancing was entertaining enough to build an entire film around. A hundred years ago, if you told someone that snoring giants did *not* cause earthquakes, they'd say you were crazy and then throw you in a lake to see whether or not you were a witch (Float? *Witch*. Sink? *Not a witch, but now dead*.).

Even in our personal lives we're adrift in a sea of uncertainty. You think you're happy, but are you really happy? You think you should get married, but are you really in love? You think you want a second dessert, but will it leave you feeling all gross and bloated?[1]

You will never know the truth, so you might as well stop trying. I knew this Yogi—an Indian holy man, not the bear—that used to hang around the arcade all day playing Frogger with these big blu-blocker sunglasses on. *(See Figure 1: Blind Arcade Yogi.)* You could tell he was very wise because he knew that if you unplugged the change machine while it was tilted at a ninety-degree angle, when you plugged it back in it would spit out a bunch of change. He was always hogging the Frogger[2] game, so one day I said to

---

(1) It will. You do.

(2) Frogger is a videogame people used to play back when all the most famous movie stars were tap dancers.

FIGURE 1: BLIND ARCADE YOGI

If you see this guy playing Frogger, just let him finish the game. Trust me. It was easy to draw this portrait from memory, because I see his face every time I close my eyes.

him, "You know, to tell you the truth, there are other people who want to play that game too." Just then he broke the Frogger high score of 100,000 points, which causes a program glitch that makes the game screen go black and emit a high-pitched warble like a screaming cat. He turned around and took off his sunglasses and I could see that his irises were covered by big, milky white cataracts; his eyes lolled at me blindly like two hard-boiled eggs and he said, "Truth is an illusion."

Right now you're probably thinking: "That story isn't true." Well guess what? It *is* true! If that doesn't convince you that truth is an illusion, then you're just being intentionally contrary, or you're my college logic professor.

The realization that truth is the dream of a sleeping butterfly shouldn't plunge you into an existential crisis, it should instead liberate you to seek more pragmatic goals. Isn't it empowering to realize that the truth is up for grabs? Even though you can't attain inner peace and harmony, there's a chance you can convince Phil in accounting—who thinks he knows everything about 70s rock-and-roll, because he was *there*, man—that Iggy Pop was more influential in the evolution of punk rock than the Sex Pistols were.

Arguing is an activity everybody engages in, but whose tactics and theories only a small percentage of people actually understand; in this way it's very similar to sex, especially if you're my ex-wife (zing!). Many people apply the tactics on this chart naturally and unconsciously; for instance, when losing an argument, it's common for the defender to change the subject, or switch to personal attacks (see tactics 17 and 18 on page 107). However, by studying and consciously applying these tactics of persuasion you will gain a huge advantage over self-taught arguers (unless they're also a rapper, in which case they will still win, because their arguments will rhyme).

The system of dialectic tricks outlined in the *How to Win an Argument* chart are based on Arthur Schopenhauer's treatise *The Art of Being Right*, which I highly recommend reading. Schopenhauer was a piercingly insightful German philosopher known for his advocacy of pessimism; some people might claim this makes him the evil twin of Gottfried Leibniz, the German polymath, philosopher, and optimism advocate. However, as we all know, Leibniz's evil twin was actually Sir Isaac Newton *(See Evil Twins, pages 68-71)*; but if you disagree, I'm certainly willing to argue the point.

FIGURE 2: SOME EXPRESSIONS TO USE OVER THE COURSE OF AN ARGUMENT, BEST EMPLOYED WHILE YOUR OPPONENT IS TALKING

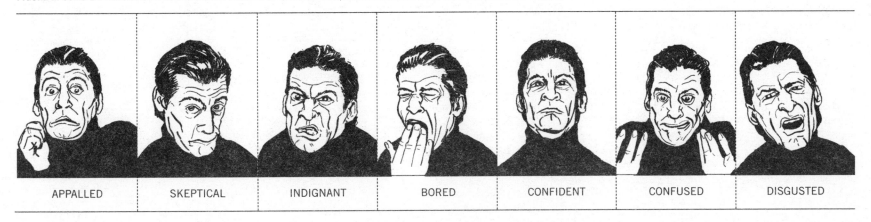

| APPALLED | SKEPTICAL | INDIGNANT | BORED | CONFIDENT | CONFUSED | DISGUSTED |

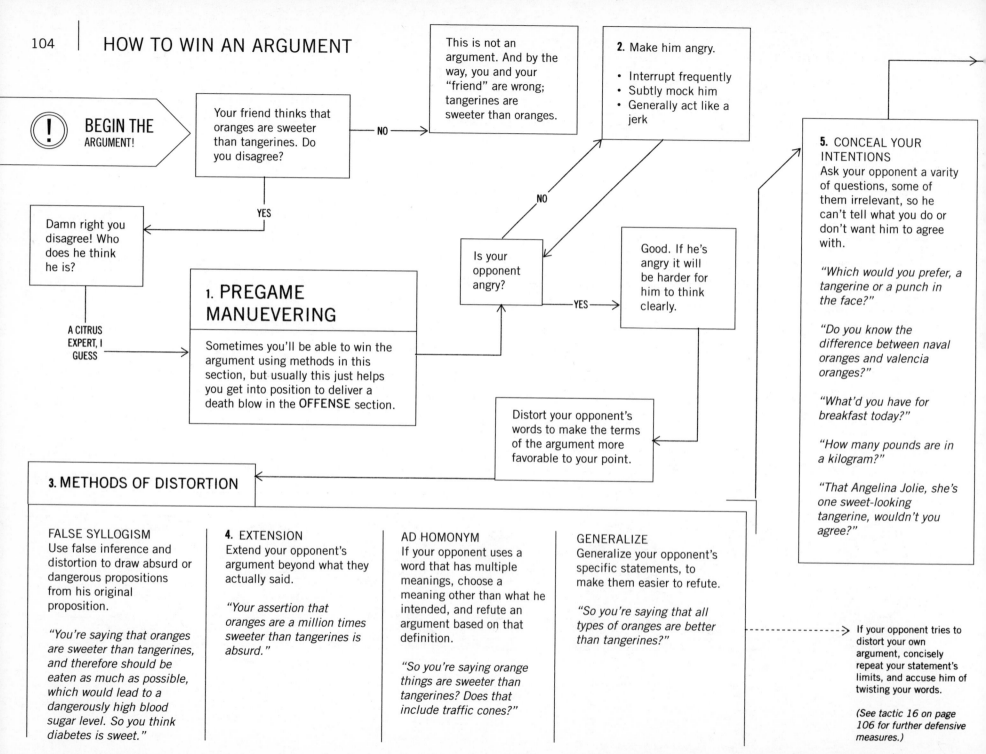

BEGIN THE ARGUMENT!

Your friend thinks that oranges are sweeter than tangerines. Do you disagree?

NO

This is not an argument. And by the way, you and your "friend" are wrong; tangerines are sweeter than oranges.

2. Make him angry.

- Interrupt frequently
- Subtly mock him
- Generally act like a jerk

NO

YES

Damn right you disagree! Who does he think he is?

A CITRUS EXPERT, I GUESS

1. PREGAME MANUEVERING

Sometimes you'll be able to win the argument using methods in this section, but usually this just helps you get into position to deliver a death blow in the **OFFENSE** section.

Is your opponent angry?

YES

Good. If he's angry it will be harder for him to think clearly.

Distort your opponent's words to make the terms of the argument more favorable to your point.

5. CONCEAL YOUR INTENTIONS

Ask your opponent a varity of questions, some of them irrelevant, so he can't tell what you do or don't want him to agree with.

"Which would you prefer, a tangerine or a punch in the face?"

"Do you know the difference between naval oranges and valencia oranges?"

"What'd you have for breakfast today?"

"How many pounds are in a kilogram?"

"That Angelina Jolie, she's one sweet-looking tangerine, wouldn't you agree?"

3. METHODS OF DISTORTION

FALSE SYLLOGISM
Use false inference and distortion to draw absurd or dangerous propositions from his original proposition.

"You're saying that oranges are sweeter than tangerines, and therefore should be eaten as much as possible, which would lead to a dangerously high blood sugar level. So you think diabetes is sweet."

4. EXTENSION
Extend your opponent's argument beyond what they actually said.

"Your assertion that oranges are a million times sweeter than tangerines is absurd."

AD HOMONYM
If your opponent uses a word that has multiple meanings, choose a meaning other than what he intended, and refute an argument based on that definition.

"So you're saying orange things are sweeter than tangerines? Does that include traffic cones?"

GENERALIZE
Generalize your opponent's specific statements, to make them easier to refute.

"So you're saying that all types of oranges are better than tangerines?"

If your opponent tries to distort your own argument, concisely repeat your statement's limits, and accuse him of twisting your words.

(See tactic 16 on page 106 for further defensive measures.)

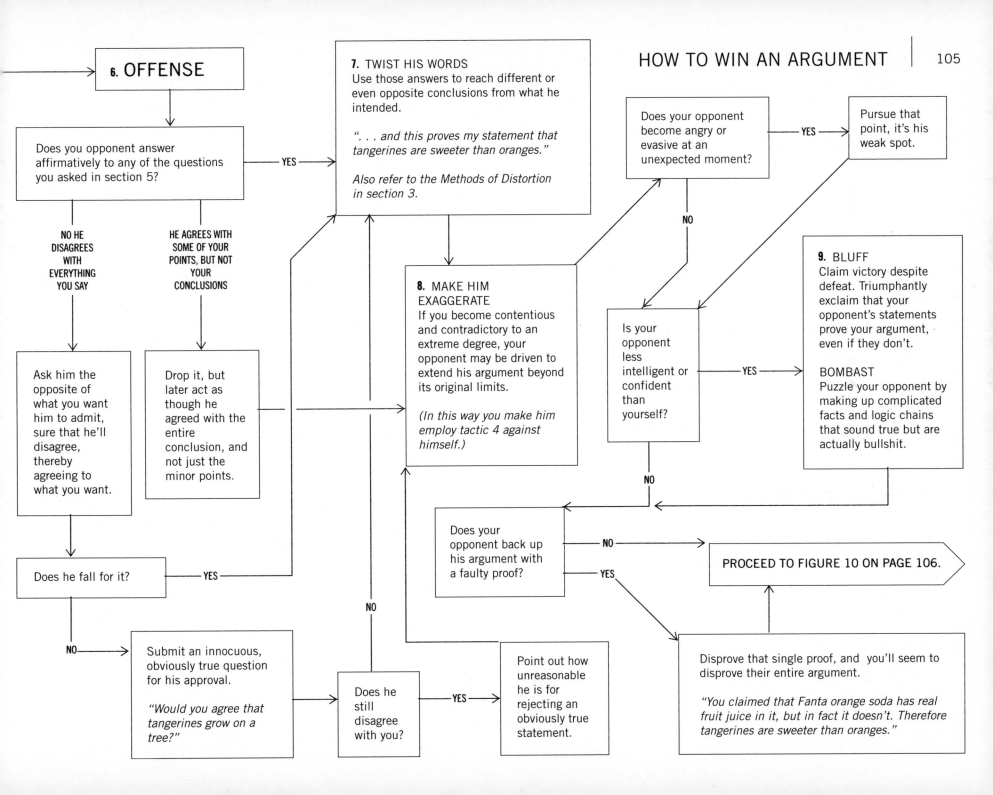

6. OFFENSE

Does you opponent answer affirmatively to any of the questions you asked in section 5?

— YES →

NO HE DISAGREES WITH EVERYTHING YOU SAY

HE AGREES WITH SOME OF YOUR POINTS, BUT NOT YOUR CONCLUSIONS

Ask him the opposite of what you want him to admit, sure that he'll disagree, thereby agreeing to what you want.

Drop it, but later act as though he agreed with the entire conclusion, and not just the minor points.

Does he fall for it?

— YES —

NO —

Submit an innocuous, obviously true question for his approval.

"Would you agree that tangerines grow on a tree?"

Does he still disagree with you?

— YES →

NO

Point out how unreasonable he is for rejecting an obviously true statement.

7. TWIST HIS WORDS
Use those answers to reach different or even opposite conclusions from what he intended.

". . . and this proves my statement that tangerines are sweeter than oranges."

Also refer to the Methods of Distortion in section 3.

8. MAKE HIM EXAGGERATE
If you become contentious and contradictory to an extreme degree, your opponent may be driven to extend his argument beyond its original limits.

(In this way you make him employ tactic 4 against himself.)

Does your opponent back up his argument with a faulty proof?

— NO →

— YES →

Does your opponent become angry or evasive at an unexpected moment?

— YES →

Pursue that point, it's his weak spot.

NO

Is your opponent less intelligent or confident than yourself?

— YES →

NO

9. BLUFF
Claim victory despite defeat. Triumphantly exclaim that your opponent's statements prove your argument, even if they don't.

BOMBAST
Puzzle your opponent by making up complicated facts and logic chains that sound true but are actually bullshit.

PROCEED TO FIGURE 10 ON PAGE 106.

Disprove that single proof, and you'll seem to disprove their entire argument.

"You claimed that Fanta orange soda has real fruit juice in it, but in fact it doesn't. Therefore tangerines are sweeter than oranges."

OFFENSE *(continued from page 105)*

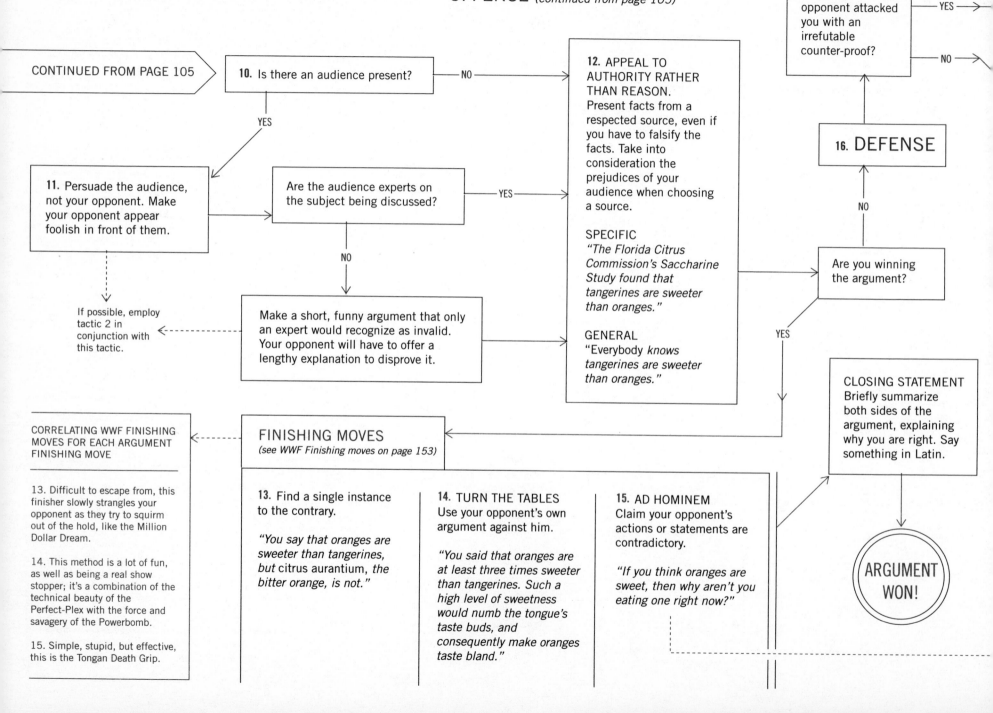

CONTINUED FROM PAGE 105

10. Is there an audience present?

YES

NO

11. Persuade the audience, not your opponent. Make your opponent appear foolish in front of them.

If possible, employ tactic 2 in conjunction with this tactic.

Are the audience experts on the subject being discussed?

YES

NO

Make a short, funny argument that only an expert would recognize as invalid. Your opponent will have to offer a lengthy explanation to disprove it.

12. APPEAL TO AUTHORITY RATHER THAN REASON.
Present facts from a respected source, even if you have to falsify the facts. Take into consideration the prejudices of your audience when choosing a source.

SPECIFIC
"The Florida Citrus Commission's Saccharine Study found that tangerines are sweeter than oranges."

GENERAL
"Everybody knows tangerines are sweeter than oranges."

Has your opponent attacked you with an irrefutable counter-proof?

YES

NO

16. DEFENSE

NO

Are you winning the argument?

YES

CLOSING STATEMENT
Briefly summarize both sides of the argument, explaining why you are right. Say something in Latin.

ARGUMENT WON!

CORRELATING WWF FINISHING MOVES FOR EACH ARGUMENT FINISHING MOVE

13. Difficult to escape from, this finisher slowly strangles your opponent as they try to squirm out of the hold, like the Million Dollar Dream.

14. This method is a lot of fun, as well as being a real show stopper; it's a combination of the technical beauty of the Perfect-Plex with the force and savagery of the Powerbomb.

15. Simple, stupid, but effective, this is the Tongan Death Grip.

FINISHING MOVES
(see WWF Finishing moves on page 153)

13. Find a single instance to the contrary.

"You say that oranges are sweeter than tangerines, but citrus aurantium, *the bitter orange, is not."*

14. TURN THE TABLES
Use your opponent's own argument against him.

"You said that oranges are at least three times sweeter than tangerines. Such a high level of sweetness would numb the tongue's taste buds, and consequently make oranges taste bland."

15. AD HOMINEM
Claim your opponent's actions or statements are contradictory.

"If you think oranges are sweet, then why aren't you eating one right now?"

Defend your position by adding a subtle distinction to your original argument.

"When I said tangerines were sweeter, I of course included clementines in that group as well."

17. Divert his attention by arguing about something only tangentially related.

"Orange oil is considered a more evironmentally friendly cleaning product than ammonia, but the orange oil extraction process releases dangerous amounts of CO2, which contributes to global warming."

Is the argument diverted?

— NO →

18. MAKE IT PERSONAL
Become insulting and rude. Attack and mock him personally. This will have the triple effect of angering him (tactic 2), diverting his attention (tactic 17), and possibly even making him look stupid in front of the audience (tactic 11).

"Your girlfriend thinks that tangerines are sweeter. At least that's what she told me last night. However, she hastened to add that they aren't as sweet as me."

Has your opponent asked you to admit something from which the point in dispute will follow?

— NO →

YES

YES

Does he continue to press his advantage?

— NO →

Return to tactic 6, Twist His Words (page 105), then proceed through the chart.

Does he take the bait and engage you in a name-calling fight?

— YES

NO

Refuse to do so, and say "You're begging the question."

LAST RESORT
Three desperate tricks.

Return to tactic 11, and stay there until the argument is over.

If your opponent asks why you aren't eating a tangerine right now:

• Smile to reveal a tangerine wedge in your teeth

• "I already at three tangerines today; they're so sweet, I can't eat a fourth."

• "Stop being so racist."

ODIOUS ASSOCIATION
Place your opponent's argument into some category; choose the category based on the prejudices of your opponent or the audience.

"What you're saying sounds like _____."

• *Racism*
• *Fascism*
• *Neo-Conservatism*
• *Reactionism*
• *Nazism*

INCOMPETENT JUDGE
Insinuate that what your opponent says is nonsense, by admitting you can't understand what he's talking about.

"What you say may be true, but I can't understand it."

Admit his premises but deny the conclusion.

"That's all very well in theory, but it won't work in practice."

Return to tactic 12, the Appeal to Authority, then proceed through the chart quickly, before everyone realizes you're full of shit.

MAFIA NICKNAMES

AS ANYONE WHO'S WATCHED *The Sopranos* knows, being in the mafia is a lot of fun; good food, flexible hours, and plenty of opportunities for upward career mobility. However, there is a dark side to the mafia that they don't want you to know about. I could probably get whacked for even talking about this, but here I go: as a member of the mafia, you are not allowed to choose your own nickname.

I found this out the hard way when I was hanging out with a bunch of mafioso and made the following mistake: I had just chopped a guy's hand off with a hatchet. This piece of shit was in our summer reading club, and he tried to tell me that he should be able to pick the next book 'cuz I had picked the last three and all of them had been from the *Bunnicula* series, which he claimed was for kids[1]. There was blood all over my face, so I asked somebody for a tissue. And everybody started calling me Tissues. I just chopped a guy with a hatchet! Why don't you call

me the Hatchet? Tommy Chops? Yackety Axe? No, *Tissues*. So I had to drop out of the mafia, which really sucked, because I haven't been able to find a good reading group since then.

My negative experience with mafia nicknames is not necessarily typical; lots of mob guys end up with awesome nicknames: the Snake, Gaspipe, the Shadow, Iceman—those are badass nicknames. However, there are also numerous examples of lackluster nicknames: Benny the Bug, Boobie, Cheesebox, and of course, the Artichoke King. The Artichoke King was the nickname of Ciro Terranova, one-time leader of the Morello crime family, who earned his bizarre nickname by selling lots of artichokes.

The Artichoke King is a perfect example of the

mafia nicknames chart's most amazing feature— 90% of the names on the chart are real mob nicknames, and 100% of the most absurd, sissy-sounding nicknames are real. Surprisingly, research has revealed that the toughness of a mobster's nickname is in inverse proportion to the toughness of the actual mobster. *(See Figure 1: Mobster Toughness Identification Scale.)* So maybe Tissues wasn't such a bad name after all.

---

(1) The three books were *Bunnicula*, *The Howliday Inn*, and *The Celery Stalks at Midnight*. All three are about a vampire rabbit who eviscerates vegetables—does that sound like kid stuff to you?

FIGURE 1: MOBSTER TOUGHNESS IDENTIFICATION SCALE

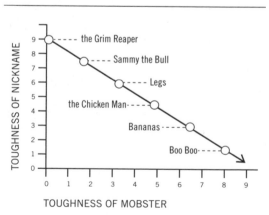

FIGURE 2: MATCH THE NICKNAME WITH THE FACE

1. Petite Pete
2. Johnny Gigabyte
3. Tony the Dame
4. Dicknose
5. Earthworm Jim
6. Bobby Bowtie
7. Louie the Dwarf
8. Tony Hitlercat
9. Babyface
10. Johnny Eggroll
11. Tony Tusks
12. Nicky the Saint
13. Pugs
14. Shakey Jake
15. the Thumb
16. Chins
17. Sammy the Jew
18. the Ghost
19. Wrinkles
20. Tommy Two-eyes

ANSWERS: 1R, 2Q, 3P, 4G, 5F, 6E, 7D, 8C, 9A, 10B, 11H, 12I, 13N, 14S, 15T, 16O, 17M, 18K, 19L, 20J

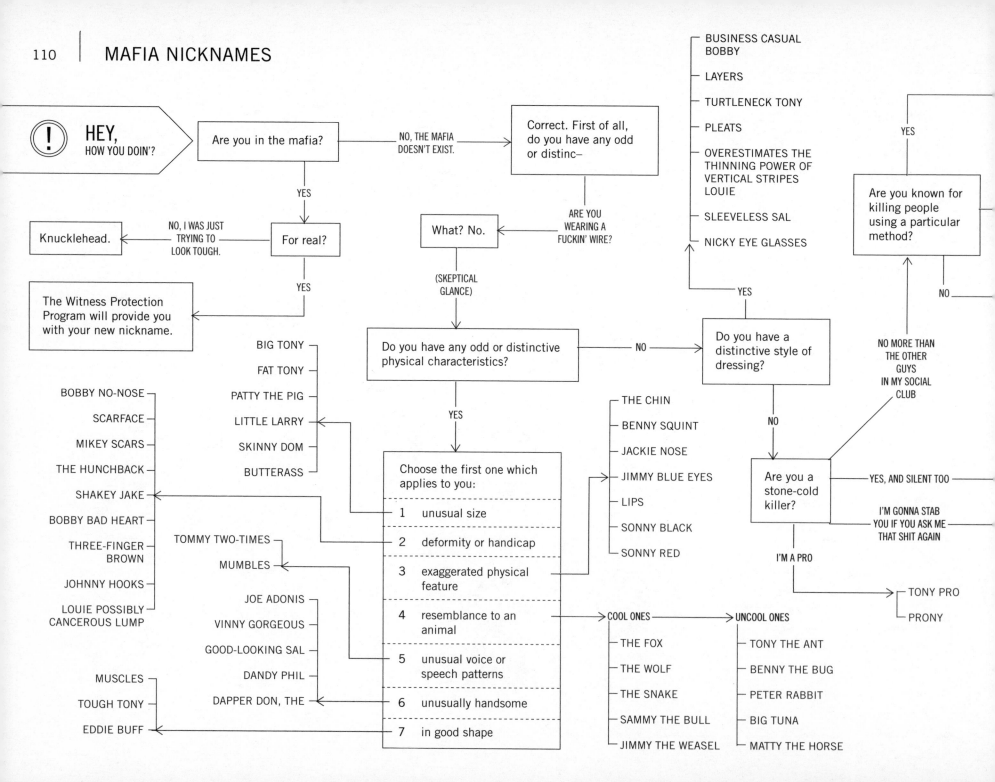

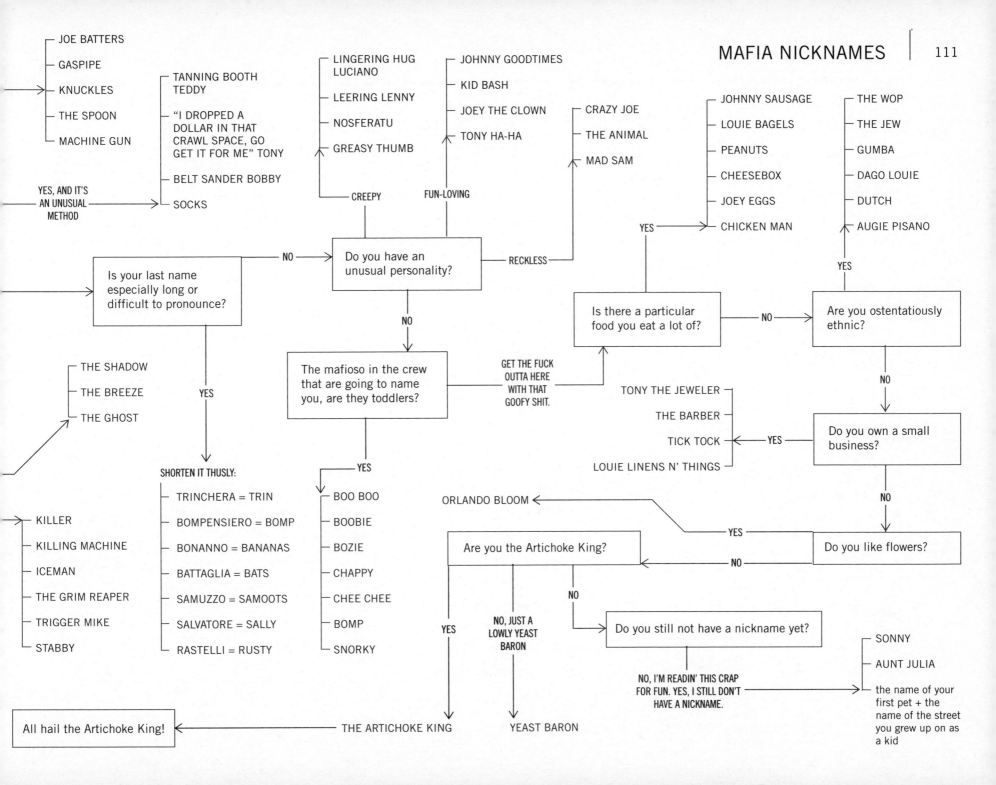

JOE BATTERS
GASPIPE
KNUCKLES
THE SPOON
MACHINE GUN

TANNING BOOTH TEDDY
"I DROPPED A DOLLAR IN THAT CRAWL SPACE, GO GET IT FOR ME" TONY
BELT SANDER BOBBY
SOCKS

YES, AND IT'S AN UNUSUAL METHOD

LINGERING HUG LUCIANO
LEERING LENNY
NOSFERATU
GREASY THUMB
CREEPY

JOHNNY GOODTIMES
KID BASH
JOEY THE CLOWN
TONY HA-HA
FUN-LOVING

CRAZY JOE
THE ANIMAL
MAD SAM

JOHNNY SAUSAGE
LOUIE BAGELS
PEANUTS
CHEESEBOX
JOEY EGGS
CHICKEN MAN

THE WOP
THE JEW
GUMBA
DAGO LOUIE
DUTCH
AUGIE PISANO

Is your last name especially long or difficult to pronounce?

NO → Do you have an unusual personality? — RECKLESS

YES → Is there a particular food you eat a lot of? — NO → Are you ostentatiously ethnic?

YES

NO

THE SHADOW
THE BREEZE
THE GHOST

YES

NO

The mafioso in the crew that are going to name you, are they toddlers?

GET THE FUCK OUTTA HERE WITH THAT GOOFY SHIT.

TONY THE JEWELER
THE BARBER
TICK TOCK
LOUIE LINENS N' THINGS

YES

Do you own a small business?

NO

SHORTEN IT THUSLY:

TRINCHERA = TRIN
BOMPENSIERO = BOMP
BONANNO = BANANAS
BATTAGLIA = BATS
SAMUZZO = SAMOOTS
SALVATORE = SALLY
RASTELLI = RUSTY

YES

BOO BOO
BOOBIE
BOZIE
CHAPPY
CHEE CHEE
BOMP
SNORKY

ORLANDO BLOOM ←

Are you the Artichoke King?

YES → NO

Do you still not have a nickname yet?

NO, I'M READIN' THIS CRAP FOR FUN. YES, I STILL DON'T HAVE A NICKNAME.

YES

Do you like flowers?

NO

KILLER
KILLING MACHINE
ICEMAN
THE GRIM REAPER
TRIGGER MIKE
STABBY

NO, JUST A LOWLY YEAST BARON

SONNY
AUNT JULIA
the name of your first pet + the name of the street you grew up on as a kid

All hail the Artichoke King! ← THE ARTICHOKE KING

YEAST BARON

SALAD DRESSING

I KNOW WHAT YOU ARE THINKING—that the inclusion of salad dressing in this book is a crude and transparent attempt to appeal to readers' baser instincts; another shameful example of the commercialization of salad dressing, an exploitation that pervades our culture like the strangling tendrils of a fleshy vine—your words, not mine. *(See Figure 1: Further Examples of Audaciously Purple Prose You've Written.)*

FIGURE 1: FURTHER EXAMPLES OF AUDACIOUSLY PURPLE PROSE YOU'VE WRITTEN

The following is an excerpt from your self-published novel *Song of the Princess's Soul*:

The turgid tangle of golden-spun, tumbling tresses trembled 'neath Tess's tiara—a tiara that weighed heavily on the pulchritudinous Princess's highborn head. The Duke glowered malevolently at her with his hooded reptilian eyes—pestiferous mustache trembling iniquitously with each poison poultice syllable that dripped from his despicable lips. "The throne . . . shall . . . be . . . mine!" he intoned with malefic glee.

Nothing could be further from the truth! The discussion of salad dressing here is meant to educate, not scintillate. Like yourself I am shocked at the ubiquity of salad dressing in the mainstream media. There is nothing inherently wrong with salad dressing when used properly; good dressing—used judiciously, applied prudently—is the glue that holds a salad together. (*WARNING: Do not put glue on your salad.*) But the wanton portrayal of salad dressing in the mainstream media is anything but healthy or prudent.

Let me describe a commercial I saw on TV the other day: Fade in on a black marble kitchen counter. A techno beat pulses tribally in the background. The camera zooms in close on a chilled salad bowl. The bowl is filled with fresh, plump produce, beaded with moisture, partying on a bed of lettuce: hothouse tomatoes lounge near the bowl's lip; twin sprigs of frisee frolic between French-slivered carrot sticks; a firm, quartered cucumber dances with a cluster of cauliflower. A husky woman's voiceover says "What's sexier than undressing?" *(Sensitive readers please stop here and proceed to Things People Say to my Dog, page 136.)*

In slow motion, a massive bottle lowers into the frame above the bowl and douses the salad in thick, creamy Ranch dressing. The veggies squeal in delight. Close-up, quick cuts of the tomatoes, the carrot sticks, a giggling gaggle of baby spinach, laughing and splashing in the gooey cream, smearing it all over each other's bodies.

The woman's voice slides in again, "What's sexier than undressing? . . . *Dressing.*" If anything hap-

---

FIGURE 2: SEXUAL EUPHEMISMS INVOLVING SALAD DRESSING

Toss your salad

All you can eat salad bar at the YWCA

French dressing

The old "oil and vinegar"

Newman's Own

pened after that, I didn't see it, because I was too busy throwing up into my bowl of popcorn.

If you think this kind of filth is only on Cinemax you are wrong. I saw this commercial at 3 p.m. on a Tuesday in the middle of *Boy Meets World*. Oh the irony of that show's title! Because these commercials are exactly how so many young people (boys) are learning about the salad dressing around them (meeting the world, so to speak). *(See Figure 3 for Full Metaphor Equation Mathematics.)* The crucial variable that separates healthy salad dressing users from dressing abusers is education, and that knowledge is exactly what the Salad Dressing chart can facilitate.

"But I don't want my kids to know about salad dressing!" you whine in a nasally voice.

Don't begrudge your children their natural salad dressing curiosity. Remember that once, not long ago, you were young and hungry too. We can all remember nights when we parked under a burnt-out streetlamp and greedily gobbled a take-out salad in the front seat of our hatchback. Or that electric summer evening when we plowed through an entire bottle of rich poppy seed dressing, *Thunder Road* blaring in the background.

The bottom line is, whether you like it or not, your kids are going to learn about salad dressing— that's not up to you. What *is* up to you is *how* your kids learn about dressing. Do you want them to learn about it by being eyeball groped by a slick TV commercial with Gwen Stefani dressed as a carrot? Or by having an uncomfortable conversation with you perched creepily on the edge of

their bunkbed? *(See Figure 5: Where are We Giving our Children the "Salad Dressing Talk?")* The choice is yours.

FIGURE 5: WHERE ARE WE GIVING OUR CHILDREN THE "SALAD DRESSING TALK?"

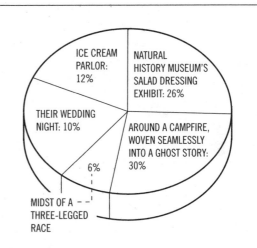

ICE CREAM PARLOR: 12%

NATURAL HISTORY MUSEUM'S SALAD DRESSING EXHIBIT: 26%

THEIR WEDDING NIGHT: 10%

AROUND A CAMPFIRE, WOVEN SEAMLESSLY INTO A GHOST STORY: 30%

6%

MIDST OF A THREE-LEGGED RACE

FIGURE 3: FULL METAPHOR EQUATION MATHEMATICS

VARIABLES DEFINED:
BOY = Young People, MEETS = Learn About = +, WORLD = Salad dressing

EQUATION:
YOUNG PEOPLE + SALAD DRESSING − EDUCATION = Teenage Wasteland

---

FIGURE 4: FIELD GUIDE TO NORTH AMERICAN DRESSINGS

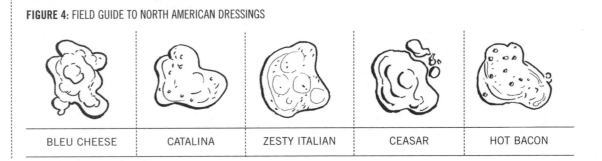

| BLEU CHEESE | CATALINA | ZESTY ITALIAN | CEASAR | HOT BACON |

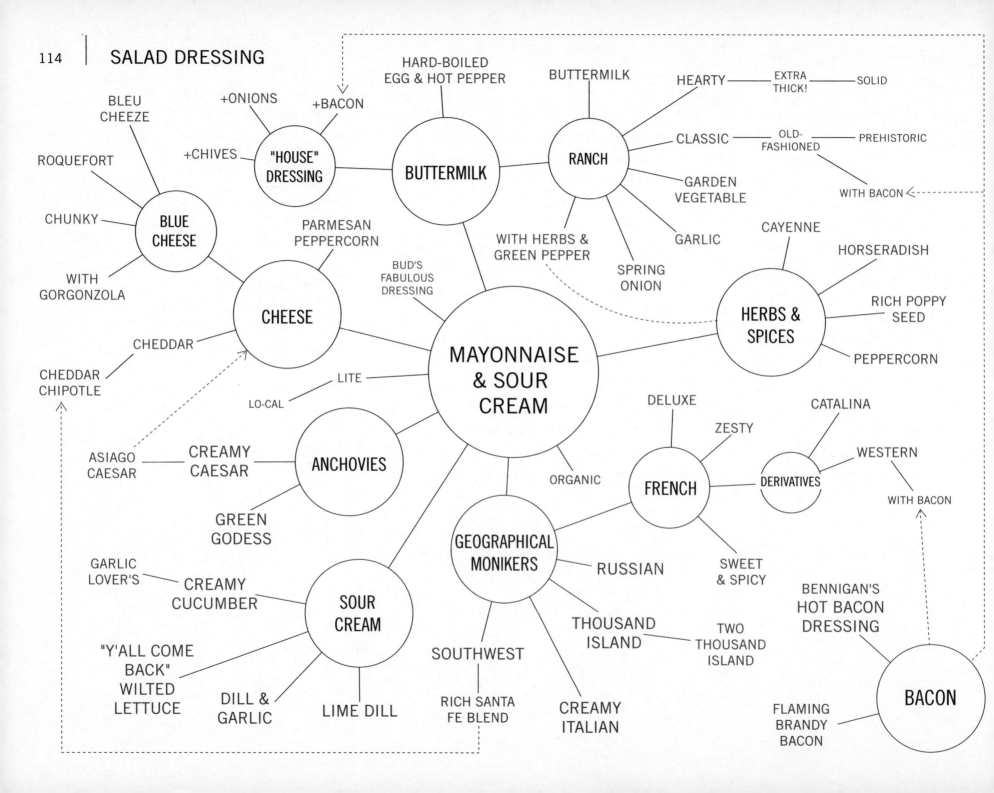

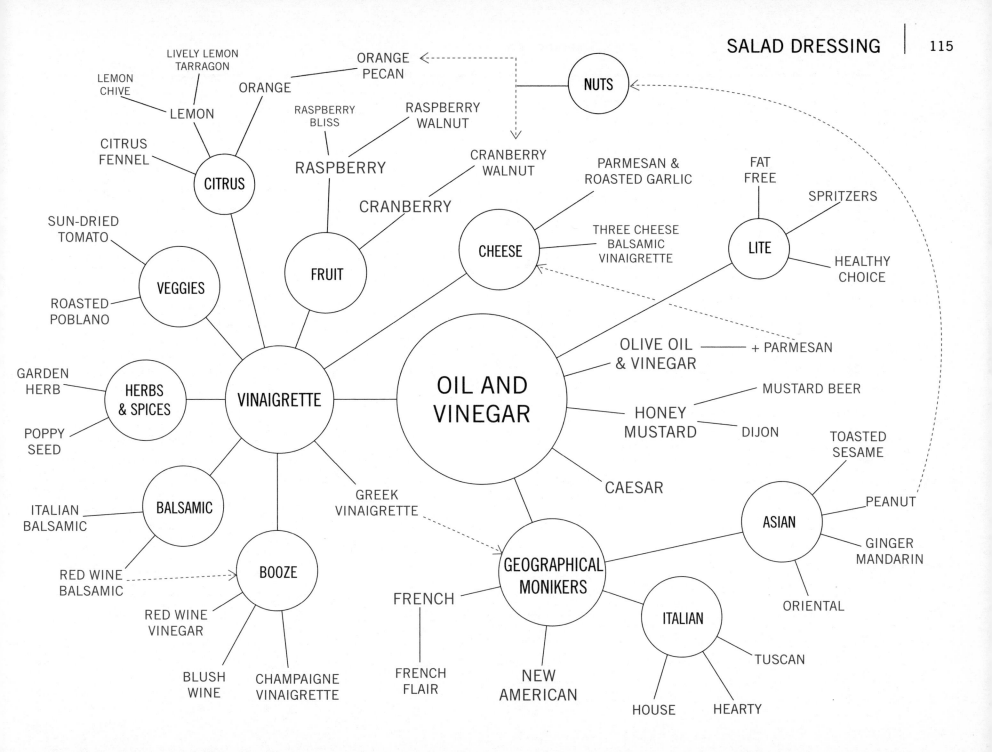

STAND-UP COMEDY

MANY PEOPLE THINK COMEDY is an art, but in actuality it is an exact science just like math, physics, or greyhound racing. As such, it has proven laws and equations that, if followed, will result in surefire laughs. I realize this may come as a surprise to you, since—to the casual observer—it seems like stand-up comedians are pouring their hearts and souls out on stage, relating unique anecdotes and observations; a small percentage of comedians actually *are*, but these suckers are doing it the hard way. Nobody likes these smarty-pants, and they always have to sit at a table by themselves in the comedy cafeteria. *(See Figure 1: Which Comedian Would you Rather Be?)*

The hilarious poet Robert Frost said it best in his poem "The Road Not Taken":

> *Two roads diverged in a wood, and I—*
> *I took the far easier road,*
> *the one with road signs,*
> *and now I'm a famous and rich comedian.*

FIGURE 1: WHICH COMEDIAN WOULD YOU RATHER BE?

A. RED SKELTON
Made funny faces, fell down a lot. Imitated an idiot named Clem Kaddidlehopper, and a toddler whose catch phrase was "I dood it!" Died rich and beloved at the age of 84.

B. LENNY BRUCE
Skewered society with his razor sharp, insightful wit. Arrested multiple times for obscenity and drug possession. Junkie. Died on a bathroom floor, ruined and penniless at the age of 41.

Correct answer: A

The Road Not Taken was the last poem Robert Frost ever wrote, because after that he was able to afford a ghostwriter. Ghostwriters are worth considering if you like to be on stage and have everyone listen to you, but don't actually care what you're screaming about.

If you insist on writing your own semi-original material, then I can deduce that you lead a tortured and tragic life, since you always insist on doing things the hard way. Well you're in luck, because having a crappy life is a surefire recipe for comedy meat loaf! (Note: everyone loves meat loaf.) It's a paradoxical truth that the sweet fruits of comedy often grow from the bitter soil of tragedy. But how do you achieve this alchemy? How do you turn the lead bricks of tragedy into comedy gold? Luckily for you there's the Tragedy to Comedy conversion chart. *(See Figure 2: Tragedy to Comedy Conversion Chart.)* That's right, two comedy charts for the price of one! Now you can turn your shitty life into shitty jokes. Who's laughing now? That's right: everybody—at you[1].

---

(1) In a good way

FIGURE 2: TRAGEDY TO COMEDY CONVERSION CHART

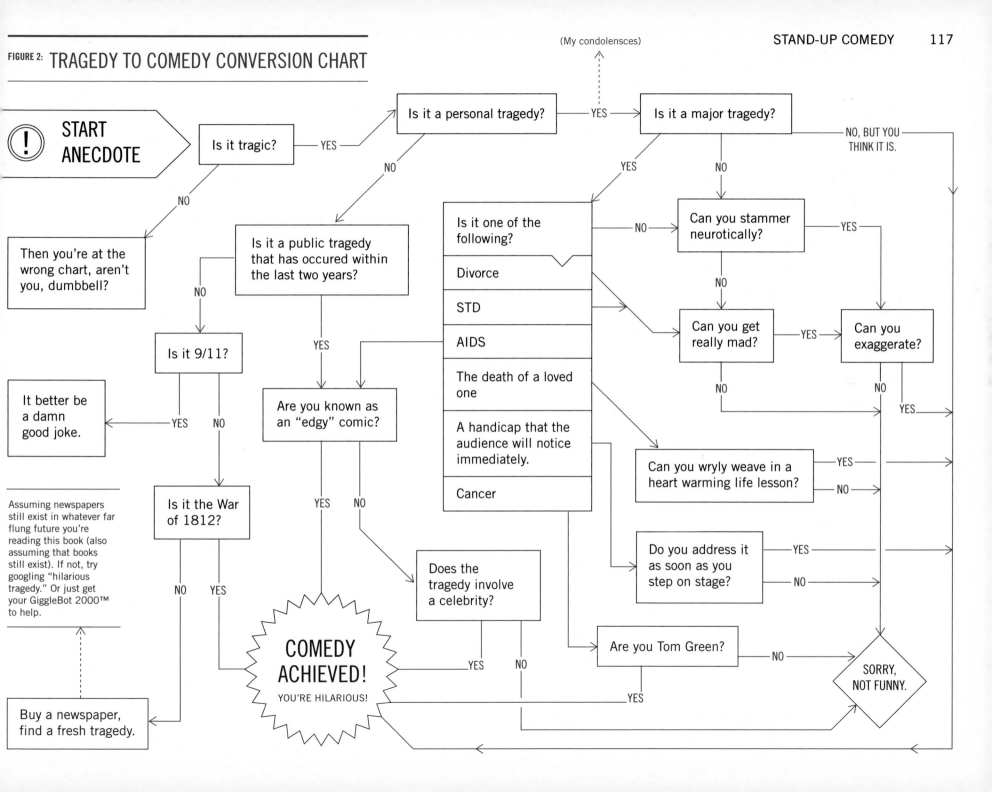

(My condolensces)

START ANECDOTE

Is it tragic? — YES — Is it a personal tragedy? — YES — Is it a major tragedy?

NO, BUT YOU THINK IT IS.

NO → Then you're at the wrong chart, aren't you, dumbbell?

NO → Is it a public tragedy that has occured within the last two years?

YES → Is it one of the following?

Divorce
STD
AIDS
The death of a loved one
A handicap that the audience will notice immediately.
Cancer

NO → Is it 9/11?

Assuming newspapers still exist in whatever far flung future you're reading this book (also assuming that books still exist). If not, try googling "hilarious tragedy." Or just get your GiggleBot 2000™ to help.

It better be a damn good joke. ← YES — NO → Is it the War of 1812?

Are you known as an "edgy" comic?

NO — Can you stammer neurotically? — YES

NO

Can you get really mad? — YES — Can you exaggerate?

NO

NO

YES

Can you wryly weave in a heart warming life lesson? — YES
NO

Do you address it as soon as you step on stage? — YES
NO

NO — YES → Is it the War of 1812?

YES → Does the tragedy involve a celebrity?

Buy a newspaper, find a fresh tragedy.

COMEDY ACHIEVED!
YOU'RE HILARIOUS!

YES — NO

Are you Tom Green? — NO

YES

SORRY, NOT FUNNY.

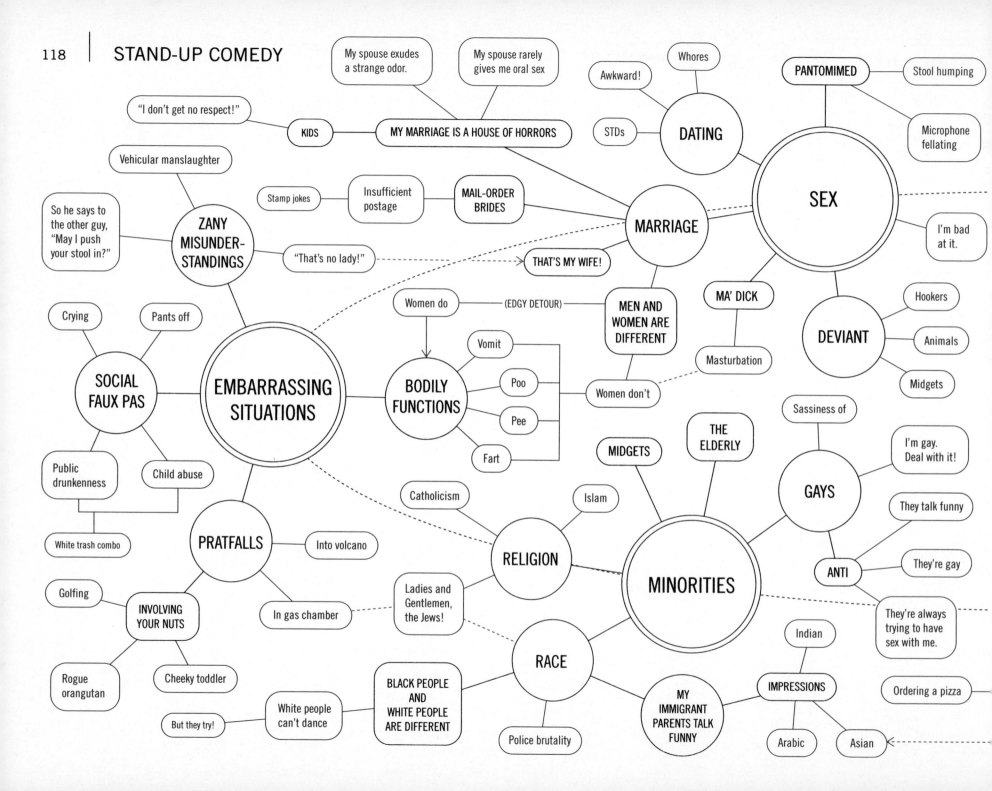

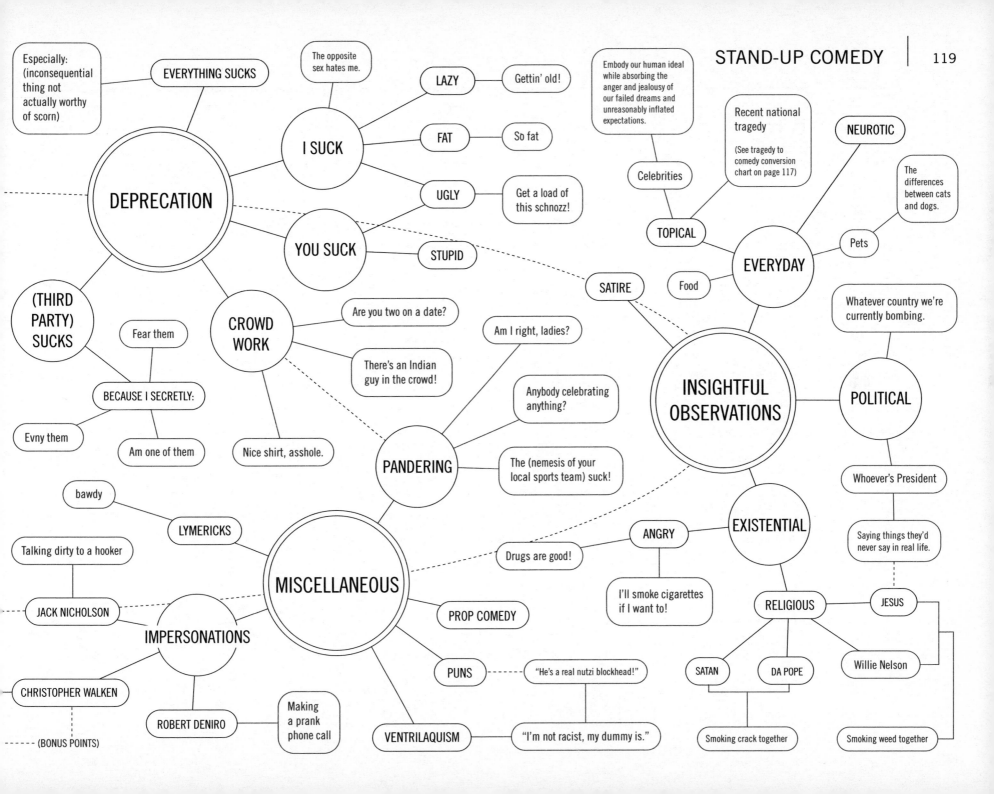

Especially: (inconsequential thing not actually worthy of scorn)

EVERYTHING SUCKS

The opposite sex hates me.

I SUCK

LAZY — Gettin' old!

FAT — So fat

UGLY — Get a load of this schnozz!

DEPRECATION

YOU SUCK

STUPID

(THIRD PARTY) SUCKS

Fear them

CROWD WORK

Are you two on a date?

There's an Indian guy in the crowd!

BECAUSE I SECRETLY:

Evny them

Am one of them

Nice shirt, asshole.

Am I right, ladies?

PANDERING

Anybody celebrating anything?

The (nemesis of your local sports team) suck!

Embody our human ideal while absorbing the anger and jealousy of our failed dreams and unreasonably inflated expectations.

Recent national tragedy

(See tragedy to comedy conversion chart on page 117)

Celebrities

TOPICAL

SATIRE

Food

NEUROTIC

The differences between cats and dogs.

Pets

EVERYDAY

INSIGHTFUL OBSERVATIONS

POLITICAL

Whatever country we're currently bombing.

Whoever's President

Saying things they'd never say in real life.

bawdy

LYMERICKS

Talking dirty to a hooker

JACK NICHOLSON

MISCELLANEOUS

Drugs are good!

ANGRY

EXISTENTIAL

RELIGIOUS

JESUS

IMPERSONATIONS

PROP COMEDY

I'll smoke cigarettes if I want to!

CHRISTOPHER WALKEN

PUNS

"He's a real nutzi blockhead!"

SATAN

DA POPE

Willie Nelson

(BONUS POINTS)

ROBERT DENIRO

Making a prank phone call

VENTRILAQUISM

"I'm not racist, my dummy is."

Smoking crack together

Smoking weed together

SUPERPOWERS

FIGURE 1: HOW ARE PEOPLE GAINING THEIR SUPERNATURAL POWERS?

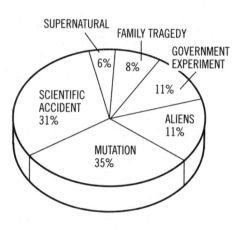

SUPERNATURAL 6%
FAMILY TRAGEDY 8%
GOVERNMENT EXPERIMENT 11%
ALIENS 11%
MUTATION 35%
SCIENTIFIC ACCIDENT 31%

FIGURE 2: WHAT SHOULD YOU DO AFTER IDENTIFYING YOUR POWERS?

1. Name yourself
2. Sew a costume
3. Fight crime/commit crime
4. Battle nemesis
5. Return to step 3

THE SPIDERMAN, BATMAN, AND OTHER super-hero documentaries have gone a long way toward fostering understanding between humans and meta-humans, but we are still worlds apart. "Can I gain superpowers during sexual intercourse?" is still a question I get asked all the time at meta human education seminars. *(See Figure 1: How Are People Gaining Their Supernatural Powers?)* Superpowers are, for better or worse, part of our world now, and it's best that you familiarize yourself with these "gods that walk among us," and their accompanying powers.

Perhaps you or someone you love are struggling with strange powers you don't want to talk to your doctor or spiritual advisor about, for fear of being sent to a superhuman government detainment facility? The Superpowers chart can help you identify your power and move on from there. *(See Figure 2: What Should You do After Identifying Your Powers?)* Superheroes hate to be "defined" by their superpower. "Oh, just because

my power is superspeed, you think I have commitment issues?" Or, "Just because I'm physically invulnerable, you think I don't have feelings?" I can't tell you how many times I've heard these complaints from superpeople I know.

Should you become a hero or a villain? Both have their advantages: superheroes win more often *(see Figure 3: How Often do Heroes and Villains Win Their Battles?)*, but supervillains have more fun. You hardly ever hear superheroes laugh maniacally after a victory, but villains can do so for hours, their manic laughter bouncing off the walls of their

BONUS FOR ASPIRING HEROES: ROYALTY-FREE ICONS YOU CAN USE ON YOUR COSTUME.

underground lairs. Although powers themselves are neither good nor bad, there are certain superhuman abilities that seem to lead to villainy, or are difficult to use in a positive manner: Mind control (possession), darkness control, poison generation, necromancy, self-detonation, disease bestowal. Superhuman intelligence especially seems to lead people down the "mad scientist route." But whichever side of the law you choose to align yourself on, you'll find the same career perks: flexible hours, excitement, and travel. *(See Figure 4: Where do Superhumans Fight Their Battles?)*

Once you figure out what your particular power is, you'll need to identify your weakness. Don't worry, it will be something very rare! Perhaps a relic from

FIGURE 4: WHERE DO SUPERHUMANS FIGHT THEIR BATTLES?

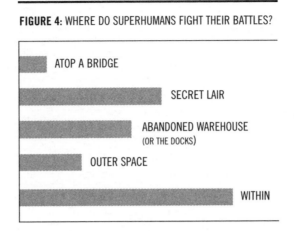

ATOP A BRIDGE

SECRET LAIR

ABANDONED WAREHOUSE
(OR THE DOCKS)

OUTER SPACE

WITHIN

your home world, a rare isotope, or the love of a pure woman. (Unless you're a member of the Green Lantern Corps., in which case your weakness will be something inanely common.) If you're unable to discover your weakness on your own, don't worry, eventually your nemesis will figure it

out. No matter what your weakness is, you will probably also be susceptible to magic, the annoying wildcard of the superpowers world. Many superheroes who are supposed to be invulnerable are still susceptible to the effects of magic. Super strength, mental powers, power negation, illusions—a magical being could have any and all of these powers. The chief drawbacks of magic are its unreliability, high prep time, and general hoakyness.

Young meta humans often argue about what power is "the best." Super strength and invulnerability are top contenders, as is mind control and super intelligence. But even if your super power is something more humble *(see Figure 5: Lamest Super Powers)* just remember, it's not the size of your power that matters, but how you use it.

FIGURE 5: LAMEST SUPER POWERS

1. Super boring
2. The ability to see 3 seconds into the past
3. Animal communication: worms only
4. Impenetrable dinner conversation
5. The strength of a dog
6. Invisibility to the opposite sex
7. Ennui
8. Heightened paranoia
9. Omnilinguism
10. Je ne sais quoi

FIGURE 3: HOW OFTEN DO HEROES AND VILLAINS WIN THEIR BATTLES?

KEY

HERO	**VILLAIN**

*The rematch battle ends in a tie 10% of the time.

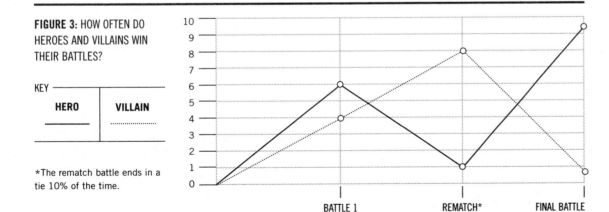

BATTLE 1   REMATCH*   FINAL BATTLE

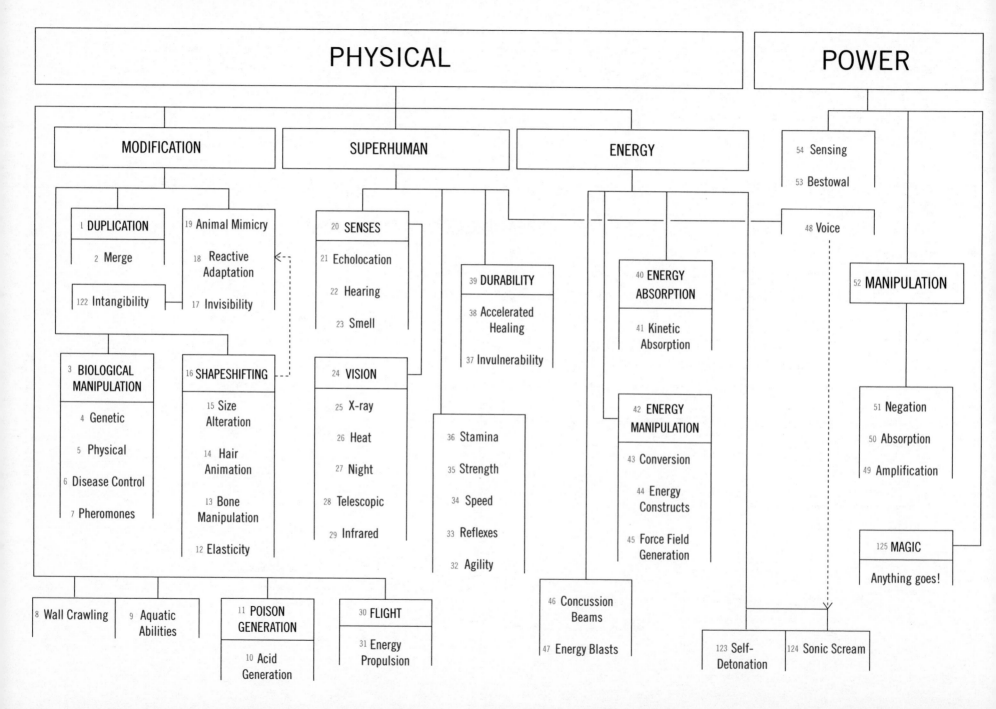

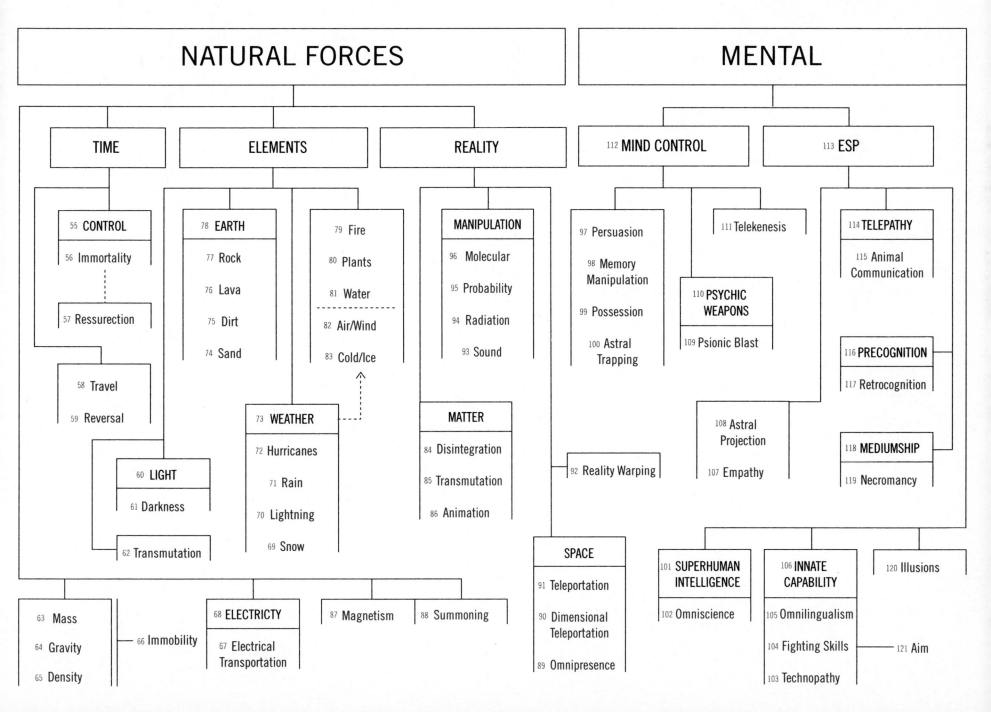

(corrolates to the Superpowers chart, page 122)

SUPERPOWER INDEX

Here's a handy list of comic book superheroes and villains whose powers correlate to the Superpowers chart on pages 122 and 123. I've tried to include a hero or villain from both the DC and Marvel universe, but in some cases was unable. Some powers listed on the chart for the sake of thoroughness (i.e., dirt control) don't have corresponding heroes in the index, because their powers are covered by a larger group (e.g., earth control).

#			#			#			#			#		
1	DC	Multiplex	9	DC	Aquaman	17	DC	Invisible Kid	31	DC	Static	45	DC	Argent
	M	Multiple Man		M	Namor		M	Invisible Woman		M	Cannonball		M	Unus the Untouchable
2	DC	B'Wana Beast	10	DC	– –	18	DC	Doomsday	32	DC	the Creeper	46	DC	Gunfire
	M	Kleinstocks		M	Man-Thing		M	Lifeguard		M	the Beast		M	Cyclops
3	DC	– –	11	DC	Cobra	19	DC	Animal Man	33	DC	Blade	47	DC	Starfire
	M	Elixir		M	Poison Ivy		M	Wolfsbane		M	Blade		M	Havok
4	DC	Slig	12	DC	Plastic Man	20	DC	Icon	34	DC	Flash	48	DC	– –
	M	High Evolutionary		M	Mr. Fantastic		M	Beast		M	Quicksilver		M	– –
5	DC	– –	13	DC	– –	21	DC	Man-Bat	35	DC	Blok	49	DC	– –
	M	Terror Inc.		M	Marrow		M	Daredevil		M	Hulk		M	Fabian Cortez
6	DC	– –	14	DC	Spider Girl	22	DC	Superman	36	DC	Captain Marvel	50	DC	Black Alice
	M	Plague (Morlock)		M	Medusa		M	Feral		M	Roughouse		M	Rogue
7	DC	Crimson Fox	15	DC	Giganta	23	DC	Timber Wolf	37	DC	Supergirl	51	DC	– –
	M	Wallflower		M	Henry Pym		M	Sabretooth		M	the Thing		M	Leech
8	DC	Night Crawler	16	DC	Chameleon Boy	24	DC	Powergirl	38	DC	Lobo	52	DC	– –
	M	Spiderman		M	Mystique		M	Silver Surfer		M	Wolverine		M	– –
						25	DC	Superman	39	DC	Solomon Grundy	53	DC	Synergy
							M	Peepers		M	Luke Cage		M	Sage
						26	DC	Superman	40	DC	Apocalypse (?)	54	DC	Nemesis Kid
							M	Universe Boy		M	Bishop		M	Caliban
						27	DC	Doctor Mid-Nite	41	DC	Growing Man	55	DC	Zoom
							M	Owl		M	Sebastian Shaw		M	Tempo
						28	DC	Lar Gand	42	DC	Captain Atom	56	DC	Vandal Savage
							M	Hyperion		M	– –		M	Mephisto
						29	DC	Doctor Mid-Nite	43	DC	Wildfire	57	DC	Immortal Man
							M	– –		M	Dazzler		M	– –
						30	DC	Black Adam	44	DC	Jade			
							M	Angel		M	Cerise			

#		DC	M
58	DC / M	Time Trapper	Trevor Fitzroy
59	DC / M	Dark Angel	--
60	DC / M	Doctor Light	Dazzler
61	DC / M	Shadow Thief	Cloak
62	DC / M	Metamorpho	Alchemy
63	DC / M	Star Boy/Starman	Black Bishop
64	DC / M	Geo Force	Alex Power
65	DC / M	Martian Manhunter	Vision
66	DC / M	--	The Blob
67	DC / M	Livewire	Electro
68	DC / M	Black Lightning	Electro
69	DC / M	--	--
70	DC / M	Captain Marvel	Thor
71	DC / M	--	--
72	DC / M	--	--
73	DC / M	Typhoon	Storm
74	DC / M	--	Sandman
75	DC / M	--	--
76	DC / M	--	--
77	DC / M	--	--
78	DC / M	Terra	Petra
79	DC / M	Fire	Pyro
80	DC / M	Floronic Man	Klara Prast
81	DC / M	Tempest	Hydro Man
82	DC / M	Red Tornado	Wind Dancer
83	DC / M	Polar Boy	Iceman
84	DC / M	Plasmus	Wither
85	DC / M	Metamorpho	Alchemy
86	DC / M	Ozymandias	Selene
87	DC / M	Doctor Polaris	Magneto
88	DC / M	Kid Eternity	Magik
89	DC / M	--	Eternity
90	DC / M	Gates	Blink
91	DC / M	Misfit	Nightcrawler
92	DC / M	Mister Mxyzptlk	Franklin Richards
93	DC / M	Fiddler	Klaw
94	DC / M	Radiation Roy	X-Ray
95	DC / M	Calamity King	Domino
96	DC / M	Firestorm	Apocalypse
97	DC / M	the Brain	Silver Fox
98	DC / M	Zatanna	Professor X
99	DC / M	Jericho	Nocturne
100	DC / M	--	Shadow King
101	DC / M	Brainiac 5	Leader
102	DC / M	Mageddon	Infinity
103	DC / M	Cyborg Superman	Iron Man
104	DC / M	Deathstroke	Taskmaster
105	DC / M	Wonder Woman	Cypher
106	DC / M	--	Forge
107	DC / M	Raven	Empath
108	DC / M	Ravager	Marvel Girl
109	DC / M	Psimon	Psylocke
110	DC / M	--	Mirage
111	DC / M	Maxima	Jean Grey
112	DC / M	Universo	Karma
113	DC / M	Maxima	Professor X
114	DC / M	Saturn Girl	Exodus
115	DC / M	Namor	Tarzan
116	DC / M	Dream Girl	Destiny
117	DC / M	--	Sway
118	DC / M	Phantom Stranger	Wicked
119	DC / M	Spectre	Dead Girl
120	DC / M	Manchester Black	Mastermind
121	DC / M	Deadshot	Bullseye
122	DC / M	Phantom Girl	Kitty Pryde
123	DC / M	Damage	Nitro
124	DC / M	Black Canary	Banshee
125	DC / M	Zattana	Doctor Strange

SUPERVILLAIN SCHEMES

FIGURE 1: PARTING OATHS

"You have not seen the last of (your name)!"

"You will rue the day you crossed (your name)!"

"Vengeance shall be mine!"

"My memory is as long as my reach!"

"I'll try harder next time!"

"Every dog has his day!"

(For added dramatic effect, repeat oath twice.)

FIGURE 2: SUPERVILLAIN SCHEME SUCCESS RATE

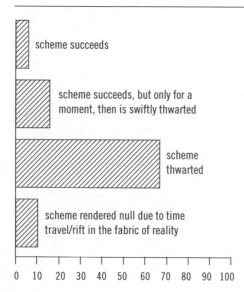

scheme succeeds

scheme succeeds, but only for a moment, then is swiftly thwarted

scheme thwarted

scheme rendered null due to time travel/rift in the fabric of reality

0 10 20 30 40 50 60 70 80 90 100

IT SUCKS TO BE A VILLAIN. How would you feel if every time one of your plans failed (that soufflé you burnt, that lopsided sweater you knitted, that monster you created that went rougue and turned against you) everybody clapped? You'd feel rotten, that's how you'd feel—and you'd swear vengeance! (*See Figure 1: Parting Oaths.*) Now, also consider the fact that supervillain schemes almost always fail (*see Figure 2: Supervillain Scheme Success Rate*), and it's easy to understand why villains spend so much time scowling from the balcony of their mountain fortress.

I know I shouldn't feel any sympathy for supervillains; that, if they had their way, I'd be toiling in the methane mines of Titan, or be just another pile of bones beneath their throne of skulls. Although you and I can't empathize with the blackhearted motivations behind their schemes, can we admit that perhaps we have more in common with supervillains than we do with superheroes? Frankly, I have little in common with either, because super isn't an adjective that describes me well. (*See Figure 3: Things Super About Me.*) Regardless, consider the evidence: How often have you swooped in, saved the day, and been carried off on the shoulders of a cheering crowd? Now, how many times have the poorly constructed plans that you dreamed about for months collapsed into shambles? I can remember clearly the rickety skateboard half-pipe I built in the backyard that broke a friend's leg, the useless philosophy degree I got in college, the awful band I formed in junior high. (We were called Leaky Stigmata. We only played one show, in the back room of a pizza shop, before a heated argument about "selling out" tore the band apart.) Personally, the only time I've come close to saving the day was when we went camping and I was the only one who remembered to bring the ingredients to make s'mores. I sincerely hope this is a keen observation I've just made about humanity at large, and not just a highly personal (not to mention embarrass-

FIGURE 3: THINGS SUPER ABOUT ME

1. Super crabby in the morning
2. Super hairy in unusual places
3. Super stumbly after drinking lots of wine
4. Super self-deprecating
5. Super shy around strangers
6. Super ambivelent about sports
7. Super average at games of chance

FIGURE 4: SCHEMES WITH IMPRESSIVE VISUAL COMPONENTS

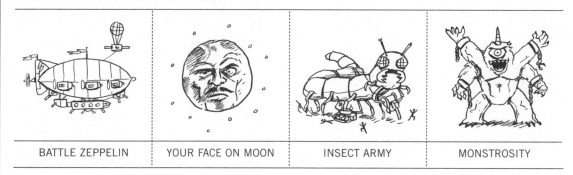

| BATTLE ZEPPELIN | YOUR FACE ON MOON | INSECT ARMY | MONSTROSITY |

ingly indulgent) admission of my own eternal underdog status—which is probably what it is. I guess I could delete these last two sentences . . . but what's the point (melodramatic sigh).

Scheming is a distinctly villainous activity. Heroes certainly don't scheme, they just wait around for the villains to do something, then stop it. Villains spend months, perhaps years, planning complex schemes—building lasers, breeding super-smart apes, searching catacombs for magical stones—and then, just when they've almost succeeded, just when their scheme is almost finally accomplished, a red light will begin blinking on the console of the superhero's crime fighting computer. The hero will put down their news-

paper, say something corny, and then fly over and punch the villain into submission. "Nice try, Dr. X! Maybe next time you should build a bigger robot." Then the hero will go on vacation, perhaps to a tropical island somewhere, and walk down the beach kicking over sand castles.

Supervillains are kind of asking for it though, since their schemes are always absurdly complicated. Why shrink the hero and make him battle a scorpion when you could just shoot him in the face? Or, if he's already shrunk, why not just squish him? Ruling the world or destroying one's nemesis isn't enough for a supervillain, he also has to accomplish it in a grandiose way. Often it seems that schemes are chosen more for their

dramatic effect than their chance of success or degree of efficacy. (*See Figure 4: Schemes With Impressive Visual Components.*)

Although this flair for the theatrical is the supervillain's Achilles' heel, it's also what separates him from run-of-the-mill hoodlums in the first place. The common thug's brilliant scheme to rob the bank by walking in and pulling out a gun—although effective—is not worthy of charting. Yes, most supervillain schemes are guaranteed to fail, but at least they will fail spectacularly, grandly—a flaming comet streaking through the night sky, hopefully hitting the town's electric factory, or something equally important.

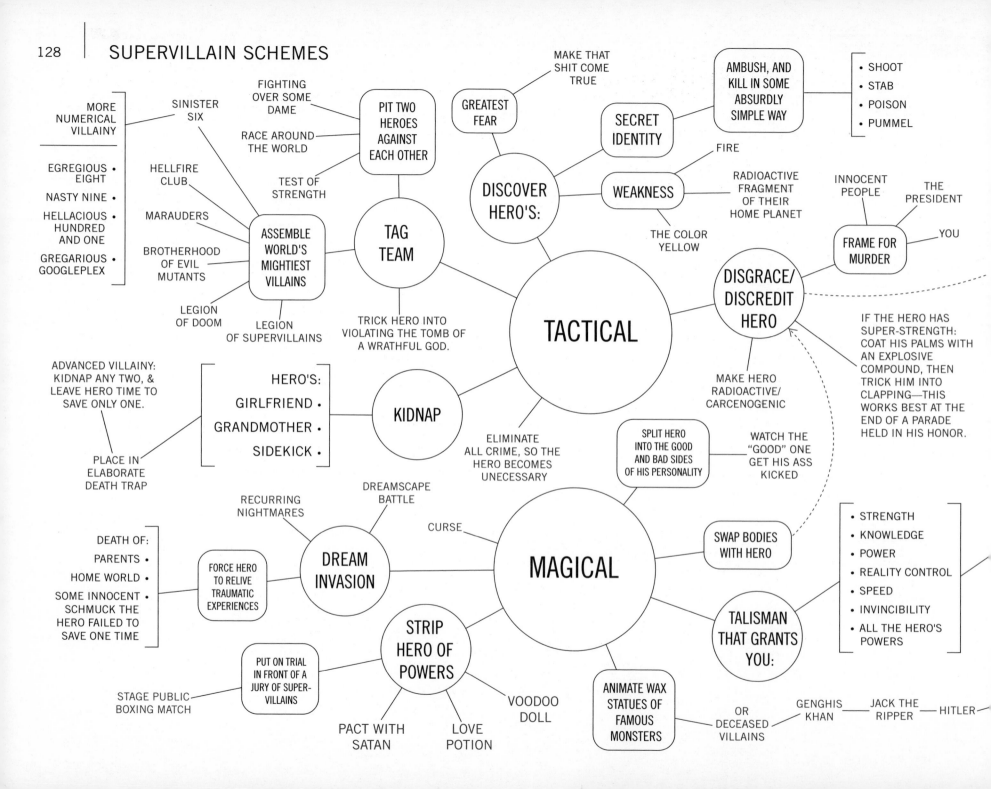

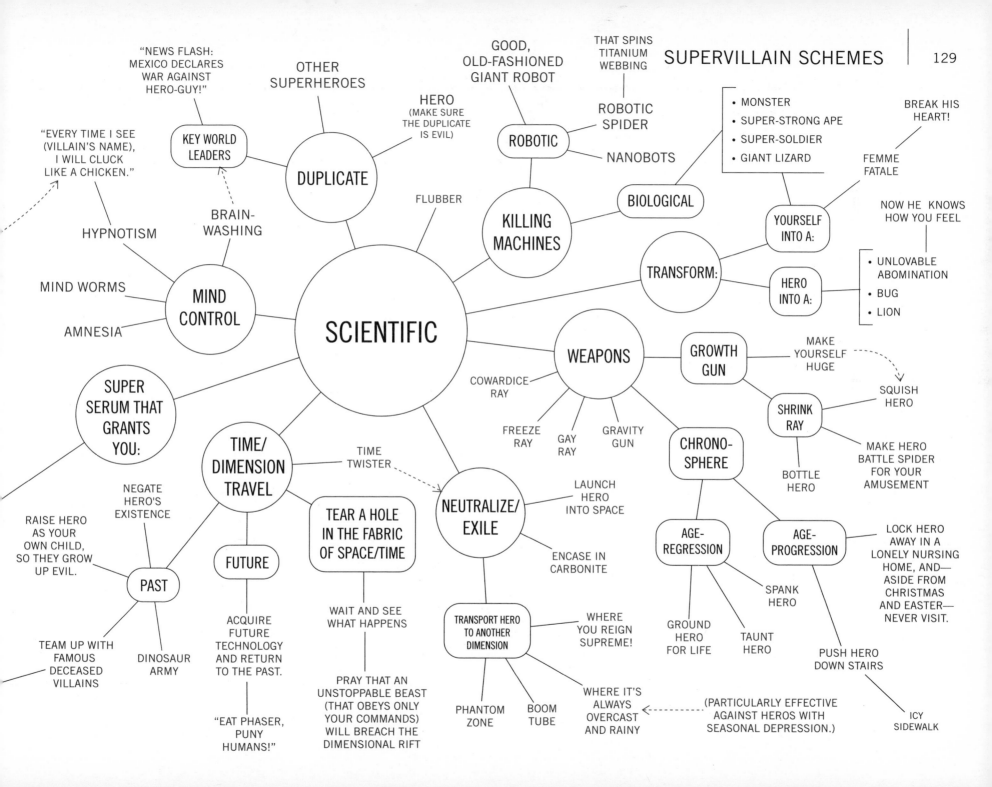

TATTOOS

YOU WANT TO GET A TATTOO, but you don't know what tattoo to get. You realize that the right tattoo could transform your life: motivate you to take that cross-country motorcycle trip, get that hot barista at Starbucks to notice you, and make your big belt buckle appear un-ironic. But you also know that the wrong tattoo could ruin your life: get you kicked out of drama club, send unintended secret messages to bisexuals, and prevent you from wearing short sleeves at family reunions.

Choosing what tattoo to get is literally the most important decision you will ever make in your entire life, and if you accuse me of hyperbole I will never forgive you in a billion years. Like most important decisions, choosing a tattoo is something you're not qualified to do on your own, which is the same reason we have the electoral college. Luckily for you there is now a flowchart to answer the question that your pastor is too holier-than-thou to help you with.

Using a combination of statistics, psychology, science, and good old-fashioned witchcraft, the Perfect Tattoo Flowchart™ is guaranteed to lead you to a tattoo that's right for you. Perhaps you're thinking "But I don't want a tattoo off a chart, I want a totally unique, one-of-a-kind tattoo, to reflect my completely unique and special-like-a-snowflake personality." I hate to break it to you, but there are no unique tattoos left, and snowflakes are an optical illusion created by swamp gas. Everything that can be tattooed onto a person (or pot-bellied pig) has been, except for the following four tattoos *(see Figure 1: The Only Tattoos that Haven't Been Used Yet)*, and depending on when you read this, those tattoos may have been taken too, probably by Johnny Depp.

Choosing a tattoo is a two-part process. You must not only choose the tattoo, but also its placement on your body, which will affect the tattoo's meaning. *(See Figure 2: Who Should Get Tattoos in the Following Places?)* If you go into the tattoo shop and don't specify where you want that ink, it could end up anywhere,

FIGURE 1: THE ONLY TATTOOS THAT HAVEN'T BEEN USED YET, BUT NOW THAT THEY'RE IN A BOOK, HAVE PROBABLY BEEN USED

| RACCOON SHARK | TONGUE DEPRESSOR | SEXY BANANA | OTTOMAN EMPIRE MAP, CIRCA 1914 |

even on someone else. Here's an example of how the same tattoo in different locations sends vastly different messages.

- **American flag on arm:** You're a proud patriot.
- **American flag on thigh:** You're a patriot, but only willing to reveal that information to certain people.
- **American flag on butt:** You're unpatriotic.
- **American flag on forehead:** You're a psycho.
- **American flag covering entire face and both fists:** You're a government engineered superhero.

People often decide to get a tattoo because of a dramatic life change—a difficult breakup, whirlwind summer in Thailand, or mob initiation ceremony. Be careful not to let the emotional turmoil of that moment cloud your tattoo judgment. Remember that that tattoo is going to be inscribed in your flesh for the rest of your life, until the day you die and are denied burial in a Jewish cemetery because you defaced your body and broke your grandmother's heart—you monster.

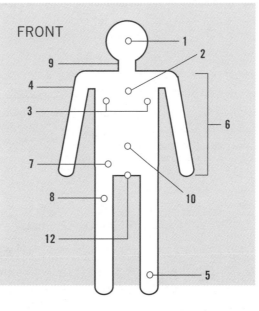

FRONT

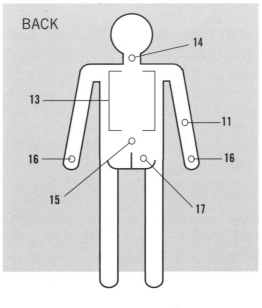

BACK

FIGURE 2: WHO SHOULD GET TATTOOS IN THE FOLLOWING BODY LOCATIONS?

1. **FACE:** Carnies, Prize Fighters, Heavy Metal Drummers, Jailhouse Snitches
2. **STERNUM:** Secret Society Members, Assassins, Prisoners, Tortured Souls
3. **BOOBS (FEMALES ONLY):** Burlesque Dancers, Exhibitionists, Crazy Bitches
4. **UPPER ARM:** Normal People, Average Joes, Plumbers
5. **ANKLE:** Islanders, Surfers, Cowards
6. **FULL SLEEVE:** Bikers, Artists, Lead Guitarists
7. **PELVIS:** Sexy Divorcees, Cock Teases
8. **THIGH:** Introverts, Bassists
9. **NECK:** Serious Customers, Thugs, Mixed Martial Arts Experts, Bus Drivers with Mysterious Pasts
10. **STOMACH:** Optimists, Rappers
11. **FOREARM:** Sailors, Baristas, Truckers
12. **GENITALS: MALE:** Perverts, Rapists, Porn Stars
    FEMALE: Dancers, Suicide Girls, my Ex-Girlfriend
13. **FULL BACK:** Yakuza, Freaky Hot Chics, Patriots
14. **BACK OF NECK:** Dystopia Worker Drones, Buddhists
15. **LOWER BACK:** Tramps, Hos, Young Naifs
16. **PALMS:** Wizards, Witches, Hypnotists
17. **BUTT:** Party Animals, Drunks, Steve O., You

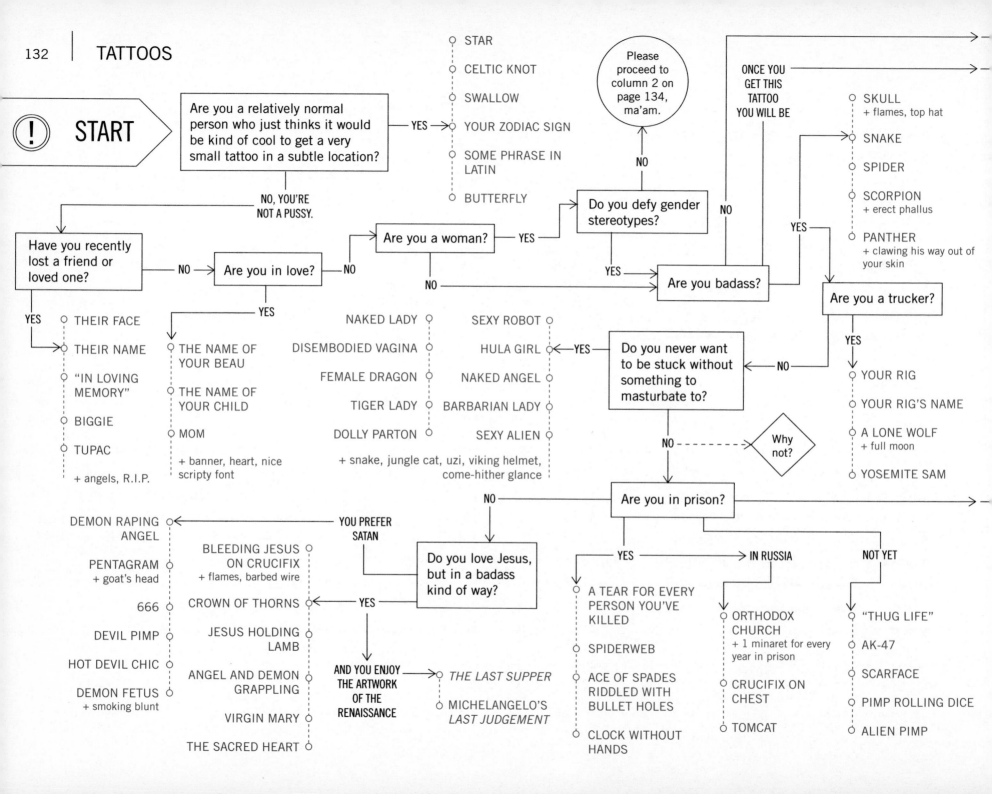

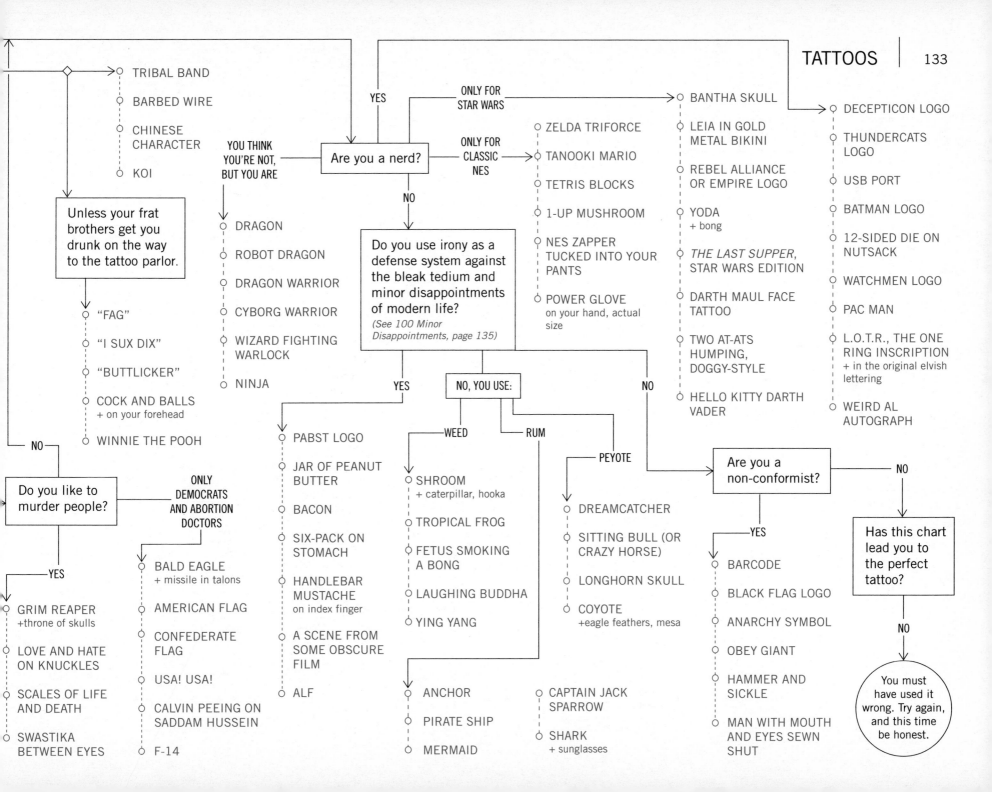

TRIBAL BAND

BARBED WIRE

CHINESE CHARACTER

KOI

Unless your frat brothers get you drunk on the way to the tattoo parlor.

"FAG"

"I SUX DIX"

"BUTTLICKER"

COCK AND BALLS
+ on your forehead

WINNIE THE POOH

YOU THINK YOU'RE NOT, BUT YOU ARE

DRAGON

ROBOT DRAGON

DRAGON WARRIOR

CYBORG WARRIOR

WIZARD FIGHTING WARLOCK

NINJA

Are you a nerd?

YES

ONLY FOR STAR WARS

ONLY FOR CLASSIC NES

NO

Do you use irony as a defense system against the bleak tedium and minor disappointments of modern life?
(See 100 Minor Disappointments, page 135)

ZELDA TRIFORCE

TANOOKI MARIO

TETRIS BLOCKS

1-UP MUSHROOM

NES ZAPPER TUCKED INTO YOUR PANTS

POWER GLOVE
on your hand, actual size

BANTHA SKULL

LEIA IN GOLD METAL BIKINI

REBEL ALLIANCE OR EMPIRE LOGO

YODA
+ bong

THE LAST SUPPER, STAR WARS EDITION

DARTH MAUL FACE TATTOO

TWO AT-ATS HUMPING, DOGGY-STYLE

HELLO KITTY DARTH VADER

DECEPTICON LOGO

THUNDERCATS LOGO

USB PORT

BATMAN LOGO

12-SIDED DIE ON NUTSACK

WATCHMEN LOGO

PAC MAN

L.O.T.R., THE ONE RING INSCRIPTION
+ in the original elvish lettering

WEIRD AL AUTOGRAPH

YES

NO, YOU USE:

NO

PABST LOGO

JAR OF PEANUT BUTTER

BACON

SIX-PACK ON STOMACH

HANDLEBAR MUSTACHE
on index finger

A SCENE FROM SOME OBSCURE FILM

ALF

WEED

RUM

PEYOTE

SHROOM
+ caterpillar, hooka

TROPICAL FROG

FETUS SMOKING A BONG

LAUGHING BUDDHA

YING YANG

DREAMCATCHER

SITTING BULL (OR CRAZY HORSE)

LONGHORN SKULL

COYOTE
+eagle feathers, mesa

Are you a non-conformist?

NO

YES

BARCODE

BLACK FLAG LOGO

ANARCHY SYMBOL

OBEY GIANT

HAMMER AND SICKLE

MAN WITH MOUTH AND EYES SEWN SHUT

Has this chart lead you to the perfect tattoo?

NO

You must have used it wrong. Try again, and this time be honest.

NO

Do you like to murder people?

ONLY DEMOCRATS AND ABORTION DOCTORS

YES

GRIM REAPER
+throne of skulls

LOVE AND HATE ON KNUCKLES

SCALES OF LIFE AND DEATH

SWASTIKA BETWEEN EYES

BALD EAGLE
+ missile in talons

AMERICAN FLAG

CONFEDERATE FLAG

USA! USA!

CALVIN PEEING ON SADDAM HUSSEIN

F-14

ANCHOR

PIRATE SHIP

MERMAID

CAPTAIN JACK SPARROW

SHARK
+ sunglasses

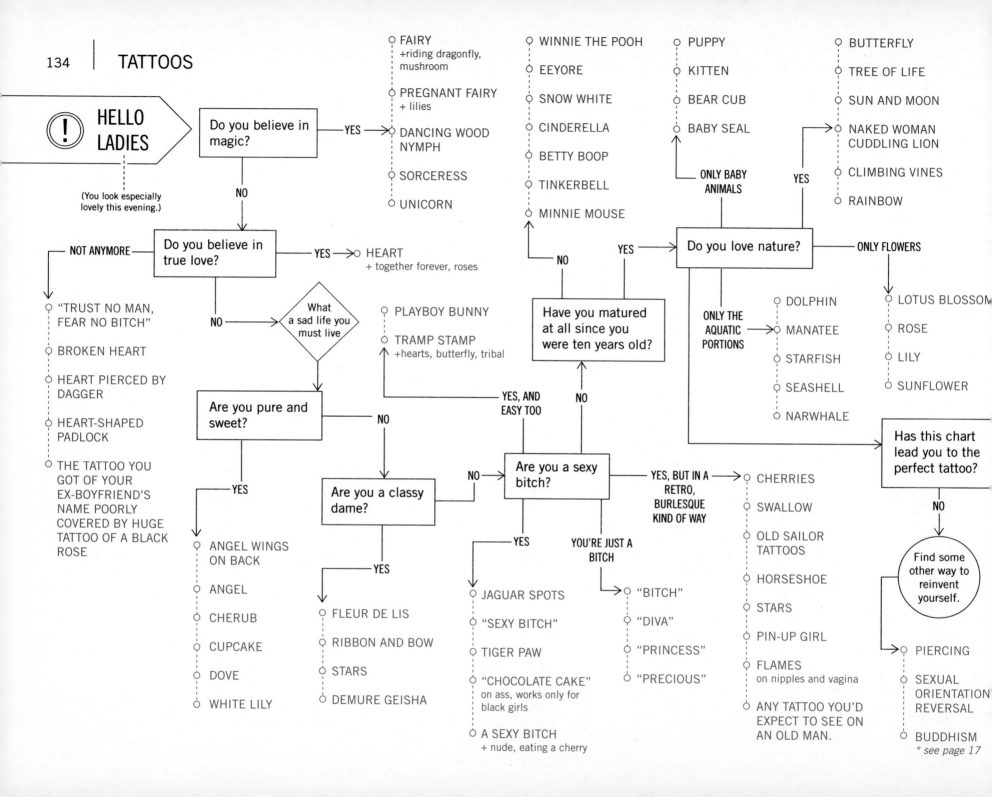

HELLO LADIES

(You look especially lovely this evening.)

Do you believe in magic? — YES →
- FAIRY +riding dragonfly, mushroom
- PREGNANT FAIRY + lilies
- DANCING WOOD NYMPH
- SORCERESS
- UNICORN

Do you believe in magic? — NO ↓

Do you believe in true love? — YES → HEART + together forever, roses

Do you believe in true love? — NOT ANYMORE →
- "TRUST NO MAN, FEAR NO BITCH"
- BROKEN HEART
- HEART PIERCED BY DAGGER
- HEART-SHAPED PADLOCK
- THE TATTOO YOU GOT OF YOUR EX-BOYFRIEND'S NAME POORLY COVERED BY HUGE TATTOO OF A BLACK ROSE

Do you believe in true love? — NO → What a sad life you must live

What a sad life you must live →
- PLAYBOY BUNNY
- TRAMP STAMP +hearts, butterfly, tribal

Are you pure and sweet? — YES →
- ANGEL WINGS ON BACK
- ANGEL
- CHERUB
- CUPCAKE
- DOVE
- WHITE LILY

Are you pure and sweet? — NO ↓

Are you a classy dame? — YES →
- FLEUR DE LIS
- RIBBON AND BOW
- STARS
- DEMURE GEISHA

Are you a classy dame? — NO →

Are you a sexy bitch? — YES →
- JAGUAR SPOTS
- "SEXY BITCH"
- TIGER PAW
- "CHOCOLATE CAKE" on ass, works only for black girls
- A SEXY BITCH + nude, eating a cherry

Are you a sexy bitch? — YOU'RE JUST A BITCH →
- "BITCH"
- "DIVA"
- "PRINCESS"
- "PRECIOUS"

Are you a sexy bitch? — YES, BUT IN A RETRO, BURLESQUE KIND OF WAY →
- CHERRIES
- SWALLOW
- OLD SAILOR TATTOOS
- HORSESHOE
- STARS
- PIN-UP GIRL
- FLAMES on nipples and vagina
- ANY TATTOO YOU'D EXPECT TO SEE ON AN OLD MAN.

Have you matured at all since you were ten years old? — YES, AND EASY TOO → (to Are you a sexy bitch?)

Have you matured at all since you were ten years old? — NO ↑
- WINNIE THE POOH
- EEYORE
- SNOW WHITE
- CINDERELLA
- BETTY BOOP
- TINKERBELL
- MINNIE MOUSE

Do you love nature? — YES → Have you matured at all since you were ten years old?

Do you love nature? — ONLY BABY ANIMALS →
- PUPPY
- KITTEN
- BEAR CUB
- BABY SEAL

Do you love nature? — YES →
- BUTTERFLY
- TREE OF LIFE
- SUN AND MOON
- NAKED WOMAN CUDDLING LION
- CLIMBING VINES
- RAINBOW

Do you love nature? — ONLY THE AQUATIC PORTIONS →
- DOLPHIN
- MANATEE
- STARFISH
- SEASHELL
- NARWHALE

Do you love nature? — ONLY FLOWERS →
- LOTUS BLOSSOM
- ROSE
- LILY
- SUNFLOWER

Has this chart lead you to the perfect tattoo? — NO ↓

Find some other way to reinvent yourself. →
- PIERCING
- SEXUAL ORIENTATION REVERSAL
- BUDDHISM

* see page 17

(from Tattoos chart, page 133)

100 MINOR DISAPPOINTMENTS

1. Fortune cookie empty
2. Antique worthless
3. Puppy too sleepy to play
4. Hot tub tepid
5. Mall Santa slightly Asian
6. Long story pointless
7. Spouse aging
8. Caricature looks nothing like you
9. Potato chips baked
10. Savages not noble
11. Picnic rained out
12. Summer camp friends drift apart in the Fall
13. Au pair not attractive; not even French
14. Vacation too short
15. Revenge hollow
16. *Indiana Jones and the Kingdom of the Crystal Skull*
17. Mentor lecherous
18. Sasquatch sighting faked
19. Outfit that looked great in the store looks not so great at home
20. Cookies eaten by roommate
21. Grandparents racist
22. Amish village touristy
23. Organic food unhealthy
24. Pancakes too filling

25. Company outing businesslike
26. Triscuits unsalted
27. Twist ending predictable
28. Crossword puzzle difficult
29. Magic eye picture not working
30. Comedian tragic
31. Birthday ignored
32. Presents crappy
33. No free refills on soda
34. Prayer unanswered
35. Nature buggy
36. Ebay bid outbid
37. Innocence slowly eroding
38. Sex anticlimactic
39. Star Wars prequels
40. Party not wild
41. "Best years of your life" okay
42. Nostalgia unwarranted
43. Foreign film hard to follow
44. New haircut funky—and not in a good way
45. Swimsuit unflattering
46. Master's degree useless
47. Foreplay cursory
48. New sweater not complimented
49. Blog unread
50. Limerick not bawdy
51. Toast burnt

52. Poem unintentionally hilarious
53. Daughter plain
54. Altoids not as intense as their marketing claims
55. Hero rude
56. Bin Laden uncaptured
57. Cat unaffectionate
58. Baby ugly
59. Sermon soporific
60. Imported cheese smelly
61. Portion too small
62. Fancy cigar tastes like a bundle of burning leaves
63. Really cute heels uncomfortable
64. Leftover french fries inedible
65. Beach crowded
66. Beloved film from your childhood not as good as you remember it
67. Three-day weekend squandered
68. Role model sexist
69. Boxing match civilized
70. Chicken salad sandwich dry
71. Dog disobedient
72. Season finale inscrutable
73. No room for dessert
74. Youth fleeting
75. Second place
76. Psychiatrist preoccupied
77. Old person not full of wisdom
78. Art unappreciated
79. Retirement boring
80. Christmas not white

81. Circus ratty
82. Fortune-teller vague
83. Effects of exercise regiment gradual
84. Solar eclipse unimpressive
85. Vending machine out of order
86. Soda flat
87. Expensive wine's taste indescernable from regular wine
88. Buffet selection limited
89. New cubicle same as old cubicle
90. Sequel not as good as original
91. Awesome dream just a dream
92. Son not good enough to play major league ball
93. Pen pal poor speller
94. Lap dance perfunctory
95. High five left hangin'
96. Scrabble triple word score word disputed
97. Inspirational quote uninspiring
98. Monkeyhouse closed for cleaning
99. Disappointment list one disappointment short

THINGS PEOPLE SAY TO MY DOG

I'M A CHARMING CONVERSATIONALIST. I read the newspaper every day to stay abreast of current events[1] and keep a special eye out for interesting stories I can use as conversation starters[2]. I have a nonthreatening physical presence, warm smile, and wear pleasant, sorbet-colored shirts. I know three different surefire ice-breakers[3], a ton of jokes, and one magic trick involving clothespins (which I always carry, just in case).

My dog walks around naked, has pee breath, and cannot speak a single word of English (or Spanish), but people still prefer talking to him than me. Squatting to poop on the sidewalk, he makes a better first impression than I do wearing a tuxedo and handing out free ice cream.

Strangers will often stop us during our walks and hold lengthy, one-sided conversations with my dog without ever acknowledging my presence, other than to ask me his name; his name is Toby, but sometimes I'll tell people his name is Doogie, so the conversation at least takes on the *illusion* of involving me. When people ask Toby questions— the same stupid questions over and over—it's unclear whether I'm supposed to answer for him or stand in dumb silence, holding his leash. It's not dissimilar from someone walking up and starting a conversation with your shoes or wristwatch.

I'd like to make it clear that I'm not jealous of my dog—seriously, I have way more friends than him[4]. And I can't help but think that the daily grooming and jaunty little bandana I put on him are integral parts of his charm. I do feel kind of bad for him, because when people talk to him, he can't talk back—although he is an eloquent non-verbal communicator. *(See Figure 1: Nonverbal Dominance Assertion.)*

Of course, dogs' inability to talk actually increases their charm. They can't judge you, challenge your politics, or condescendingly question your employment status. (For the record, I wasn't fired, I'm on furlough.) If people actually wanted talking dogs, we would have them. It's an open secret that the technology to read certain animals' minds, including dogs, has been around since the 1960s, when the government developed it as part of their Cold War Bovine Interrogation Program. I know that sounds unbelievable, and I'd explain the mechanics to you, but it would be way over your head. *(See Figure 2: Other Stuff You Wouldn't Understand, Even if I Explained it to You.)*

---

(1) Orlando Bloom's New Gal Pal!

(2) Scientists discover that dolphins name themselves!

(3) Did you hear about the overweight polar bear? He broke the ice. (Extend hand.) Hi, my name's Doogie.

(4) If you don't count his Facebook friends. He especially makes a big deal out of the fact that he's Facebook friends with Mr. T, even though I doubt it's the real Mr. T.

Anyway, what scientists discovered is that dogs are pretty much thinking what you assume they are, although they're surprisingly snarky when it comes to questions about their pedigree.

Personally, my favorite aspect of talking to dogs is that it's one of the few crazy behaviors you can safely indulge in public (other than freaking out over organized sports). You can walk up to a stranger's dog and talk to them in a weird high-pitched voice as you stroke their face and—surprisingly, illogically—it's socially acceptable. Same thing with babies. That baby can't understand a word you say, but nobody would let that

stop them from complimenting his hat, asking if he wants to be a fireman when he grows up, or pretending to steal and eat his nose. *(See Figure 3: How Crazy are You for Talking to the Following People, Animals, and Inanimate Objects?)*

FIGURE 2: OTHER STUFF YOU WOULDN'T UNDERSTAND, EVEN IF I EXPLAINED IT TO YOU

1. Atoms
2. Anti-matter
3. Electrolytes
4. Floam
5. The opposite sex
6. Nuclear whatever
7. Rap music
8. Lasers
9. Imaginary numbers
10. Gaydar

FIGURE3: HOW CRAZY ARE YOU FOR TALKING TO THE FOLLOWING PEOPLE, ANIMALS, AND INANIMATE OBJECTS?

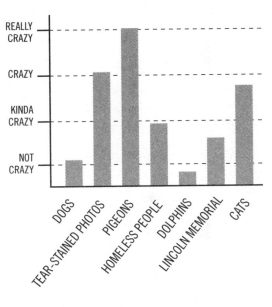

FIGURE 1: NONVERBAL DOMINANCE ASSERTION

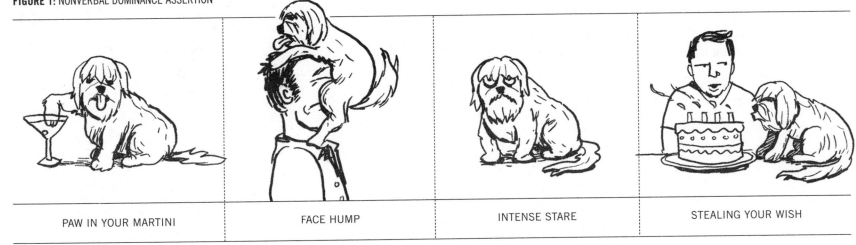

| PAW IN YOUR MARTINI | FACE HUMP | INTENSE STARE | STEALING YOUR WISH |

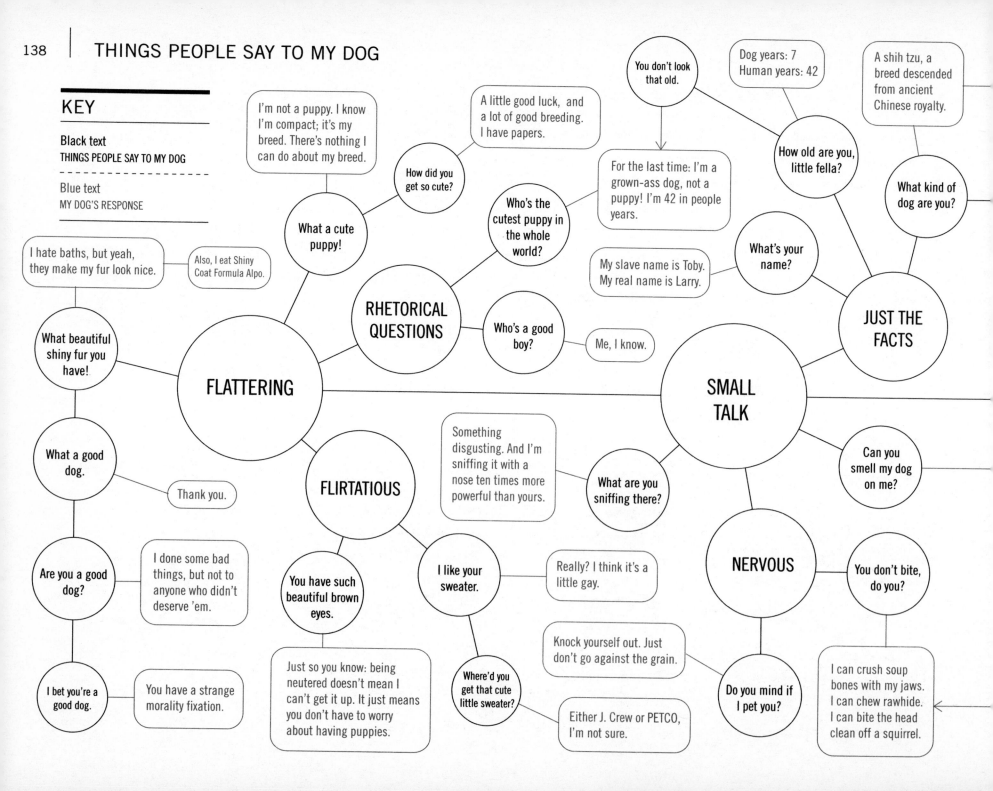

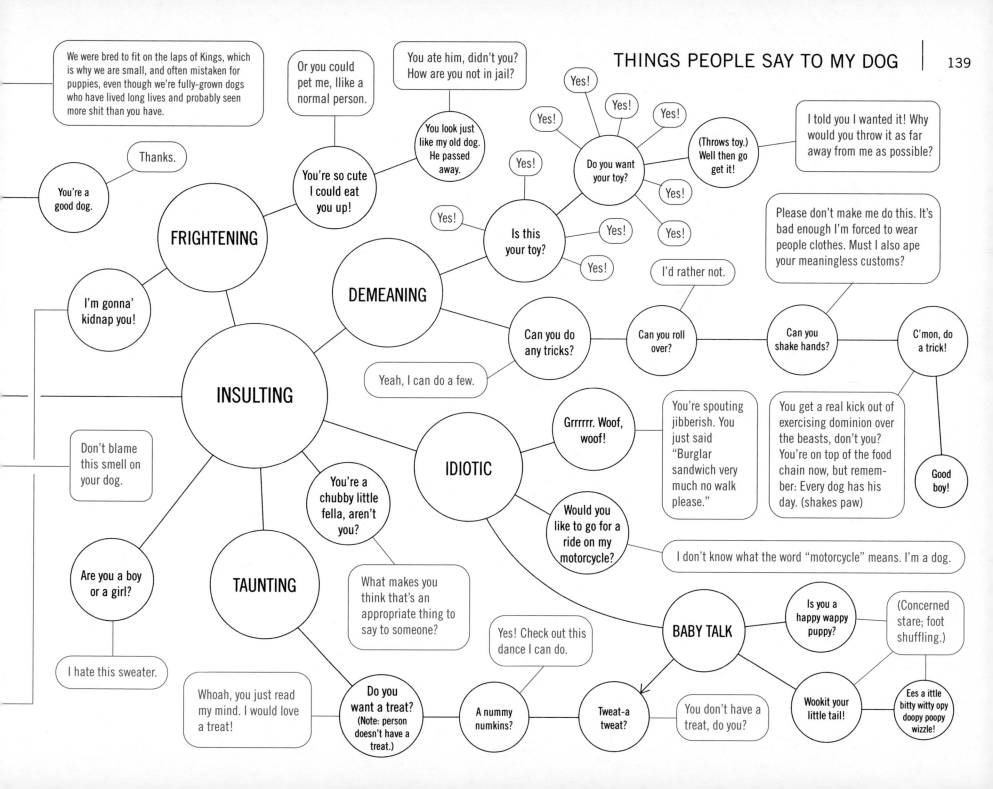

THINGS TO SAY DURING SEX

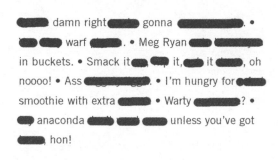

OFTEN, IN THE HEAT OF THE MOMENT, it's difficult to find the right words to express how you feel. Let's face it, we aren't all poets like Emily Dickinson[1] and Jimmy Shakespeare. We've all blurted out off-putting pillow talk, or brayed like a donkey when we meant to roar like a lion[2]. *(See Figure 1: Which Animals Make Sexy Sounds?)*

Why is this chart entitled "Things to Say During Sex," rather than "Things You Say During Sex"? There are two reasons: First of all, the things you say during sex *(see Figure 2: Things You Say During Sex)* are so far beyond the boundaries of common decency, there's no way they could be reprinted in this book unless it was sold under the counter with a brown paper wrapper. And secondly, I didn't want to embarrass you.

You'll notice that the chart is divided into two

(1) Historical evidence suggests that Emily Dickinson was probably a lesbian.
(2) When I say "we" I of course mean "you."

██ damn right██ gonna █████████. • ████ warf ████. • Meg Ryan ████ █████ in buckets. • Smack it██, ██ it,██ it ██, oh noooo! • Ass █████████. • I'm hungry for██ smoothie with extra ████ • Warty ██████? • ██ anaconda ████ ██ ██ unless you've got ██, hon!

sections: good and bad. It thereby offers not only examples of appropriate pillow talk, but also ill-chosen boudoir banter you may currently be using, not realizing it's inappropriate.

The good and bad hemispheres of the chart are very similar to each other in structure, almost achieving bilateral symmetry. Not only is there structural symmetry, but the five tertiary categories on either side of the vertical axis of attraction are identical. There are multiple reasons for this.

1. The structural and editorial symmetry of the chart emphasize the minor differences that separate good pillow talk from bad. Cadence alone separates the sexy "No, don't stop," from the date-rapey "No . . . Don't . . . STOP!" The very nature of love is similarly tenuous, the things that attract us—a scent, a glance, the nape of a neck—fragile as a summer's sigh . . . or a butterfly . . . or a dandelion patch. Your hair looks incredible in this light[3].

2. The bilateral symmetry of the "Things To Say During Sex" chart reflects the physical symmetry of most animals, including humans. Viewed thusly, the chart provides a metaphorical manifestation of human existence. Also, it kind of looks like a pair of fallopian tubes (if you squint), or two testicles with lots of crazy hairs. *(See Figure 2: Kind of a Rorschach Test, But Not Really.)*

Foreign languages are a popular genre for amorous whisperings, since they lend a whiff of the exotic. Not all foreign tongues are equally attractive though. French, for instance, is far sexier than German. Its superior seductiveness is partially due to the linguistic cadence and rhythms of the language, however the main reason lies in the two countries' respective shapes. France is shaped like a sexy little strawberry mark on your lover's lower back (also known as "angel kisses" on newborns), while Germany is shaped more like a gravy stain on the rented sheets of a turnpike Motel. *(See Figure 3: France and Germany.)*

One category that surprises some people is "Rhetorical questions." Why are rhetorical questions better than actual questions? Well, questions can be risky because they cause the logical part of your partner's mind to kick into action. This is the last thing you want, because there is nothing logical about making love—getting naked, sticking your "you know what" in some stranger's "there you have it," possibly creating a tiny human being with your awkward thrustings—yuck. Nothing is more distracting than asking your partner how to get stains out of silk sheets in the middle of hot and heavy gettings on[4].

---

(3) I'm not just saying that. I mean it.

(4) I love you.

FIGURE 2: KIND OF A RORSCHACH TEST, BUT NOT REALLY

A silhouette of one half of the *Things to Say During Sex* chart, fallopian tubes, and testicles, when stacked on top of each other, kind of looks like a funny man whose head is surrounded by a swarm of hornets. Discuss the implications of this with your partner (and then have sex).

FIGURE 3: FRANCE AND GERMANY

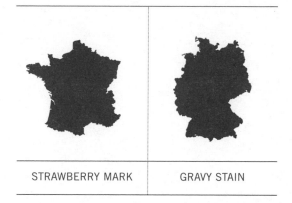

| STRAWBERRY MARK | GRAVY STAIN |

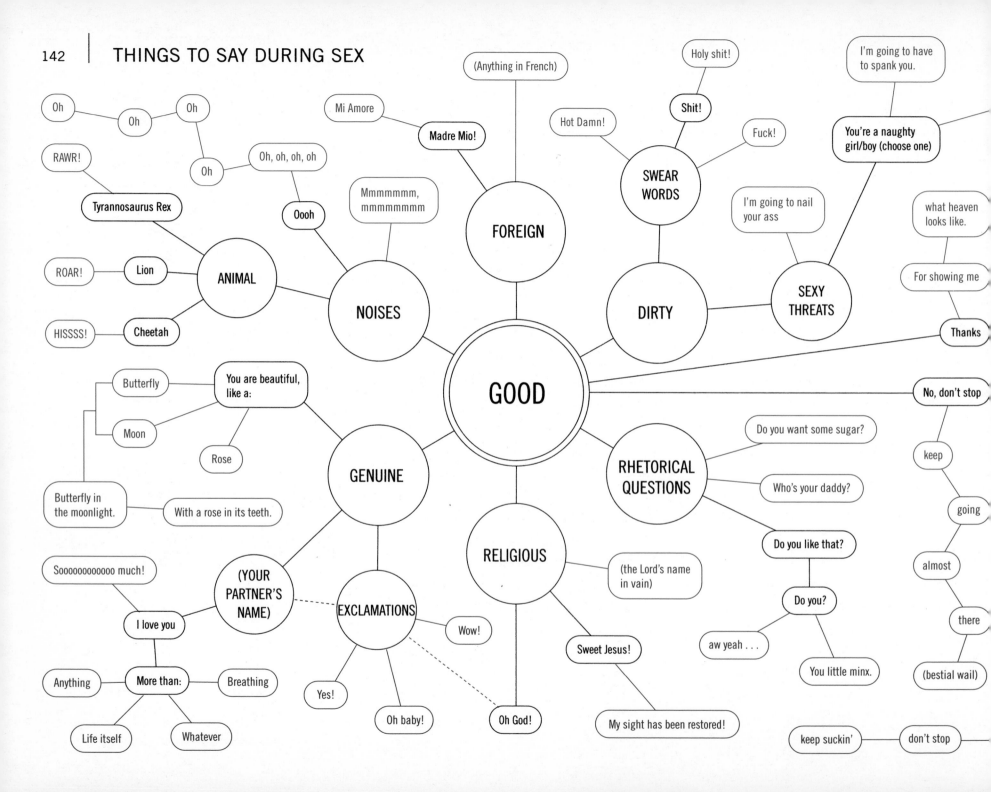

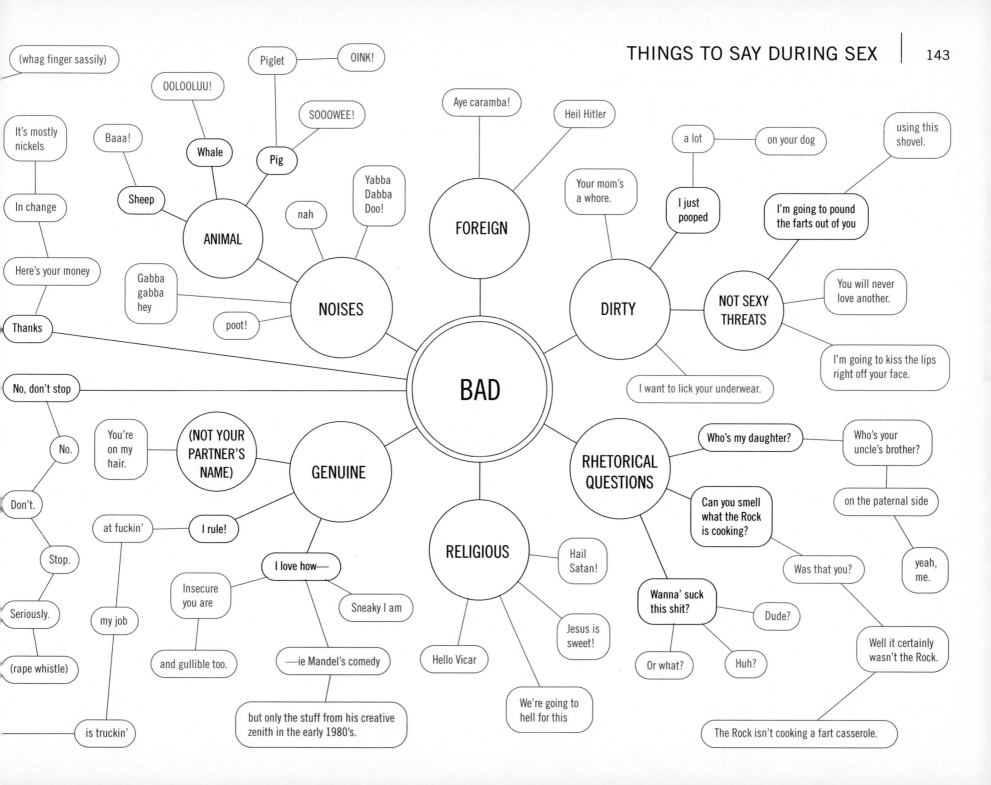

U.S. PRESIDENTIAL RUMBLE

JOHN ADAMS WAS THE SECOND President of the United States, and consequently the first U.S. President who was able to challenge George Washington to a fight, which he did on the eve of his inauguration.

Washington initially demurred, but as he turned his back to leave, Adams kicked him in the ass. Washington whirled around and Adams kicked him again—this time in the stomach—so hard that Washington's false teeth flew out. The first Presidential Fight had begun, and although Adams didn't realize it, he was starting a tradition that would last up until the present day. *(See Figure 1: Gilbert Stuart's Famous Portrait of Washington, Painted Days After his Beating by Adams.)*

The next presidential fight was between Adams and Jefferson. The two men were already bitter political rivals, and their fight proved far more cutthroat than the one between Adams and

FIGURE 1: GILBERT STUART'S FAMOUS PORTRAIT OF WASHINGTON, PAINTED DAYS AFTER HIS BEATING BY ADAMS

Washington. Although at this time the presidential rumble was not yet a tradition, Jefferson suspected Adams might challenge him to a fight on inauguration day and therefore ambushed him a week ahead of time. (It's also possible that Jefferson was unaware of the Presidential Fight tradition and battered Adams over an unrelated beef.) Whatever the instigation, their rumble was so violent that it ignited a political war that culmi-

nated with Jefferson's vice-president, Aaron Burr, shooting Alexander Hamilton for no good reason.

After this everybody conceded that things had gone too far. Congress forced Burr to write a nice letter to Hamilton's widow, and also to mow her lawn once a week for the rest of his life (although he just got a slave to do it). The presidential fights became far less violent and primarily ceremonial; the actual form of the fight was left up to the sitting president, who usually chose something like a vigorous debate about tariffs, a thumb-wrestling match, or a brief game of mercy. *(See Figure 2: Some Presidential Fights.)*

Although the presidential fights didn't involve actual fisticuffs anymore, political satirists and notable wits nevertheless speculated whether the incoming or outgoing president would win in a fight, and these fantasy fights became quite popular with the common rabble. Prominent writers of the day would often pen short stories about these

FIGURE 2: SELECTED PRESIDENTIAL FIGHTS

1801	Cowboys and Indians, played using actual people
1829	Name that amendment
1854	Bean bag toss
1861	Guess a number between 1 and 4 score and 7 years
1877	Paper, Rock, Congressional Filibuster
1889	Game of touch football: Senate vs. House of Representatives
1929	Three legged race, each president tied to a one-legged WWI veteran
1945	The Fire Bombing of Nagasaki
1953	Full-contact rhetoric
1961	Guess which cabinet member farted
1974	Truth or impeachment (with a specific *no nudity* clause)
1977	Staring contest
1981	Laser tag
1989	Cannonball dive contest (measured by splash height, no extra points for "style")
1993	Pokemon Battle

imagined fights, such as Mark Twain's lively and humorous *Punch, Presidents, Punch!: an Apology to Harrison's Widow* (1898), and Mickey Spillane's hard-boiled thriller *The Oval Ring* (1953).

FIGURE 3: NOTABLE PRESIDENTS, AND THEIR FIGHTING STYLES

GROVER CLEVELAND	ULYSSES S. GRANT	FRANKLIN ROOSEVELT	WILLIAM H. TAFT
tag team luchadore	*drunken boxing*	*master blaster*	*sumo*

It is in this long tradition of fantasy presidential pugilism that I have constructed the following chart. I've tried to make the chart as historically accurate as possible, and limited any speculation or flights of fancy. I remember reading Hunter S. Thompson's account of the imagined death battle between Lyndon Johnson and Richard Nixon and being annoyed by one part where he said that Nixon's dog, Checkers, would tear out Johnson's throat. Checkers is a cocker spaniel! How's he going to reach Johnson's throat, with a ladder? The freak ticket indeed!

Regarding the chart's organization: the presidents have been split into four conferences and seeded to facilitate maximum equity of competition, just like in college basketball. In other words, the strongest presidents have been spread out. I have also included extensive footnotes, which can be found on page 151, to help clarify things in case you aren't well-versed in presidential history—which is really the history of your country, and which you should feel deep shame for not knowing in more depth.

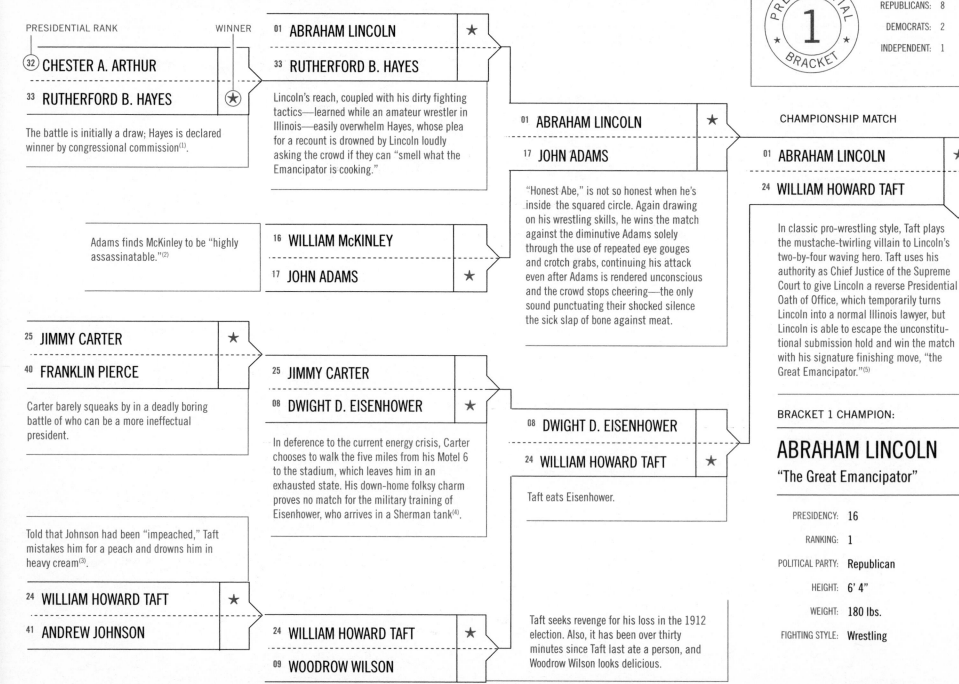

PRESIDENTIAL RANK   WINNER

(32) CHESTER A. ARTHUR

33 RUTHERFORD B. HAYES ★

The battle is initially a draw; Hayes is declared winner by congressional commission[1].

01 ABRAHAM LINCOLN ★

33 RUTHERFORD B. HAYES

Lincoln's reach, coupled with his dirty fighting tactics—learned while an amateur wrestler in Illinois—easily overwhelm Hayes, whose plea for a recount is drowned by Lincoln loudly asking the crowd if they can "smell what the Emancipator is cooking."

Adams finds McKinley to be "highly assassinatable."[2]

16 WILLIAM McKINLEY

17 JOHN ADAMS ★

01 ABRAHAM LINCOLN ★

17 JOHN ADAMS

"Honest Abe," is not so honest when he's inside the squared circle. Again drawing on his wrestling skills, he wins the match against the diminutive Adams solely through the use of repeated eye gouges and crotch grabs, continuing his attack even after Adams is rendered unconscious and the crowd stops cheering—the only sound punctuating their shocked silence the sick slap of bone against meat.

25 JIMMY CARTER ★

40 FRANKLIN PIERCE

Carter barely squeaks by in a deadly boring battle of who can be a more ineffectual president.

25 JIMMY CARTER

08 DWIGHT D. EISENHOWER ★

In deference to the current energy crisis, Carter chooses to walk the five miles from his Motel 6 to the stadium, which leaves him in an exhausted state. His down-home folksy charm proves no match for the military training of Eisenhower, who arrives in a Sherman tank[4].

08 DWIGHT D. EISENHOWER

24 WILLIAM HOWARD TAFT ★

Taft eats Eisenhower.

Told that Johnson had been "impeached," Taft mistakes him for a peach and drowns him in heavy cream[3].

24 WILLIAM HOWARD TAFT ★

41 ANDREW JOHNSON

24 WILLIAM HOWARD TAFT ★

09 WOODROW WILSON

Taft seeks revenge for his loss in the 1912 election. Also, it has been over thirty minutes since Taft last ate a person, and Woodrow Wilson looks delicious.

CHAMPIONSHIP MATCH

01 ABRAHAM LINCOLN ★

24 WILLIAM HOWARD TAFT

In classic pro-wrestling style, Taft plays the mustache-twirling villain to Lincoln's two-by-four waving hero. Taft uses his authority as Chief Justice of the Supreme Court to give Lincoln a reverse Presidential Oath of Office, which temporarily turns Lincoln into a normal Illinois lawyer, but Lincoln is able to escape the unconstitutional submission hold and win the match with his signature finishing move, "the Great Emancipator."[5]

BRACKET 1 CHAMPION:

ABRAHAM LINCOLN
"The Great Emancipator"

PRESIDENCY:	16
RANKING:	1
POLITICAL PARTY:	Republican
HEIGHT:	6' 4"
WEIGHT:	180 lbs.
FIGHTING STYLE:	Wrestling

PRESIDENTIAL **1** BRACKET

REPUBLICANS:	8
DEMOCRATS:	2
INDEPENDENT:	1

REPUBLICANS: 2.5
DEMOCRATS: 4
WHIGS: 2
DEMOCRATIC-REPUBLICANS: 1
BULL MOOSE: .5

PRESIDENTIAL BRACKET **2**

CHAMPIONSHIP MATCH

★ 04 THEODORE ROOSEVELT

21 GROVER CLEVELAND

An avid big game hunter who had bagged lions and bears, Roosevelt longed to hunt the most dangerous animal—man. Cleveland's head is now mounted on Roosevelt's wall between Kaiser Wilhelm II and an unknown Spaniard. Teddy has the ivory from Grover's tusks made into some *bully* cufflinks which he distributes among the Rough Riders as Christmas presents.

BRACKET 2 CHAMPION:

THEODORE ROOSEVELT

"Rough and Ready Teddy"

PRESIDENCY: 26

RANKING: 4

POLITICAL PARTY: Republican/Bull Moose

HEIGHT: 5' 10"

WEIGHT: 200 lbs.

FIGHTING STYLE: Big Game Hunting

★ 04 THEODORE ROOSEVELT

13 ANDREW JACKSON

Roosevelt refuses to recognize Jackson's *Roosevelt Removal Act of 1830*, which would require him to walk the 600 miles back to his homeland in New York City. Jackson fires at Roosevelt with a musket, but—perhaps due to humidity—the powder doesn't ignite. Roosevelt punches Jackson in the heart, dislodging a musket ball left there from a previous duel and killing Jackson instantly.[6]

05 HARRY S. TRUMAN

★ 21 GROVER CLEVELAND

Truman defeats Grover Cleveland almost too easily. As he stands over his foe's dead body he remembers too late that Cleveland was the only president to serve two non-consecutive terms in office. He feels a gun muzzle pressed into the small of his back and turns around to see the second-term Cleveland standing there, his tusks dripping with blood.

★ 04 THEODORE ROOSEVELT

38 GEORGE W. BUSH

While in high school, a young Roosevelt took up boxing, eventually becoming the runner up in the Harvard boxing championship. While in high school, a young Bush was on the cheerleading squad, eventually becoming the runner up in the Harvard recreational cocaine use championship.

★ 13 ANDREW JACKSON

20 JAMES MADISON

37 MILLARD FILLMORE

★ 05 HARRY S. TRUMAN

A puzzled Fillmore stands in an empty ring, waiting for Truman to arrive, when he hears the drone of an airplane overhead and looks up just in time to see an atomic bomb plummeting towards him. At a press conference in a cement bunker a safe distance away, a smiling Truman holds up a newspaper whose headline reads "Fillmore Defeats Truman."[7]

12 JAMES K. POLK

★ 21 GROVER CLEVELAND

WINNER | PRESIDENTIAL RANK

29 ZACHARY TAYLOR

★ 38 GEORGE W. BUSH

Before the match, in the parking lot of the stadium, Bush accidentally hits Taylor with his car while driving under the influence.[8]

Jackson gives Madison a "special blanket," which, unbeknownst to Madison, is contaminated with smallpox.[9]

28 JAMES GARFIELD

★ 37 MILLARD FILLMORE

Garfield the president refuses to fight and sends in his second, Garfield the cat. Fillmore retaliates by sending in his second, Mallard Fillmore the duck, who eviscerates Garfield with a scathingly unfunny op-ed column.

Polk initially laughs at Cleveland's walrus-like mustache, until Cleveland smiles and reveals that he has walrus-like tusks as well, which he savagely buries in Polk's throat.[10]

BRACKET 3 CHAMPION:

GEORGE WASHINGTON
"Dollar Bill"

PRESIDENTIAL RANK

WINNER

(31) MARTIN VAN BUREN (★)

34 HERBERT HOOVER

Hoover's use of *laissez-faire* fighting tactics consist of him trying to ignore how badly Van Buren's repeated kicks and punches hurt. The Secret Service has to hold back the surly crowd, who pelts Hoover with rotten food and death threats. After the first round Hoover declares he never wanted to be president in the first place and leaves to go fishing.[11]

02 GEORGE WASHINGTON ★

31 MARTIN VAN BUREN

The debate over the truthfelness of Washington's "cherry tree" story is ended as Washington enters the ring wielding an axe. Thirty seconds later a panting Washington admits, "I cannot tell a lie, it was I who severed Van Buren's head. Shwickity-shwack!"

15 BILL CLINTON ★

18 GEORGE H.W. BUSH

Shouldn't have called him Bozo.[14]

02 GEORGE WASHINGTON ★

15 BILL CLINTON

"Wow, George Washington?! I can't believe I'm actually meeting the first president of the United States! Your farewall address was a huge inspiration to me as a young man. My name is William Jefferson Clinton, I'm the 42nd president of the—say, what's with the axe? OH GOD NO, PLEASE STOP! AHHHHHHHHHH!"

PRESIDENCY: 1

RANKING: 2

POLITICAL PARTY: None

HEIGHT: approx. 6' 2"

WEIGHT: approx. 175 lbs.

FIGHTING STYLE: Wild, relentless axe-chopping

CHAMPIONSHIP MATCH

02 GEORGE WASHINGTON ★

10 RONALD REAGAN

"Hey there young feller, I don't believe I know your name. Sorry, but I have a touch of Alzheimers so I'm not too good and remembering people. Say, that's a nice axe you have there—OH GOD NO! PLEASE DON'T! AHHHHH!"

26 CALVIN COOLIDGE ★

39 WILLIAM HENRY HARRISON

Once again, coolage proves to be the death of William Henry Harrison.[12]

26 CALVIN COOLIDGE

07 THOMAS JEFFERSON ★

The two men conspicuously ignore each other in a stalemate of silent aloofness until Jefferson uses his 100 slaves to win the match for him.[15]

Reagan uses his acting skills to do a spot-on impersonation of Lincoln and frees Jefferson's slaves. Jefferson is left exposed to an attack from Reagan's simian co-star from *Bedtime for Bonzo*, who rips Jefferson's face off.[16]

07 THOMAS JEFFERSON

10 RONALD REAGAN ★

Grant arrives reeking of whiskey, wearing only one boot and dragging his suspenders behind him. Buchanan is vividly reminded of his own alcoholic father, and the fight becomes a psychological war of attrition, as Grant wears Buchanan down with verbal abuse while Buchanan cries in the corner.[13]

23 ULYSSES S. GRANT ★

42 JAMES BUCHANAN

23 ULYSSES S. GRANT

10 RONALD REAGAN ★

Grant is transfixed by a jar of jelly beans that Reagan is eating. Since the candy didn't exist while Grant was alive, he mistakes the brightly-colored candies for a symptom of the d.t.'s and downs a hog's head of bourbon in an attempt to counter the perceived withdrawal.

PRESIDENTIAL **3** BRACKET

REPUBLICANS: 8

DEMOCRATS: 2

INDEPENDENT: 1

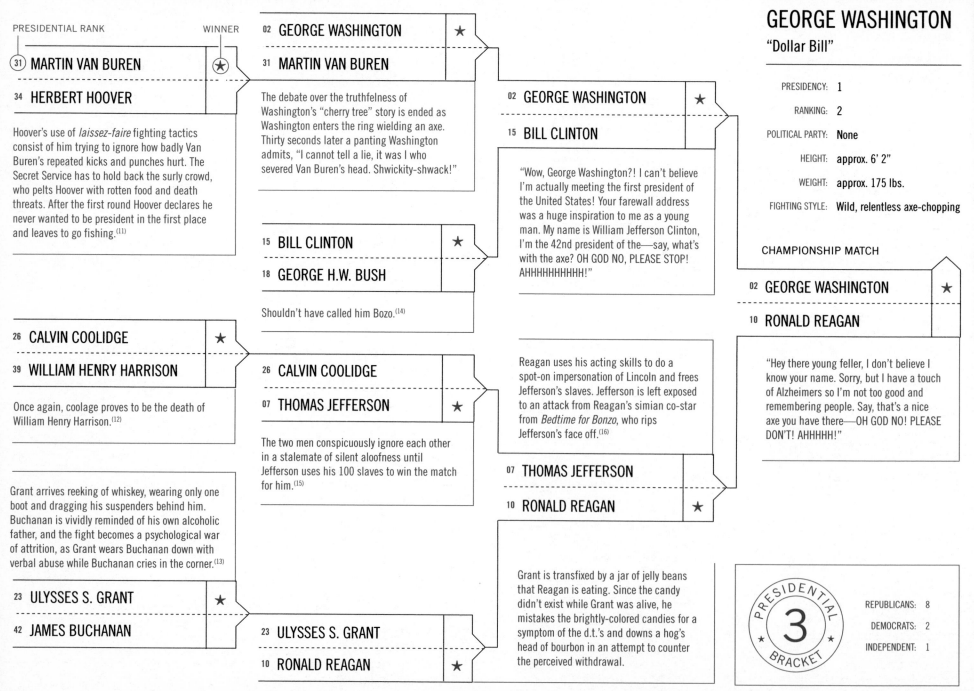

JAMES MONROE

"Dr. Feelgood"

PRESIDENCY: 5

RANKING: 14

POLITICAL PARTY: Democratic-Republican

HEIGHT: 6'

WEIGHT: 180 lbs.

FIGHTING STYLE: Psychological warfare

CHAMPIONSHIP MATCH

★ 14 JAMES MONROE

06 JOHN F. KENNEDY

Lyndon Johnson comes out of nowhere with a CIA assasination squad and shoots Kennedy in the head. Monroe, also armed, is the second shooter. Johnson challenges Monroe to a title fight, but then Jack Ruby rushes from the crowd and shoots Johnson. Ruby immediately dies of cancer, and all eyewitnesses to the fight die of various completely natural causes within the next two years.[17]

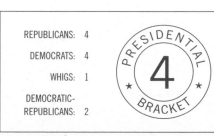

REPUBLICANS: 4

DEMOCRATS: 4

WHIGS: 1

DEMOCRATIC-REPUBLICANS: 2

PRESIDENTIAL 4 BRACKET

03 FRANKLIN D. ROOSEVELT

★ 14 JAMES MONROE

Monroe uses his mutant ability to exude calming pheremones—the same ability that allowed him to mantain the national "Era of Good Feelings" from 1817-1825—to lull Eleanor into a deep slumber. He then pushes Franklin's wheelchair down the steps of the Capitol Building in an obvious homage to the famous baby carriage scene in *Battleship Potemkin*.[18]

Kennedy and Obama merely being in the same room together exposes everyone in attendence to a lethal overdose of hope. Obama flings his Nobel Peace Prize at JFK, but the medallion bounces off Kennedy's charisma shield and strikes Obama in the eye.

★ 06 JOHN F. KENNEDY

43 BARACK OBAMA

Johnson accuses Obama of being a Communist and mounts a massive troop offensive against him, including sustained aerial bombardment. However all of the bullets and bombs bounce harmlessly off Obama's Nobel Peace Prize. Johnson slinks out of the ring amid the jeers of student protestors.[19]

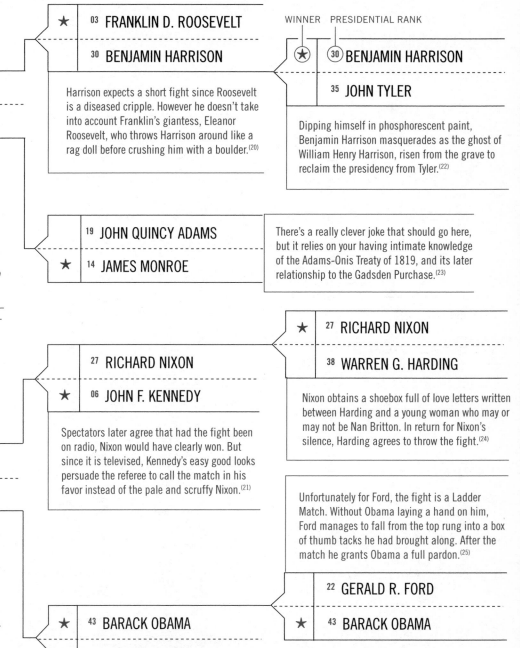

★ 03 FRANKLIN D. ROOSEVELT

30 BENJAMIN HARRISON

Harrison expects a short fight since Roosevelt is a diseased cripple. However he doesn't take into account Franklin's giantess, Eleanor Roosevelt, who throws Harrison around like a rag doll before crushing him with a boulder.[20]

19 JOHN QUINCY ADAMS

★ 14 JAMES MONROE

27 RICHARD NIXON

★ 06 JOHN F. KENNEDY

Spectators later agree that had the fight been on radio, Nixon would have clearly won. But since it is televised, Kennedy's easy good looks persuade the referee to call the match in his favor instead of the pale and scruffy Nixon.[21]

★ 43 BARACK OBAMA

11 LYNDON B. JOHNSON

WINNER   PRESIDENTIAL RANK

★ 30 BENJAMIN HARRISON

35 JOHN TYLER

Dipping himself in phosphorescent paint, Benjamin Harrison masquerades as the ghost of William Henry Harrison, risen from the grave to reclaim the presidency from Tyler.[22]

There's a really clever joke that should go here, but it relies on your having intimate knowledge of the Adams-Onis Treaty of 1819, and its later relationship to the Gadsden Purchase.[23]

★ 27 RICHARD NIXON

38 WARREN G. HARDING

Nixon obtains a shoebox full of love letters written between Harding and a young woman who may or may not be Nan Britton. In return for Nixon's silence, Harding agrees to throw the fight.[24]

Unfortunately for Ford, the fight is a Ladder Match. Without Obama laying a hand on him, Ford manages to fall from the top rung into a box of thumb tacks he had brought along. After the match he grants Obama a full pardon.[25]

22 GERALD R. FORD

★ 43 BARACK OBAMA

THE FINAL FOUR

FIGHT!

ABRAHAM LINCOLN

ODDS 2:1

	1	2	3	4	5
STRENGTH					
SPEED					
FIGHTING SKILLS					
INTELLIGENCE					
DURABILITY					

THEODORE ROOSEVELT

ODDS 1:2

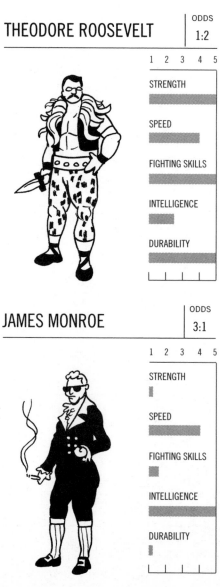

	1	2	3	4	5
STRENGTH					
SPEED					
FIGHTING SKILLS					
INTELLIGENCE					
DURABILITY					

GEORGE WASHINGTON

ODDS 1:1

	1	2	3	4	5
STRENGTH					
SPEED					
FIGHTING SKILLS					
INTELLIGENCE					
DURABILITY					

JAMES MONROE

ODDS 3:1

	1	2	3	4	5
STRENGTH					
SPEED					
FIGHTING SKILLS					
INTELLIGENCE					
DURABILITY					

---

01 ABRAHAM LINCOLN

04 THEODORE ROOSEVELT ★

During their lives, Roosevelt and Lincoln had both been attacked by assasins with guns—Lincoln while in office, Roosevelt while on the campaign trail. The attack on Lincoln was, of course, fatal. Roosevelt, however, went on to give a ninety-minute speech immediately after being shot, because he's bulletproof. With no armor piercing rounds in his arsenal, Lincoln is forced to concede the fight.

02 GEORGE WASHINGTON

14 JAMES MONROE ★

Washington attempts to suprise Monroe by attacking on Christmas night; but instead of crossing an icy river, he dresses as Santa and goes down the chimney, in an obvious homage to *Silent Night Deadly Night*. Unknown to Washington Monroe is an athiest, and also an insomniac. Instead of finding Monroe asleep from too much holiday revelry, a soot-covered Washington finds Monroe sitting in front of the fireplace cleaning his gun.[26]

CHAMPIONSHIP MATCH

04 THEODORE ROOSEVELT

14 JAMES MONROE ★

The Monroe Doctrine leads to the Roosevelt Coronary.[27]

GRAND CHAMPION:

JAMES MONROE

DEAL WITH IT!

FIGURE 4: U.S. PRESIDENTIAL RUMBLE FOOTNOTES

---

(1) In the presidential election of 1876, Hayes lost the popular vote but won the electoral vote. Consequently his victory was highly disputed.

(2) McKinley was assassinated by an anarchist in 1901.

(3) In 1868 Johnson became the first president to be impeached. William Howard Taft was very fat, and liked peaches.

(4) On inauguration day, Carter covered the mile and a half from the Capitol to the executive mansion by walking instead of driving, in deference to the energy crisis.

(5) After his presidency, Taft became Chief Justice of the Supreme Court, the only president to ever do so. One of the Chief Justice's duties is administering the Oath of Office to entering presidents.

(6) *The Indian Removal Act of 1830* forced thousands of Native Americans to leave their tribal lands and walk hundreds of miles West to find new homes, an emigration which became known as the *Trail of Tears*.
   An assassination attempt was made on Jackson in 1833, but the assassin's muskets misfired.
   Jackson lived most of his life with a musket ball lodged near his heart, a wound from a duel.

(7) Truman authorized the use of the atomic bomb on Japan in 1945.
   Truman was such an underdog in the election of 1948 that the *Chicago Tribune* prematurely ran the headline *Dewey Defeats Truman*, although Truman ended up winning the election.

(8) In 1976 George W. Bush was arrested for a DUI.

(9) The Native Americans were given smallpox-infected blankets by the U.S. Government. There's a possibility that this wasn't accidental.

(10) Grover Cleveland looked like a walrus.

(11) Laissez-faire economics is an approach to regulating the economy by limiting government intervention— essentially, doing as little as possible to control it. During the Great Depression, Hoover was criticized for his use of laissez-faire economic policies.

(12) Harrison delivered his exceptionally long (two hour) inaugural speech in the cold rain without hat or coat, and died one month later of pneumonia.

(13) Grant was an alcoholic.

(14) H.W. Bush famously referred to Clinton as "Bozo" during the '92 campaign.

(15) As the principal author of the Declaration of Independence, Jefferson was one of the most influential proponents of liberty. He also owned slaves, which some people think is ironic.

(16) Before becoming one of the handsomest presidents, Reagan was an actor who starred in films such as *Bedtime For Bonzo*, a comedy about a monkey.

(17) Although the Warren Commission concluded that Oswald acted alone in the assassination of JFK, many people have speculated that there was a second shooter, and that the assassination was a conspiracy that the CIA and perhaps even Lyndon Johnson were complicit in. Lee Harvey Oswald was shot by Jack Ruby before he was able to stand trial.

(18) Monroe presided over an unusually calm period of American politics known as the *Era of Good Feelings*.
   Battleship Potemkin is a 1925 Polish film. The

film's most famous scene takes place on the *Odessa Steps*; among general mayhem and violence, a baby stroller careens out of control down the steps.

(19) Lyndon Johnson's presidency was defined by his escalation of the Vietnam War, which ultimately made him the target of widespread protesting.

(20) FDR was paralyzed from the waist down. His wife Eleanor was 5' 11.5".

(21) The Nixon/Kennedy debates of the 1960 election were the first televised debates. While Kennedy appeared tan, confident, and comfortable, Nixon looked gaunt, pale, and uncomfortable.

(22) John Tyler ascended to the presidency from the position of vice-president, following the untimely death of William Henry Harrison.

(23) Nope, I won't explain it here either.

(24) Harding was plagued by rumors of various extra-marital affairs, some of which were undoubtedly true. Harding and the Republican National Committee paid hush money to various women over the years.

(25) Gerald Ford was notoriously clumsy, and was parodied by Chevy Chase on *Saturday Night Live*, often falling off ladders or tripping over things.
   Ford attained the presidency after Nixon's resignation, and granted Nixon a full pardon for any crimes he may have committed during the Watergate scandal.

(26) On the night of December 25, Washington surprised the Hessians at Trenton by crossing the Delaware; James Monroe was among his troops.

(27) In 1904, Teddy Roosevelt added the Roosevelt Corollary to the Monroe Doctrine. In 1919 Roosevelt died of a heart attack, otherwise known as a coronary.

WWF FINISHING MOVES

FINISHING MOVES ARE NOT all equally awesome, but all awesome wrestlers must have a finishing move. Without a finishing move, a wrestler is just the wrestler in the blue trunks that gets smacked around by the Honky Tonk Man while Honky waits for the Ultimate Warrior to take the Intercontinental Belt from him in an embarrassingly brief match (32 seconds). The best finishing moves embody a defining characteristic of the wrestler who invented them, and are thereby indelibly linked to them: The DDT's stunning speed mirrored Jake the Snake's viper like quickness and cunning; the Perfect-Plex showcased Mr. Perfect's technical prowess; and Junkyard Dog's DogButt—where he would crawl on all fours, repeatedly headbutt his opponent, and then pantomime urinating on them—vividly illustrated his belief that he was a dog[1].

This chart isn't a comprehensive list of every WWF finishing move. I limited its scope to important or influential wrestlers who were active between Wrestlemania I and XIII, a golden age of wrestling bookended by the wrestling boom of the 1980s and the Attitude Era of the late 90s. The Attitude Era officially began at the 1996 King of the Ring, when America embraced redneck heel "Stone Cold" Steve Austin's victory over Jake "the Snake" Roberts, a willful act of stupidity with strong parallels to the 2000 presidential election[2].

You may notice that Crush's Heart Punch is missing from the chart, as is the British Bulldog's Running Power Slam, Dusty Rhode's bionic elbow, and Doink the Clown's Whoopie Cushion. If you did notice any of these omissions, congratulations! You're a bigger wrestling nerd than I am. Also, the Heart Punch is a lame finishing move, Doink is *literally* a clown, the Running Power Slam is just a standard power slam with a running start, and while I liked Dusty Rhodes, he had big yellow polka dots on his singlet, and a doughy physique like one of those Hollywood character actors that always plays a hot dog vendor. So, although I tried to make this chart as comprehensive as space allows, it's also skewed toward my personal preferences. *(See Figure 1: Why Isn't my Favorite Wrestler on This Chart?)*

You might have noticed that this essay is more serious than the other essays in the book[3]. That's because there is nothing funny about professional wrestling—unless you think muscle-men playing dress-up, smacking each other, and rolling around on the ground together is funny.

---

(1) Incidentally, my favorite WWF entrance music is Junkyard Dog's original song, *Grab Them Cakes*.

(2) This is one of two instances in the book where I compare Al Gore to Jake "the Snake" Roberts. See if you can find the other one!

(3) You might have also noticed that none of the essays have a clear thesis statement, that the charts are riddled with curse words, and that this is the worst baby shower gift you've ever received.

FIGURE 1: **WHY ISN'T YOUR FAVORITE WRESTLER ON THIS CHART?**

START GRIPING

Is your favorite wrestler one of the following?

- Fighter Hayabusa
- Starman
- King Corn Karn
- Giant Panther
- The Amazon
- King Slender
- Great Puma

— YES →

I always thought that, in a fight between the Great Puma and Mike Tyson from Punch Out, the Great Puma would win. However, the Great Puma and all the other wrestlers on that chart were characters in the NES videogame Pro Wrestling, not real wrestlers.

— THEY SEEMED REAL TO ME. →

Great graphics for the time, I agree, but they still weren't real.

I ESPECIALLY LIKED STARMAN'S SOMERSAULT KICK.

Cool . . .

I HAD A TOUGH CHILDHOOD. MY FOLKS WERE DIVORCED. AT NIGHT I'D CRY MYSELF TO SLEEP AND DREAM THAT STARMAN WOULD SHOW UP AND SOMERSAULT KICK ALL MY PROBLEMS AWAY.

— NO →

Was your favorite wrestler active in the WWF between Wrestlemania I-XIII?

— NO →

I limited the chart to that era because it encapsulates my favorite period in WWF history, and was also considered by many people to be the Golden Age of WWF, before the attitude era kicked in the late 90s.

— YES →

Is your favorite wrestler Jake "the Snake" Roberts?

— NO →

Is your favorite wrestler Sid Justice?

— YES →

He's on the chart as well. The powerbomb is under slams and suplexes.

WHAT ABOUT THE CHOKE SLAM?

I remember him more for the powerbomb than the choke slam.

YEAH, BUT HE PRACTICALLY INVENTED THE CHOKE SLAM!

— NO →

Is your favorite wrestler Brutus "the Barber" Beefcake, Greg "the Hammer" Valentine, or Hercules Hernandez?

— YES →

Their finishing moves are already on the chart, I just didn't credit multiple wrestlers for each move.

— YES →

He's on the chart. The DDT (my favorite finisher) is under slams and suplexes.

WHAT ABOUT THE PART WHERE HE DRAPED HIS SNAKE OVER HIS OPPONENT'S UNCONSCIOUS BODY?

I considered that aspect "theatrics," like Ted DiBiase stuffing another wrestler's mouth full of money; it's not an essential component of the finisher.

— YEAH, BUT IT'S MY FAVORITE PART. →

— NO →

Is your favorite wrestler Andre the Giant?

— NO →

— YES →

He didn't have a finishing move, unless you count the head crush.

→ Guess what? Your favorite wrestler probably sucked.

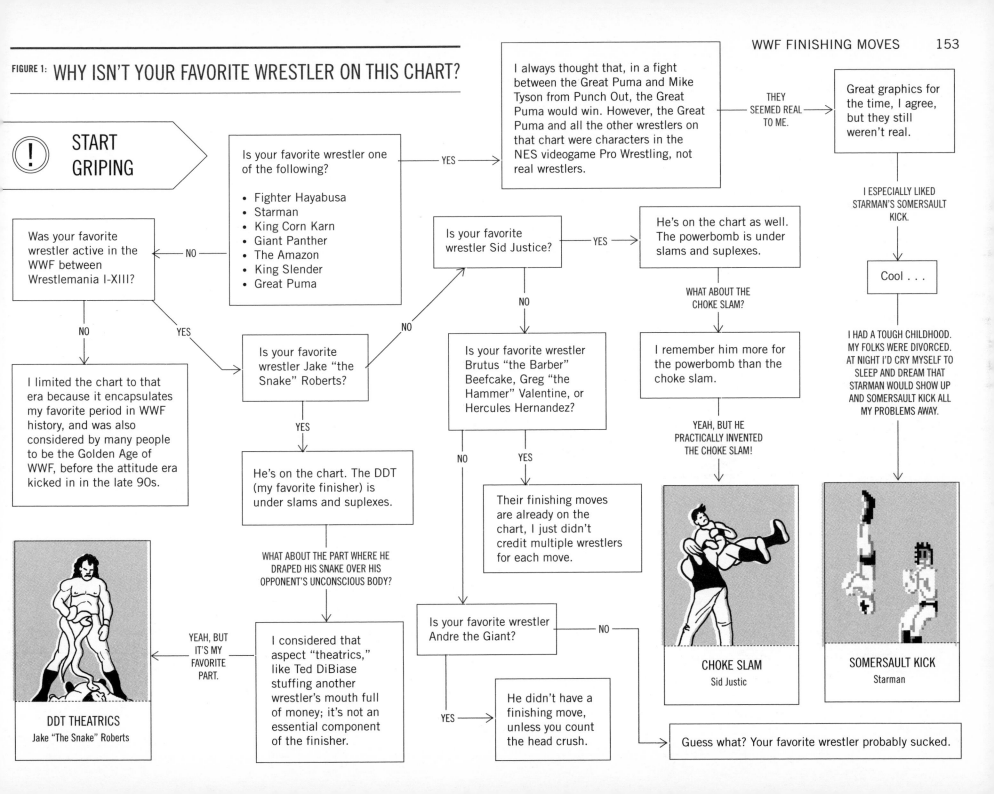

DDT THEATRICS
Jake "The Snake" Roberts

CHOKE SLAM
Sid Justic

SOMERSAULT KICK
Starman

SUBMISSION HOLDS

The wrestler focuses pressure or stress on a part of his opponent's body, usually by stretching, forcing his opponent to tap out or submit.

CAMEL CLUTCH
Iron Sheik

FIGURE FOUR LEGLOCK
Ric Flair

SHARPSHOOTER
Bret "The Hitman" Hart

BOSTON CRAB
"The Model" Rick Martel

CROSSFACE CHICKEN WING
Bob Backlund

FULL-NELSON
Billy Jack Haynes

SLEEPER HOLDS

The wrestler cuts off blood to his opponent's brain, thereby rendering him unconscious.

COBRA CLUTCH
Sgt. Slaughter

MILLION DOLLAR DREAM
Ted DiBiase

TRADITIONAL SLEEPER
"Rowdy" Roddy Piper

TONGAN DEATH GRIP
Haku

OFF THE ROPES

The wrestler leaps off the wrestling ring turnstyle and strikes his opponent with all of or part of his body.

SUPERFLY SMASH
"Superfly" Jimmy Snuka

CROSSBODY BLOCK
Ricky "The Dragon" Steamboat

FLYING ELBOW DROP
Randy "Macho Man" Savage

FLYING HEAD BUTT
Bam Bam Bigelow

OFF THE ROPES (FOR FAT DUDES)

The overweight wrestler lumbers up to the highest rung of the turnstyle he can reach (or sometimes just stands on the mat) and then falls down.

BANZAI DROP
Yokozuna

AVALANCHE
The Canadian Earthquake

BIG SPLASH
King Kong Bundy

NECKBREAKERS

The wrestler uses a throw or slam that focuses its force on his opponent's neck. The Rude Awakening is a reverse neckbreaker, while the Shake, Rattle, and Roll is a swinging neckbreaker.

RUDE AWAKENING
"Ravishing" Rick Rude

SHAKE, RATTLE, AND ROLL
The Honky Tonk Man

SUPLEXES AND SLAMS

A wrestler picks his opponent up, then slams him back down on the mat. With suplex variants the wrestler uses his own weight to increase the impact.

DDT
Jake "The Snake" Roberts

GHOSTBUSTER
Koko B. Ware

PERFECT PLEX
"Mr. Perfect" Curt Hennig

SIDE SUPLEX
Dino Bravo

END OF THE TRAIL
Tatanka

RAZOR'S EDGE
Razor Ramon

POWERBOMB
Sid Justice

GORILLA PRESS SLAM
Ultimate Warrior

PILEDRIVERS

A wrestler flips his opponent upside-down and drives his head into the mat.

TOMBSTONE PILEDRIVER
The Undertaker

MEMPHIS PILEDRIVER
Jerry "The King" Lawler

STRIKES

A wrestler strikes his opponent with a specific part of his body, either with a running start or from a standing position.

FOOTBALL CLOTHESLINE
"Hacksaw" Jim Duggan

SWEET CHIN MUSIC
Shawn Michaels

FOREARM SHIVER
Lex Luger

SERIES OF HEAD BUTTS
Junkyard Dog

ATOMIC LEG DROP
Hulk Hogan

ZEPPELIN WARFARE

ZEPPELINS ARE LIGHTER-THAN-AIR aircraft with a rigid internal structure. Other lighter-than-air crafts such as blimps or hot-air balloons have no internal structure and maintain their shape solely using air pressure. The zeppelin's rigid structure allows it to be much larger than a blimp or balloon, and thereby enables it to kill far more passengers when it inevitably falls from the sky in a terrifying conflagration. *(See Figure 1: The Zeppelin in its Natural State.)*

FIGURE 1: A ZEPPELIN IN ITS NATURAL ST...

Zeppelins are massive, majestic flying machines, but they are also notoriously fragile: Strong winds cause considerable difficulties for zeppelins, landing is dangerous even in perfect weather and requires a large ground crew, and of course early zeppelins were filled with highly flammable hydrogen gas. Some zeppelins were known to burst into flames if a passenger ordered their Bloody Mary with extra tabasco, or said a word that sounded similar to "fire." During a routine flight to Switzerland, a young zeppelin intentionally smashed itself against a mountain peak because it was going through a difficult breakup.

Considering how vulnerable zeppelins were to everyday dangers, it's surprising anybody thought they could survive the deadly atmosphere surrounding a war zone, but that's exactly what the Germans attempted in WWI. One look at a zeppelin though and you can understand the Germans' misplaced confidence, because you have to admit, zeppelins look badass. And they certainly appeared badass to the Londoners who looked up and saw them floating overhead during the German bombing raids that began in 1915 (although their bombing accuracy proved very low). Allied firepower was ineffective against zeps because regular bullets passed harmlessly through the hull. But that changed once the British figured out to use incendiary bullets—which burn upon firing—and the zeppelin's advantage disintegrated like the flammable surface of a hollow hull filled with 7 million cubic feet of hydrogen (metaphorically speaking). All allied pilots had to do was hit the zeppelin *anywhere* along the 500 foot long span of its hull and it would explode. War zeppelins ultimately proved more likely to kill the zeppelin's crew than anyone on the ground, and they inevitably joined the long list of failed and obsolete weapons. *(See Figure 2: Obsolete Weapons of War.)*

Sadly, zeppelins' beauty didn't outweigh their uselessness. Most things in the world exist either because they're beautiful or useful. *(See Figure 4: Existence Validity Scale.)* If you examine the scale, you'll notice that the vast majority of objects reside in either the upper right or bottom left quarter; they're either a combination of useful and ugly or beautiful and useless—it's difficult to make useful things beautiful, and if something's useless and ugly as well, we usually don't keep it around. Pity the tragically flawed zeppelin! Floating alone in the upper right corner: extremely beautiful, but relatively useless—right next to babies.

FIGURE 2: OBSOLETE WEAPONS OF WAR

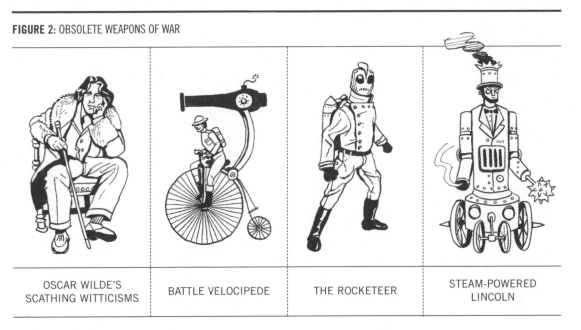

| OSCAR WILDE'S SCATHING WITTICISMS | BATTLE VELOCIPEDE | THE ROCKETEER | STEAM-POWERED LINCOLN |

FIGURE 3: MORE OBSOLETE STUFF

1. Chivalry
2. Horses
3. Pencils
4. Telephones that can't give you directions to the nearest Thai restaurant
5. Top hats
6. Nature
7. Grammar
8. Vaudeville
9. Shame
10. Sanctity of Marriage
11. Trolleys
12. Monocles
13. Edison wax cylinders
14. Mail
15. Samurai
16. Abacus
17. Books full of charts
18. Tap dancing
19. Medicinal leeches
20. Anything that isn't the Internet

FIGURE 4: EXISTENCE VALIDITY SCALE

1. Spoons
2. Flyswatters
3. Rich heiresses
4. Men's underwear
5. Roman numerals
6. Zeppelins
7. Bowties
8. Babies
9. Breasts
10. Fire hydrants
11. Me
12. Chivalry
13. Car alarms
14. Kabuki Theater
15. Toenails
16. Concrete
17. Earmuffs
18. Monocles
19. Garden gnomes
20. Irony
21. Your appendix
22. Hairless cats

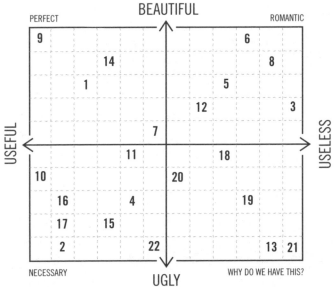

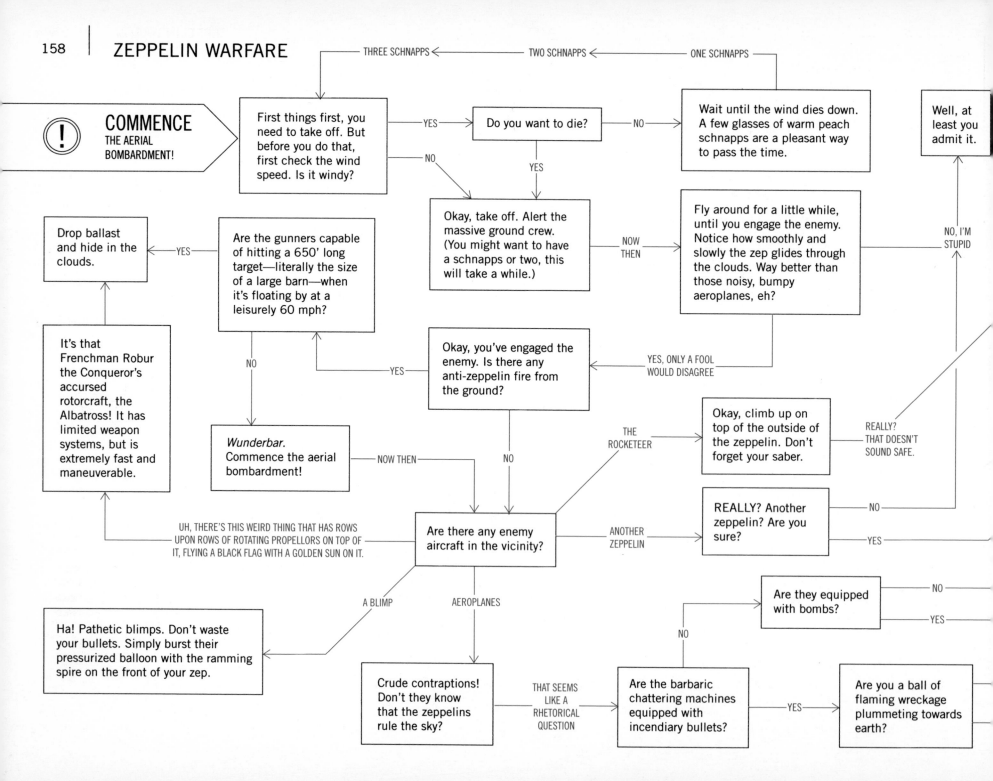

THREE SCHNAPPS ← TWO SCHNAPPS ← ONE SCHNAPPS

COMMENCE THE AERIAL BOMBARDMENT!

First things first, you need to take off. But before you do that, first check the wind speed. Is it windy?

— YES → Do you want to die? — NO → Wait until the wind dies down. A few glasses of warm peach schnapps are a pleasant way to pass the time.

Well, at least you admit it.

Do you want to die? — YES ↓ — NO →

Okay, take off. Alert the massive ground crew. (You might want to have a schnapps or two, this will take a while.)

— NOW THEN → Fly around for a little while, until you engage the enemy. Notice how smoothly and slowly the zep glides through the clouds. Way better than those noisy, bumpy aeroplanes, eh?

NO, I'M STUPID

Drop ballast and hide in the clouds.

— YES — Are the gunners capable of hitting a 650' long target—literally the size of a large barn—when it's floating by at a leisurely 60 mph?

It's that Frenchman Robur the Conqueror's accursed rotorcraft, the Albatross! It has limited weapon systems, but is extremely fast and maneuverable.

Okay, you've engaged the enemy. Is there any anti-zeppelin fire from the ground?

— YES, ONLY A FOOL WOULD DISAGREE

Okay, climb up on top of the outside of the zeppelin. Don't forget your saber.

REALLY? THAT DOESN'T SOUND SAFE.

NO ↓

Wunderbar. Commence the aerial bombardment!

— NOW THEN —

THE ROCKETEER

REALLY? Another zeppelin? Are you sure? — NO —

UH, THERE'S THIS WEIRD THING THAT HAS ROWS UPON ROWS OF ROTATING PROPELLORS ON TOP OF IT, FLYING A BLACK FLAG WITH A GOLDEN SUN ON IT.

Are there any enemy aircraft in the vicinity?

— ANOTHER ZEPPELIN → — YES —

A BLIMP / AEROPLANES

Ha! Pathetic blimps. Don't waste your bullets. Simply burst their pressurized balloon with the ramming spire on the front of your zep.

Are they equipped with bombs? — NO — / — YES —

Crude contraptions! Don't they know that the zeppelins rule the sky?

— THAT SEEMS LIKE A RHETORICAL QUESTION → Are the barbaric chattering machines equipped with incendiary bullets? — YES → Are you a ball of flaming wreckage plummeting towards earth?

NO

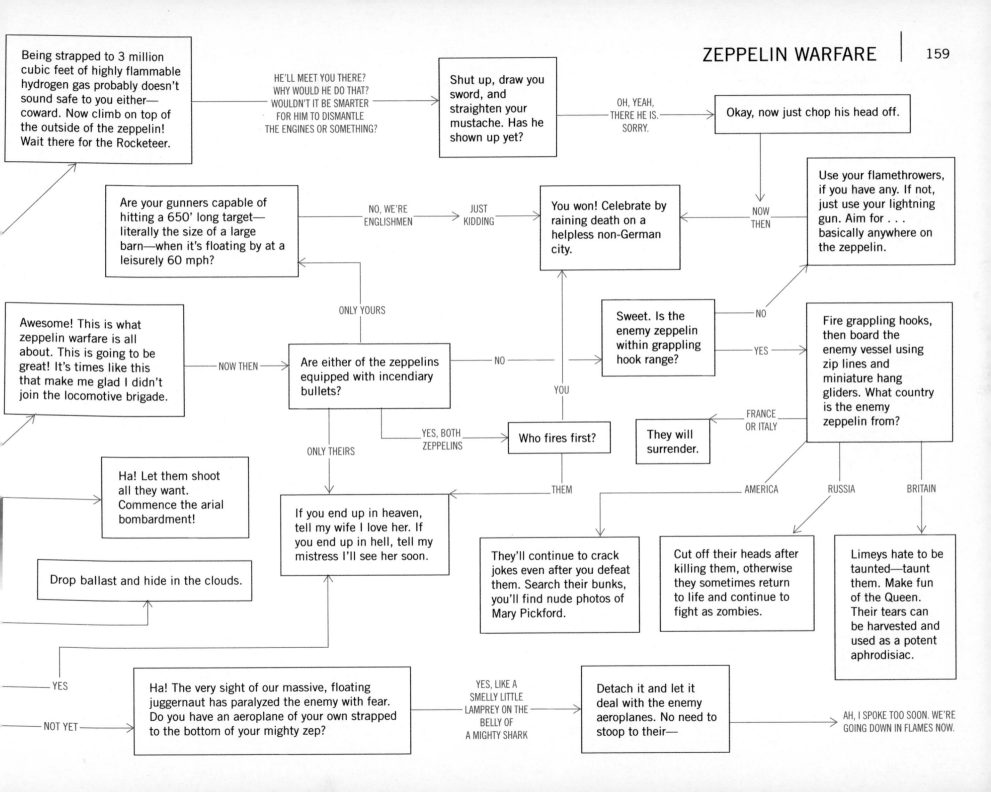

Being strapped to 3 million cubic feet of highly flammable hydrogen gas probably doesn't sound safe to you either—coward. Now climb on top of the outside of the zeppelin! Wait there for the Rocketeer.

HE'LL MEET YOU THERE? WHY WOULD HE DO THAT? WOULDN'T IT BE SMARTER FOR HIM TO DISMANTLE THE ENGINES OR SOMETHING?

Shut up, draw you sword, and straighten your mustache. Has he shown up yet?

OH, YEAH, THERE HE IS. SORRY.

Okay, now just chop his head off.

Use your flamethrowers, if you have any. If not, just use your lightning gun. Aim for . . . basically anywhere on the zeppelin.

Are your gunners capable of hitting a 650' long target—literally the size of a large barn—when it's floating by at a leisurely 60 mph?

NO, WE'RE ENGLISHMEN

JUST KIDDING

You won! Celebrate by raining death on a helpless non-German city.

NOW THEN

Awesome! This is what zeppelin warfare is all about. This is going to be great! It's times like this that make me glad I didn't join the locomotive brigade.

NOW THEN

Are either of the zeppelins equipped with incendiary bullets?

NO

Sweet. Is the enemy zeppelin within grappling hook range?

NO

YES

Fire grappling hooks, then board the enemy vessel using zip lines and miniature hang gliders. What country is the enemy zeppelin from?

ONLY YOURS

YOU

YES, BOTH ZEPPELINS

Who fires first?

They will surrender.

FRANCE OR ITALY

ONLY THEIRS

Ha! Let them shoot all they want. Commence the arial bombardment!

THEM

AMERICA

RUSSIA

BRITAIN

Drop ballast and hide in the clouds.

If you end up in heaven, tell my wife I love her. If you end up in hell, tell my mistress I'll see her soon.

They'll continue to crack jokes even after you defeat them. Search their bunks, you'll find nude photos of Mary Pickford.

Cut off their heads after killing them, otherwise they sometimes return to life and continue to fight as zombies.

Limeys hate to be taunted—taunt them. Make fun of the Queen. Their tears can be harvested and used as a potent aphrodisiac.

YES

NOT YET

Ha! The very sight of our massive, floating juggernaut has paralyzed the enemy with fear. Do you have an aeroplane of your own strapped to the bottom of your mighty zep?

YES, LIKE A SMELLY LITTLE LAMPREY ON THE BELLY OF A MIGHTY SHARK

Detach it and let it deal with the enemy aeroplanes. No need to stoop to their—

AH, I SPOKE TOO SOON. WE'RE GOING DOWN IN FLAMES NOW.

ACKNOWLEDGMENTS

I WAS ORIGINALLY going to make this section another chart, instead of an essay, and then I realized: Who am I trying to impress?

This book wouldn't have passed the proposal phase without the encouragement of my friend and table tennis nemesis Greg Jones. Greg also introduced me to Frank Weimann, without whom this book wouldn't have found its way into the capable hands of Matthew Benjamin and the other fine people at HarperCollins. I'm also indebted to Jason Rekulak for the wealth of writing advice he's given me over the years.

The very funny Luke Giordano collaborated on a bunch of the charts. That list of copyright-free heavy metal band names on page 87? He came up with all of those. The Presidential Rumble? He devised the whole framework for that. The Heroes and Villains section? He had nothing to do with that, and I think it's the best part of the book. Coincidence? *Luke, I'm just kidding!*

These charts required extensive research, and I was fortunate to have the help of Gregg Gethard and Meg Favreau. Gregg didn't even have to do any research for the WWF chart, all that information was already in his brain. Meg summarized mountains of dusty books and sacred scrolls into the concise data used for the afterlife charts.

A lot of friends looked at charts in development and offered invaluable advice: Nolan Gilbride, Rob Baniewicz, Steve Gerben, Chip Chantry, Valerie Temple, Pat Kelly, Dale Archdekin, O.J., Margaret McGuire, Scott Horner, Tabitha Vidaurri, Kent Haines, Mike Reali, and most of the comedians in Philadelphia. Mom, Dad, and Anya, I love you, too!

Special thanks to Dave Walk for posting my original charts online, and to Quirk for being awesome. Extra special thanks to my wife, Jen, for finding out how many people Shaft killed, and also for being my wife.

ABOUT THE AUTHOR

photo by Jimi Robinson

DOOGIE HORNER is a stand-up comedian, writer, and graphic designer. His writing has been featured in *McSweeney's Joke Book of Book Jokes* and he is the author of *Dirty Jokes Every Man Should Know* and *The First Timer's Kit*. His book design has been featured in *Print* and *How*, and was awarded Amazon's cover of the year for *Pride and Prejudice and Zombies*. He lives in Philadelphia where he hosts the monthly comedy show the Ministry of Secret Jokes.

For more charts, visit
WWW.DOOGIEHORNER.COM